Royal
Horticultural
Society

GROW YOUR OWN FRUIT

Royal
Horticultural
Society

GROW YOUR OWN
FRUIT
Carol Klein

With Simon Akeroyd and Lucy Halsall, for the RHS

MITCHELL BEAZLEY

GROW YOUR OWN FRUIT
Carol Klein

With Simon Akeroyd and Lucy Halsall, for the RHS

First published in Great Britain in 2009 by
Mitchell Beazley, an imprint of Octopus Publishing
Group Ltd,
2–4 Heron Quays, London E14 4JP
An Hachette Livre UK Company
www.octopusbooks.co.uk

Published in association with the Royal Horticultural Society

ISBN 978 1 84533 4345

A CIP record of this book is available from the British Library.

Commissioning editor: Helen Griffin
Editorial director: Tracey Smith
Art director: Tim Foster
Designer: Lizzie Ballantyne
Project editor: Georgina Atsiaris
Copyeditor: Joanna Chisholm
Senior production controller: Lucy Carter
Proofreader: Jo Murray
Indexer: Sue Farr
Fruit consultant: Jim Arbury
RHS consultant: Simon Maughan

Set in Frutiger, Glypha, and Interstate

Colour reproduction by United Graphics, Singapore
Printed and bound by Estella

The Royal Horticultural Society is the UK's leading gardening charity
dedicated to advancing horticulture and promoting good gardening.
Its charitable work includes providing expert advice and information,
training the next generation of gardeners, creating hands-on
opportunities for children to grow plants and conducting research
into plants, pests and environmental issues affecting gardeners.
For more information, visit:
www.rhs.org.uk or call 0845 130 4646.

Contents

Why grow fruit?

To grow fruit is to enjoy living. We give our garden our noble labours in the wilful pursuit of desire, fully aware that we will inevitably give in to temptation. We yearn to create our own Garden of Eden, knowing full well that we will wantonly savour the tempting apples and all the other delectable fruit we have so lovingly nourished and cared for.

Fruit in the garden

Fruit is a reward. You plant a fruit bush or tree, look after it, and you are presented once a year with a gift of something so beautiful to look at and so pleasing to eat and so full of goodness for your body that you couldn't invent anything better. An alien from outer space would marvel at the elegance of the arrangement. If you were to plant your apple pips or your plum stone afterwards, you would join the circle and uphold your part of the bargain, just as a blackbird with a blackberry or a monkey with a fig does. Planting up a fruit garden, or just a patch, or a pot or two is the modern equivalent available to us in normal life. It is completely natural to focus on the reward, but the "doing of" can bring immense pleasure and fulfilment, in itself and for itself. Hopefully, the guidance in this book will empower you to have a go and give you the confidence to cultivate fruit really well.

To be able to grow at least some of your own fruit is very satisfying, and knowing it is fresh, healthy, unadulterated, and untainted by pesticides, fungicides, weedkillers, preservatives, irradiation, and wax coatings is very reassuring and a compelling reason to garden organically. It will also taste better, full of active flavours and subtle nuances you only discover as you eat – a rare privilege in a world of commercial uniformity. The wanton appearance and enveloping perfume of your own ripe fruit will seduce you away from the under-ripe, tasteless mountains of supermarket fare, where the emphasis is on fruits with a uniform appearance and size and which can be provided at any time of year.

Fruit and us

Before our ancestors started farming, humans hunted and foraged for food. To come across fruit was a delight. Nature had endowed fruit with sweet flesh to support the seed, and the birds, insects, reptiles, and mammals had willingly helped the plant spread itself around by seed in return for the reward of delicious nourishment. It was then only a matter of time before humans discovered fruit for

TO COME ACROSS FRUIT in a garden is a delight. These strings of shiny redcurrant 'Redpoll' are as tempting as sweets.

FILLING A BASKET WITH FRUIT, especially if you have grown it yourself, is incredibly satisfying. Think what a delicious pie these blackberries would make!

themselves. They probably noticed the enthusiasm with which other creatures devoured it. Think of monkeys descending on a wild fig tree or a grizzly bear guzzling on a cranberry bush.

We might nowadays consider wild fruit to be unbearably sour because our palates are irreversibly corrupted by the expectation of sugary sweetness. Yet in comparison with anything else that could find its way into their mouths, our ancestors would have found fruit a revelation – refreshingly and energizingly sour, yes, but with a fruity sweetness like no other. The desire to have fruit always available would have prompted them to have their own supply and that meant holding territory that already had fruiting trees as well as letting the sucked off seeds grow on after germination. Fruit became traded and fruit trees became portable. Thus the art of fruit cultivation began among different people in different places.

Today we may do our foraging at a supermarket, and fruit production is an industrial enterprise conducted

far out of sight. But to come across some fruit on a tree, bush, or vine, ripe and ready for eating, triggers in us the same delight our ancestors felt. Even if we have grown it ourselves, by our own efforts, to pick the fruit is to feel sudden glee at our luck.

Fruit in nature

Fruit is so bright and pretty. Isn't it wonderful that it's so colourful? Not just exotic tropical fruit but also bright red and green apples, blushing apricots and nectarines, garish red strawberries, translucent purple plums, and glowing, glistening red currants all attract our eye. Western industrial food is all brown and beige – high fat, high salt and sugar, and stodgy and floury. The bright colours in fruit advertise the nutrients within, and the friendly shapes and forms invite our interest.

Some fruits have contours that remind us of the human form, like the soft cheeks of peaches and plums. The velvet skins of peaches or the soft bloom on grapes have become ideals of beauty shared with the human form. Fruits become metaphors for the sensuality and sexuality of women, embodiments of desire and fertility, witnessing hope, fulfilment, and cruelty in the passage of time.

The story of most fruit and most people follows the same path – desirable female flowers brushed by the luckiest male pollen, the swelling female fruit giving birth to a new generation of seedlings. Whereas humans have to do it by following cultural norms and dictates, or by falling in love, fruit usually use the agency of flying insects, and especially bees. Successful pollination of fruit is finely balanced between the readiness of the blossom, the presence of active bees, and the weather – frost in particular. Even if the blossom and pollen are ready, the bees are needed to introduce them together, while an overnight frost could destroy the blossom and dash all hopes of fertilization. To keep your garden on their map right throughout the year, provide bees with areas of rough ground for shelter and nectar-rich flowers as food. It is as important for your fruit as anything else you can do.

POLLINATION, such a vital aspect of fruit growing, is helped if you can encourage bees and other beneficial insects to your garden with mixed, flower-rich plantings.

Planning and preparation

- Growing in a small space
- Know your plot
- Planning what to grow
- A year in the fruit garden
- Preparing for planting

Carol's fruit notebook

" Once you are motivated to grow fruit, practicalities loom large. Decisions have to be made at the outset and dealing with them successfully can make all the difference as to how well the fruit does for years to come: a fruit bush struggling in the wrong place or a barren tree sulking year after year is harder to put right than trying a different variety of carrot next year. Knowing the realities of your planting plot will establish what you can grow – its aspect and orientation to the path of the sun through the sky, its levels of sunshine, shade, and frost, its exposure to the wind at different times of the year, the soil type and structure, water retention, and drainage.

Fruit trees and bushes are like any other perennial or tree in that they follow the maxim "right plant, right place". Your most important choice is then the particular variety. Not only does it have to be viable for you to grow it and be of the right type – be it a cooking or dessert fruit – but it must also possess the flavour and texture you will appreciate. Varieties that are specific or traditional in your locality are worth discovering because they may have evolved or have been selected to suit and thrive in the same conditions that you have. Just as importantly, you might be able to give continuity to local biological diversity or social history.

The effort you put into getting the planting site ready, to make your fruit feel at home, is rewarded by the flying start the plants make. An aerated, weed-free patch with the right level of organic matter and nutrients, with plenty of natural soil organisms and fertility well established, is the ideal. To my mind, a desire to have successful fruit crops does not justify damaging the local ecology, and I always advocate hand weeding or smothering to remove competing weeds – however insidious they are – if at all possible. In my mind, the toxic consequences of weedkillers are insidiously cumulative, for you, your garden, and your innocent wild residents and visitors. "

Growing in a small space

Like many gardeners, you may dream of having a large garden, but in reality you may well have to make the most of a smaller plot of land, if any at all. But just because there isn't a huge area of land to cultivate, you can still grow fruit crops – you just need to approach things slightly differently and see the opportunities that your space has to offer.

THESE STRAWBERRIES WILL GROW happily in a hanging basket provided they're kept well fed and watered. The basket should be hung in a sunny spot at a height that makes picking easy yet is not dangerous for passers-by.

Benefits of a container garden

Growing fruit in containers is often the only option for those of us with restricted space, but far from being a limiting factor this method of fruit cultivation offers many benefits (see pages 48–49 for cultivation advice on container fruit growing). You can control the size of a plant by restricting its roots in a pot, which also forces the plant to crop more quickly than a tree or shrub in the open ground whose roots have unlimited access to the soil. This is particularly useful if space is limited in your garden because it allows you to maximize your plants' cropping potential. It also makes tree fruits much more accessible for harvesting because they rarely grow above head height when planted in containers.

A container-grown plant can easily be moved – using a sack trolley for heavier pots – to a frost-free spot for winter if it or its flowers or fruits are likely to be damaged by frosts. Figs, for example, need their embryonic fruits protected from extremes of winter cold if they are to bear a successful crop in cool-temperate climates; plants growing directly in the garden soil have to be wrapped up with insulation material such as horticultural fleece packed with straw or bracken (see page 131). Moving potted plants under cover is much simpler.

Another benefit is easier pest and disease protection. Peaches, nectarines, and other stone fruits that are vulnerable to the fungal disease peach leaf curl can be protected from infection by keeping the stems and emerging foliage dry between early winter and late spring. It is virtually impossible to cover large free-standing trees and time-consuming to cover fan-trained plants (see page 106), but you can easily move a dwarf, pot-grown peach tree into your greenhouse. Similarly, transferring a strawberry or blueberry plant to an unheated porch or greenhouse while the fruits are ripening is an extremely simple yet effective way to keep birds away from the ripening fruits. Just remember when moving plants under cover that many crops rely on insects to pollinate their flowers for a fruit set, so place flowering plants outside, or else make contingency plans such as hand pollination or opening vents and doors to allow insects access to the blooms.

Another relatively specialist gardening task that can be made much simpler if crops are pot-grown is that of forcing plants such as strawberries so they crop earlier than normal. Early in the growing season, the containers can readily be moved into a warmer area for a few weeks, thereby allowing them to come into fruit much earlier than if grown outside. This enables you to consume home-grown fruits at a time when their prices are often inflated in the shops.

Container growing allows you to meet the specific cultivation requirements of plants with specialist needs. For example, blueberries, lingonberries, and cranberries require an acidic soil that many gardens don't offer, but you can provide these crops with exactly that by planting them in a pot of ericaceous compost. These crops also require a continual moisture supply. Although container-grown plants can be more demanding in their watering needs than those in open ground, keeping a few pots of blueberries or other moisture-loving crop close to the house allows you to keep an eye on their watering requirements. Many houses have a water butt against one of their walls, and this can readily supply these ericaceous plants with rainwater, which has a neutral or acidic pH, as and when it is needed.

Fruit growing on balconies

Many residents in flats have balconies as their only outdoor space. Far from being a place devoid of suitable growing areas this offers many opportunities to the fruit gardener. Not only do balconies often provide a sheltered environment but they also, by their very nature, have plenty of vertical wall space, which can be adapted to fruit cultivation. Restricted tree forms (see page 74) such as fans, espaliers, and

PROBLEMS WITH LATE FROSTS can be avoided by growing crops in pots. These flowering strawberries can be easily moved under cover if necessary while they are in flower, as can the frost-tender citrus plant.

Making the most of small spaces

The main limiting factor most gardeners face is space, and that governs the decision over what to grow and what to buy. Luckily, however, there are a variety of ways to help the fruit gardener get the most from his or her plot.

Pruning methods

Certain fruits, notably autumn raspberries, can be forced to crop for longer than normal by adjusting their pruning regime (see page 147). Autumn raspberry canes are traditionally pruned down to ground level in late winter. However, if some of the canes are pruned back only by half their height, the remaining lower half of those canes will still bear fruit (see page 147). Because they are more advanced in growth these stems will crop two months or more before the younger canes, which have to grow, flower, and develop fruit all in one season. This technique allows gardeners to grow just one variety yet force it to crop both in summer and autumn.

Long-season crops

Some varieties of fruit crop for longer than others, so by choosing these you can extend the fresh harvest period by weeks if not months. For example, by growing perpetual strawberry varieties (also known as everbearers) such as 'Mara des Bois' and

'Albion' you will be provided with a steady supply of fresh fruits from early summer until midautumn, rather than a sudden peak in early or midsummer, as is often the case with conventional summer-fruiting varieties. This also helps to avoid gluts and dearths of produce because longer-cropping varieties may offer a lower weekly yield yet they crop more consistently over a longer period.

Storage potential

Although most fruits freeze well and many can also be dried and made into preserves (see page 28), this often limits their use thereafter because they are no longer in their fresh state. By choosing varieties that have an extended storage life you can continue to eat them raw, which also allows you to benefit from their maximum vitamin content. Apples, pears, and quinces are the most versatile crops for fresh storage, and provided you have a simple fruit store area such as a cool shed or garage, any of these crops can be enjoyed fresh until midspring.

A selection of fruits with long storage periods

Apples	Type	Season of use
'Belle de Boskoop'	Dual-purpose	Midautumn to midspring
'Bramley's Seedling'	Cooker	Late autumn to early spring
'Court Pendu Plat'	Dessert	Early winter to midspring
'Edward VII'	Cooker	Early winter to midspring
'Idared'	Dual-purpose	Early winter to late spring
'Tydeman's Late Orange'	Dessert	Early winter to midspring
Pears	Type	Season of use
'Black Worcester'	Cooker	Midwinter to midspring
'Catillac'	Cooker	Midwinter to midspring
'Moonglow'	Dual-purpose	Early autumn to midwinter
'Glou Morceau'	Dessert	Early winter to midwinter
'Santa Claus'	Dessert	Early winter to midwinter
'Vicar of Winkfield'	Dual-purpose	Early winter to late winter

Plant protection

The fresh harvest period of fruit can be extended at either end of the growing season by the use of cloches, frames, greenhouses, or conservatories. This is particularly useful for lower-growing crops such as strawberries and blueberries, which can easily be covered by a cloche or frame, and for fruits in pots that can readily be moved under cover. Extra protection in spring can allow fruits to be harvested three or four weeks earlier than those uncovered, and a protective covering at the end of the season will shield later-maturing varieties right up until the first hard frosts. Crops grown in containers can also be forced into early production, thereby extending the seasons even more because of the extra heat that can be provided by a greenhouse or conservatory.

Dual-purpose varieties

The more uses you can get out of a particular fruit the better, especially if space is an issue. Some fruits – notably apples, pears, plums, gooseberries, and cherries – have dual-purpose varieties that are suitable for both cooking and eating raw (see page 15). By focusing on growing these more versatile varieties you can maximize use of your space.

Pollination

Some fruit varieties are self-fertile – that is, their flowers can be pollinated with that plant's own pollen – while other varieties need to be pollinated by a different variety of the same plant in order to develop fruit (these are called self-infertile varieties, see individual fruit entries for details). Self-incompatibility can be a problem on some fruits such as plums. Therefore, where space is so limited that a gardener can grow just one fruiting plant, it's a good idea to choose self-fertile crops, such as currants and gooseberries. However, you can have more than one variety of apple, pear, plum, peach, or nectarine on a small plot by growing what's known as a "family tree". This is a rootstock onto which compatible fruits have been grafted, giving the gardener maximum crop variability from minimum space. For example, you can have an early dessert apple, a late-keeping dessert apple, and a cooking apple variety grafted onto one tree provided they are in compatible pollination groups.

NATURALLY COMPACT FRUIT TREES like this Ballerina apple are excellent choices for gardens with limited space.

Naturally compact fruits

Plant breeders have developed many naturally compact varieties and dwarfing rootstocks, mainly because commercial growers can then harvest a greater fruit yield per hectare. However, home gardeners can also enjoy their benefits by growing these varieties and rootstocks. For example, blueberry 'Sunshine Blue' or 'Misty', nectarine 'Nectarella', and peach 'Bonanza' are all compact varieties, as are the Ballerina apple trees 'Charlotte', 'Maypole', 'Telamon', 'Trajan', and 'Tuscan', which have spur systems concentrated on a main vertical stem (for more information on dwarfing rootstocks see individual tree fruit entries).

Restricted forms

A major difference between fruit and vegetable gardens is the longevity of the crops they contain. The majority of vegetables are treated as annuals, whereas most fruit crops are woody or herbaceous perennials. Woody perennials can be trained to develop a permanent framework of compact growth on which fruiting spurs develop, which adds ornamental value as well as saving space. Cordons, fans, espaliers, stepovers, and festooned trees all make maximum use of the space that they are in, and certain bush fruit can also be trained in these ways (see page 74).

cordons are perfectly suited to such locations, the shelter of a wall often encouraging much better fruit set and ripening than an open, exposed site.

Frosts are less of a problem on balconies, again because of the sheltered location, so tender crops that a larger, windier location may not be able to ripen are an ideal choice for balcony owners. Many flats and balcony gardens are in cities or coastal areas. Often these locations have an extremely mild climate because of either a southerly coastal location or the "urban heat island" effect (where the radiant heat and shelter provided by high-rise buildings and the waste heat generated by metropolitan activities raises the temperature by a few extra degrees). This gives gardeners with balconies the opportunity to cultivate crops that would otherwise struggle to do well in temperate areas. Citrus, pomegranate, banana, and pineapple are all worth trying in such mild locations. Growing grapevines up balcony supports offers shade in the summer and creates an ornamental feature, as well as providing a high yield of fruit. Balconies, however, are often quite windy, and this could cause problems with fruit set and yields because many fruit crops are insect-pollinated and insects are unlikely to venture into windy sites. Therefore, hand pollination is needed to ensure a good yield is obtained (see page 106).

Using courtyards and patios

The advantage of courtyards and patios is that they often have more free space than balconies, and so can provide gardeners with a wider range of crops. Again, these gardens offer similar benefits to balconies in that they are often surrounded by plenty of vertical wall space. By default some of these areas will be in the shade but there are plenty of fruits that will tolerate, or even thrive, in areas with limited sunlight. Gooseberries and red and white currants make excellent wall-trained cordons or fans on a shaded wall, and if you have space for something larger an acid cherry would be an ideal choice. For gardeners with more limited plots, ground-cover plants that often reside under the shade of taller shrubbery and tree canopies will work well. Alpine strawberries, cranberries, lingonberries, and compact blueberry varieties such as 'Sunshine Blue' will all produce good crops in the shade.

THIS APPLE 'DISCOVERY' has been festooned to encourage it to bear a large number of fruits, while keeping the size of it relatively small.

CROPS FAVOURED BY BIRDS, such as these strawberries, can easily be moved out of temptation's way when they are grown in containers.

Fruit in small gardens

For those of us lucky enough to have a garden the scope for growing fruit becomes even more extensive. The increased amount of space has obvious advantages, not least the potential to cultivate a much greater number of plants compared to smaller spaces. Another major benefit is that, because of the lack of hard surfaces, crops can be grown directly in the ground. By cultivating plants in the soil rather than in containers, maintenance is reduced because watering and feeding demands are less rigorous for plants whose roots have free access to a large volume of soil. Depending on its shape, your garden may contain some open, unshaded spaces in which most fruit will benefit from the warmth and light provided by a sunny location. Other crops, however, may be happy in shade.

Growing fruit in larger plots

Gardeners with larger gardens or allotments have the opportunity to grow a much wider selection of varieties, so issues such as pollination groups and training restricted forms become less important. With more space there can be a separate area of the garden dedicated to fruit growing, meaning that fruit cages can be erected to ward off birds, rabbits, and squirrels, which may try to damage your crop. Allotment holders occasionally have restrictions in their terms and conditions, which either limit or prohibit tree planting, but home gardeners can readily accommodate open-centred fruit trees grown on semivigorous rootstocks. The scope for including an attractive design also becomes greater where there is extra space. Gardens can be sectioned off with rows of fan-trained or espalier trees, creating a highly ornamental feature.

INCORPORATING TREE FRUITS into fences or other boundaries by training them as a stepover, fan, or espalier makes maximum use of space in your garden and creates an attractive feature as well.

Know your plot

While you may be able to adapt the layout of your garden to accommodate certain crops, its geographical location is more difficult to adjust. Local factors such as soil type, sun and shade levels, and wind and frost exposure all influence the crops that can be grown. However, there are various techniques you can adopt to lessen their effects.

A good understanding of the geographical aspects of your site is essential if you want to grow fruit crops successfully. Planting moisture-loving crops in dry soils, acid-loving crops in alkaline soils, or sun-loving crops in shady locations will result in weak, unproductive growth that is more vulnerable to nutrient deficiencies and disorders, and less resilient to pest or disease attack. Unlike vegetable crops, which are predominantly annuals, most fruit crops are perennials and therefore grow in the same piece of ground for years or even decades. Making sure they are in a suitable location initially is crucial, because moving them is impractical and impacts on their health and yield. For these reasons you must assess your potential fruit garden site before undertaking any major cultivations or plantings.

Assessing your soil

Healthy soil is essential if you want to grow plants directly in it rather than in containers. Ideally fruit gardeners require soil that is well aerated, relatively fertile, and has a neutral to slightly acidic pH. This will sustain the majority of crops with minimal effort. Fortunately, if your soil isn't ideal you can improve it.

One of the most important things to identify is your soil's texture, because it influences many physical and chemical characteristics of your plot such as nutrient availability, moisture-retention, drainage, fertility, and aeration. You therefore need to know whether your soil is made up of clay, sand, or silt particles. Most soils are a mixture of these three particles: for example, your soil may be a sandy loam or a silty clay. There are quick ways to identify your predominant soil type and so establish a better understanding of your plot's abilities and limitations (see box, below).

The structure of your soil (for example, whether it is over a shallow chalk subsoil or derived from an acidic material) will influence its pH. This in turn affects the nutrient availability of your site: for example, very acid soil tends to make magnesium unavailable

TYPES OF SOIL

A quick way to identify your soil type is by taking a handful of the soil in your garden, then wetting it slightly and moulding it in your hands. Then notice the characteristics of the "lump" in your hand.

Predominantly sandy soils

- warm up quickly in spring;
- hold onto nutrients poorly;
- drain very quickly;
- don't compact easily;
- are easy to dig and make a seedbed;
- are well aerated.

Predominantly silty soils

- warm up relatively quickly in spring;
- hold onto nutrients well;
- drain quite slowly;
- can easily become compacted;
- are relatively easy to dig, although seedbeds can cap;
- are generally sufficiently aerated.

Predominantly clay soils

- warm up slowly in spring;
- hold onto nutrients very well;
- can easily become waterlogged;
- are very prone to becoming compacted;
- can be very heavy to dig and cap easily;
- can be poorly aerated.

SANDY SOILS feel gritty between your fingers and won't easily stick together to form a ball.

SILTY SOILS feel silky to the touch and they can be rolled into a ball or cylinder relatively easily.

CLAY SOILS feel sticky and heavy, and can be rolled into a pencil-thick sausage and then bent into a ring.

AN OPEN GARDEN SUCH AS THIS ONE may be particularly exposed to frosts, so ensure you listen regularly to the weather forecast and take precautions when frosts are expected. This is especially important when crops are in flower.

whereas alkaline soil often makes plants deficient in manganese. Soil pH is measured on a scale of one to 14, with seven being pH neutral (that is, neither acid or alkaline), above seven being alkaline, and below seven being acidic. The majority of fruit crops prefer an acidic or neutral soil, so carrying out a soil test is important to establish whether you need to adjust the soil pH, limit the crops you grow in your plot, or adopt a tailored feeding regime. The more acidic or alkaline a soil is, the more difficult it becomes to change its pH, not least because this reading is measured on a logarithmic scale. Nature can only bend so far – it's much easier and more successful to grow acid-loving blueberries in a container of ericaceous (acidic) compost than to try to adjust a soil with a pH of 8.5 to a more suitable pH6. Simple pH testing kits can be purchased from garden centres, and these will provide adequate results for the fruit grower's needs. The decision can then be made whether or not to add further acidic materials such as sulphur chips to lower the pH, or use alkaline (chalky) additives such as garden lime or mushroom compost to raise the soil pH.

Tackling soil drainage

The texture and structure of a soil, along with other physical characteristics, can affect how well moisture percolates through it. Even those fruit crops that prefer a moist site, such as blueberries, cranberries, and lingonberries, will struggle to do well on a site that has poor drainage and is therefore permanently waterlogged. Other crops, such as cherries and apples, are naturally shallow-rooted because they need to be in the upper, more aerated part of the soil. Consequently they would quickly fade and die on a waterlogged plot. The provision of good drainage is therefore essential for fruit growing.

Temporary poor drainage, shown as puddles that quite rapidly drain away, often occurs when the soil surface becomes compacted. This is especially common on clay soils that have been dug or walked on while they are wet. To alleviate this, dig plenty of bulky organic matter, such as composted bark, plus a 7.5cm (3in) layer of horticultural grit into the soil to a depth of half a spade blade. More permanent drainage problems such as those caused by a sloping site or high water table require more substantial treatment, such as the digging of a soakaway or installation of a herringbone system of drainage pipes. These often involve a lot of effort and/or money to install so in such cases it's frequently more economical to use raised beds or to plant fruit crops into containers.

Weather and climate

One factor that will influence the positioning of specific fruit crops is the site and aspect of your plot, with elements such as light, temperature, and exposure all having an important impact on the selection of crops you can grow. Gardeners with a courtyard or garden surrounded by walls or fences should also be aware of "rain shadows". The base of such vertical structures is vulnerable to becoming very dry, even in rainy weather. Therefore, a plant using a wall or fence as a support can succumb to drought stress, unless adequate irrigation is provided to its roots.

Some fruits are perfectly happy to crop in a shady spot whereas others require sunlight to yield a decent harvest. Those gardeners with balconies or courtyard gardens may have to cope with a shady, north- or east-facing site – this will support fruits such as alpine strawberries, acid cherries, red and white currants, and gooseberries. Sunny, south- or west-facing aspects on the other hand are ideal for sun-loving fruits such as grapes, figs, peaches, nectarines, and apricots. Mapping out your garden to note key areas of shade and full sun will be essential before you start planting.

Minimum temperatures are also an important consideration. While the effects of climate change are enabling some gardeners to experiment with a wider range of fruits (see box, right), only truly hardy plants will crop reliably in gardens in which the temperature frequently falls below freezing during the winter months. Those wanting to grow tender crops such as citrus, pineapples, or passion fruit will need the protection of a conservatory or heated greenhouse (see individual crop entries for details). Local horticultural societies, weather station data (on official forecasting websites), or neighbours are all ideal starting points if you need to obtain details of annual temperature extremes in your area.

MANY FRUIT CROPS RELY ON INSECTS to pollinate their flowers, so for good yields it's important to site plants in a sheltered spot rather than in a windy, exposed location.

CLIMATE CHANGE

It is now widely believed that the average temperature will rise across the planet by a crucial few degrees in the 21st century, this in turn having a knock-on effect on the world's climate. Irregular weather patterns have already been experienced globally, with many countries suffering climatic extremes. If milder winters are more commonplace this would bring obvious benefits to fruit gardeners wanting to grow more exotic crops. However, it could also yield problems for more temperate fruits. Many of these hardier crops require a certain period of cold weather in order to initiate flower buds and break dormancy, so growth and yield could be impaired. This is a prime time for experimentation with cultural techniques, the effects of which are continually developing.

The majority of tree fruits flower early in the year and so require a sheltered site that attracts pollinating insects (predominantly bees) that are already on the wing. If these beneficial creatures are discouraged from visiting flowers by strong winds the fruits' flowers won't be pollinated and resulting fruit set will be very poor. Therefore, if your garden is exposed in any direction, it is a good idea to erect artificial, semipermeable windbreaks to reduce the wind's force, or plant screening trees such as holly, hawthorn, or alder to provide shelter.

Frost damage

Aside from pest and disease attack, damage from frosty weather is the most problematic issue for fruit gardeners. A badly timed late frost can destroy all blossoms open at that time and any fruitlets, reducing potential yield significantly. Frost can also damage the soft shoots and foliage of various crops, which can result in more serious plant failure.

Because most fruit crops have to flower, fertilize, swell, and ripen fruits all in one season they come into blossom comparatively early in the year. This is especially true of peaches, nectarines, apricots, plums, and pears, all of which are frequently in full blossom during late winter and early spring. Both

flowers and the young fruitlets can be damaged by frosts, which are very irregular yet prevalent during late winter and early spring. This can result in the fruits developing brown, corky, circular patches around the base or the flowers being partially or completely killed.

Protection against frost damage

The ideal method of protection is to avoid planting vulnerable crops in frost-prone areas, which has obvious limitations because most of us have to work with the plot we've inherited. If possible, however, avoid frost pockets (see box, below) .

For the majority of gardeners the main method of minimizing frost damage is to protect vulnerable plants during subzero temperatures. This can be done by moving containerized plants to a more sheltered, frost-free position or by covering plants *in situ* with protective materials. Figs, however, can be manipulated to produce frost-resistant, embryonic fruit by October. These will be small enough to survive a winter unscathed, giving them a long season in which to grow and ripen (see page 130).

Comparatively hardy crops such as kiwifruits and grapevines are vulnerable to frost damaging their

FROST POCKETS

Areas where cold air collects are known as frost pockets, and it is important to avoid growing fruit in these because flowers that emerge very early in the year can be damaged or even killed. Cold air will naturally sink to and collect in the lowest point it can reach, so sloping sites are most at risk. If your garden is in a natural valley do not plant fruit trees at the bottom of it, where there will be a natural frost pocket. You can also inadvertently create frost pockets on sloping sites by impeding the downward flow of cold air with a hedge, fence, or other impenetrable barrier. The cold air gets trapped on the upper side of such barriers, creating a pocket of cold air. Consequently if you are on a steep slope erect such structures only if absolutely necessary. Where they do exist, don't plant fruiting plants directly above them.

FLOWERS AND YOUNG FRUITS such as these apricots can be damaged or even killed by late frosts, so try to avoid planting in vulnerable areas such as frost pockets.

soft shoots and woody stems. A kiwifruit coming into leaf in spring can easily have all its foliage burnt off by a late frost, so it should be covered with a tent of horticultural fleece during this period.

Conversely the soft, unripened stems of a grapevine can be damaged by the first frosts of autumn, causing them to die back. In this case it helps to position vines in a sunny, sheltered spot to help ripen and mature the wood as much as possible before the onset of winter. Damaged stems can be pruned out once the vine comes into full leaf in late spring.

The only option for truly tender crops such as pineapples and passion fruit is to provide them with a frost-free greenhouse or conservatory for winter.

Moving plants

By far the easiest method of frost protection is moving vulnerable plants to a frost-free spot. This could be as luxurious as a heated greenhouse or conservatory, or as minimal as a sheltered cold frame or porch. While conservatories will often be double glazed and heated via a domestic system, greenhouse heating systems can be less fail-safe. Ensure your greenhouse heater works via a thermostat, which should be set a couple of degrees above freezing. While electric heaters produce no harmful emissions, greenhouses containing paraffin or gas heaters should be well ventilated. Insulating part or all of the greenhouse with bubble plastic will help retain any heat generated and keep fuel costs down.

Cold frames should also be lined with similar insulation and positioned against a sheltered wall to provide maximum protection. It is more difficult to keep cold frames frost-free because they often lack sufficient space for a heater, but they will offer a few valuable degrees of protection.

Protecting plants *in situ*

If you don't have a frost-free area, or if your fruit trees are planted out permanently, then *in situ* protection is the only option. Polythene, horticultural fleece, or glass cloches are useful for protecting the blossom of early strawberries, whereas fences or walls supporting fan-trained, cordon, or espalier fruit trees can have a double layer of horticultural fleece attached to them and draped over the plant to be

A GREENHOUSE ALLOWS GARDENERS to grow fruits, such as melons, more successfully by providing protection against cold.

COLD FRAMES ARE ALSO USEFUL for providing shelter from the cold, and they don't cost as much to purchase or maintain as a greenhouse.

protected (see page 106). When using fleece be sure to erect a tent of canes around the plant to hold the fleece away from the blossom – if touching, it will allow the cold to penetrate through to the flowers.

Whichever method of frost protection you choose remember to use it only when frosts are forecast and the plant is in blossom. Many temperate fruits need exposure to cold weather to break their seasonal dormancy, and pollinating insects need to be able to access the flowers during the day.

Planning what to grow

Because most fruit crops will be in the ground for many years it's important to plan your fruit garden thoroughly – after all, you want it to be as productive and tailored to your tastes as possible. Space restrictions, continuity of supply, garden microclimates, and aesthetic design are all important considerations that shouldn't be rushed.

CAREFUL PLANNING WILL ALLOW YOU to harvest a steady supply of fruit for most months of the year, and it also helps avoid huge gluts of one particular crop.

Deciding what to grow

A good starting point when planning a fruit garden is to compile a list of what you do and don't want to grow yourself, and more importantly the quantity of these. For example, many people love dessert grapes, but to grow them yourself is quite time consuming and requires a large greenhouse. On the other hand, a few strawberry plants brought into a porch or cold frame in midwinter would provide you with a punnet of fresh berries when prices in the shops are high – indulgent but easy to achieve. Continuity of supply is important, too: don't choose fruit crops that all mature in early summer if they don't also store well. Also when choosing particular varieties of any one crop make sure that they have different harvest times, and that some, if possible, have good storage characteristics. For those that don't store well consider if they can be frozen or made into preserves. The yield of a crop can be difficult to estimate, so an approximate guide can be useful (see table, page 28).

Settling on a design

Fruit can take on many appearances in the garden or allotment. One of the big questions to ask is whether you want to integrate or isolate your fruiting plants. A fully isolated fruit garden can make an extremely attractive feature, but not many of us have the space to plant one. A mixed fruit and vegetable plot, or a potager incorporating cut flowers, herbs, and ornamental edging plants, might be a more achievable design. Alternatively, you might prefer to plant isolated fruit trees or bushes in your garden, positioning them in and among your ornamental plants so they blend into an overall design.

Arches and pergolas can all be made more decorative with the use of climbing fruits such as grapevines, kiwifruits, or black- and hybrid berries, whereas a wall or fence can be an ideal backdrop for a feature fan- or espalier-trained fruit tree. This ornamental value of fruit shouldn't be neglected. An established fan-trained cherry in full blossom or a pergola clad in a grapevine in full autumn colour is a beautiful feature in any garden.

Fruit production chart

Unless you have lots of grateful neighbours or a large freezer it can be frustrating to experience the gluts and dearths of a fruit garden's harvest. Careful planning at the outset and use of various storage methods can, however, keep these peaks and troughs to a minimum.

Crop	J	F	M	A	M	J	J	A	S	O	N	D	Freeze	Jam & Jelly	Dry	Yield
Apples	✿	✿	✿	✿				*	*	*✿	✿	✿	✕[1]	✕[2]	✕	9–13.5kg[t]
Pears	✿	✿	✿	✿				*	*	*✿	✿	✿	✕[1]		✕	9–13.5kg[t]
Quinces	✿	✿							*✿	✿	✿		✕[1]	✕	✕	9–13.5kg[t]
Medlars									✿	✿	✿			✕		13.5–18kg[t]
Plums						*	*						✕	✕	✕	9–27kg[t]
Damsons						*	*						✕	✕		9–13.5kg[t]
Gages						*	*						✕	✕	✕	9–22.5kg[t]
Bullaces							*	*					✕	✕		9–13.5kg[t]
Peaches						*	*	*					✕		✕	9–22.5kg[t]
Nectarines						*	*	*					✕		✕	9–22.5kg[t]
Apricots						*	*	*					✕		✕	9–18kg[t]
Cherries					*	*	*						✕	✕		9–22.5kg[t]
Citrus	*	*✿	✿						*	*			✕	✕	✕	2–7kg[t]
Figs							*	*					✕		✕	4.5–9kg[t]
Strawberries					*	*	*	*	*	*			✕	✕	✕	0.5–1kg[p]
Raspberries						*	*	*	*	*	*		✕	✕		1–1.5kg[p]
Blackberries							*	*	*				✕	✕		2kg[p]
Hybrid berries							*	*					✕	✕		2kg[p]
Mulberries							*	*					✕	✕		4.5kg[t]
Blueberries							*	*	*				✕	✕	✕	2–4.5kg[b]
Cranberries									*	*			✕	✕	✕	0.5kg[p]
Ligonberries									*	*			✕	✕	✕	0.5kg[p]
Kiwifruit									*	*✿	✿			✕	✕	2kg[v]
Blackcurrants							*	*					✕	✕		4.5kg[b]
Red currants							*	*					✕	✕		4.5kg[b]
White currants							*	*					✕	✕		4.5kg[b]
Gooseberries						*	*	*					✕	✕		3.5kg[b]
Grapes							*	*	*						✕	2–3.5kg[v]
Melons							*	*	*	*						2–3.5kg[v]
Almonds	✿								*	*✿	✿	✿				4.5–7kg[t]
Cobnuts	✿								*	*✿	✿	✿				4.5–7kg[t]
Filberts	✿								*	*✿	✿	✿				4.5–7kg[t]

* fresh from plant ✿ from storage [1] best when cooked first [2] use as a bulking/setting agent [t] per tree [p] per plant [b] per bush [v] per vine

Freezing Many fruits such as raspberries and currants freeze very well, and can be defrosted then used in their fresh state. Lay such fruits on a tray so they're not touching, then freeze them; once frozen, bag them up. Others fruits such as plums and gages can be frozen raw but are best cooked before eating, while yet others such as apples and pears are best frozen in their cooked state.

Preserves The majority of fruits make excellent jams and jellies. If doing this to use up a glut, don't wait until the fruits are over-ripe because this can impair their setting ability. However, adding fruits with a naturally high pectin content such as apples can assist setting, especially for fruits such as strawberries that contain low levels of this carbohydrate.

Drying Drying fruits is a very useful way to preserve them. The fruits once dehydrated can be used in cakes, breads, or similar foodstuffs, or eaten on their own as naturally sweet snack. A food dehydrator is ideal piece for this job – the slatted trays having warm air blown over them for a set period. Alternatively, use a domestic oven on its lowest setting, leaving the door slightly ajar.

Yield The expected yield given is for a mature, healthy plant. For tree fruits in particular the yield can be extremely variable depending on the training method chosen – for example, an apple bush will yield much more fruit than an apple cordon. Fruit yield is also very dependent on the year's weather. Consequently a figure has been provided only as a rough guide.

Practical considerations

The extent to which you want your fruit garden to be practical often comes down to the amount of time you want to spend maintaining it. While integrating fruit plants into ornamentally biased designs can look attractive, it takes far less time and effort to carry out pruning or pest and disease control if those fruits with similar cultivation needs are grouped together. A fruit cage is the ultimate way to keep birds and larger mammals away from your fruits, but it may not suit your garden's style or you may not have the space for one.

Growing acid-loving blueberries in pots may be the only option if you have a chalky soil, but when cultivated in this way such container-grown fruit will require much more frequent watering and feeding than those plants set in the open ground. The least effort can be achieved by working with what your plot has to offer in the way of soil and aspect. In order to determine this, you should draw a plan of shady and sunny aspects in your garden, along with an indication of soil conditions. You can then choose crops that will thrive with minimal effort in those areas and conditions.

Buying plants

Once you have decided which plants you want to grow in your garden the next step is to source them. There are many specialist fruit growers supplying an excellent range of fruit types and varieties both at the nursery and via mail order. The best time to plant up a new garden is in midautumn, when plants are able to root quickly into the warm, moist soil and have at least six months before the onset of hot, summer weather. Failing this, any time up until and including early spring will produce good results, bearing in mind that the later you plant the less time the fruit will have to establish before the summer.

Fruit can be purchased as: bare-root; containerized (lifted and planted in a pot); or container-grown (having spent its whole life in a pot). Bare-root plants are available to buy only between midautumn and midspring but they are much less expensive than potted plants and establish just as well if not better. This is ideal if you require large numbers of plants or are on a limited budget. They are occasionally sold

CONTAINER-GROWN PLANTS, such as this blackberry are more versatile as they can be planted at almost any time of year, but they are more expensive than bare-root plants.

as root-wrapped bundles – as with raspberry canes, for example. Plants in pots are more costly but they have the advantage that they can be planted at any time of year – useful if you need to plant in summer. However, they too will establish considerably better if planted between midautumn and midspring.

When choosing your fruit plants always check that varieties of the same crops are in compatible pollination groups, should cross-pollination be required for that particular variety to set fruit. Those with smaller plots should also opt for naturally dwarfing varieties or those grafted onto dwarfing rootstocks to restrict their final size.

A year in the fruit garden

If you own a productive fruit garden each month will bring its own set of jobs to complete. Pruning, feeding, watering, planting, training, and harvesting are activities that can bring immense satisfaction as you watch your efforts pay off. Unlike vegetable gardening where crops are cleared annually, the fruit garden matures over years, resulting in a continually productive plot.

Early spring

General
- Apply a mulch around fruit trees, nuts, and bushes as long as the ground isn't frozen.
- Control aphids on various fruits but don't spray when in blossom.
- Last chance to winter wash.
- Get on top of weed control if not done in late winter and continue through to summer.
- Repot or top-dress container-grown fruits if required.

Tree fruits
- Protect almond, peach, apricot, and nectarine blossom from frost, but make sure insects can access blooms or else hand pollinate flowers.
- Carry out formative pruning of newly planted stone fruits if the weather is dry.
- Protect cherry blossom from frost.
- Apply nitrogen feed to plums, cherries, cooking apples, and pears as they're hungry feeders.
- Switch to citrus summer feed.
- Increase watering of citrus as growth resumes.

Soft fruits
- Pollinate strawberry flowers under glass by brushing over them with your hands.
- Plant cranberries and lingonberries.
- Mulch raspberries, blueberries, cranberries, and lingonberries with well-rotted farmyard manure (not mushroom compost).
- Apply high nitrogen feed to blackcurrants.
- Prune blueberries.
- Apply sulphur chips to beds of blueberries, lingonberries, and cranberries if required.
- Plant cold-stored strawberry runners.
- Sow seeds of alpine strawberries.
- Untie canes of black- and hybrid berries that have been bundled together in cold districts for the winter, and train into arches before the buds burst.

Vine fruits
- Never prune grapevines in early spring to avoid sap "bleeding".

Nuts
- Prune cobnuts and filberts if this was not done in late winter.

ONCE THIS NEW BED of raspberry canes has been planted make sure you apply a mulch to keep down weeds, keep roots cool, and retain valuable soil moisture.

Midspring

General
- Avoid using insecticides on crops in flower.

Tree fruits
- Last chance to plant bare-root fruit trees, and ideally plant container-grown forms too.
- Liquid feed fruit trees in pots with a balanced feed.
- Graft fruit trees.
- Start applying apple and pear scab controls.
- Deal with aphids, apple sucker, pear sucker, pear midge, caterpillars, and powdery mildew.
- Protect plum and pear flowers from frost but allow insects to access them.
- Damp down or mist citrus regularly when flowering begins and maintain a minimum temperature of 14°C (57°F).

Soft fruits
- Deblossom spring-planted strawberries in their first year.
- Pick forced strawberries under heated glass (midspring onwards).

- Last chance to plant bare-root bushes so they can establish well before summer.
- Look out for glasshouse red spider mite and aphids on strawberries under glass.
- Ventilate strawberries under cloches so insects can access them and mulch with straw.
- Start treating American gooseberry mildew.

Vine fruits
- Sow indoor melon seeds, one per 7.5cm (3in) pot in a heated propagator.
- Raise indoor grapevine rods once leaf buds have burst.

Late spring

General
- Avoid using insecticides on crops when they are in flower.
- Pull off suckers appearing around the base of fruit and nut trees.
- Make sure fruits aren't drought stressed at this time of year, especially those in containers, against a wall, or newly planted.
- Make sure bees can access caged and cloched fruit flowers.
- Keep an ear out for late frost forecasts and protect blossom as necessary.

Tree fruits
- Liquid feed fruit trees growing in pots with a balanced feed.
- Get a fruit specialist to ring-bark overvigorous fruit trees.
- Remove lean-to frost protection from fan-trained peaches, nectarines, apricots, and almonds.
- Control plum sawfly one week after petal-fall.
- Be aware of cherry run-off (see page 116).
- Remove wayward shoots on fan-trained trees and tie in better placed ones.
- Deal with apple sawfly and capsid bug, prevent blossom wilt if it struck last year.
- Deal with pear and cherry slugworm.
- Erect codling moth traps.

Soft fruits
- Deal with spur blight, cane spot, and cane blight on raspberries and black- and hybrid berries.
- Pick forced strawberries under heated glass.

BARE-ROOT FRUIT TREES AND BUSHES, like this red currant, need to be planted by midspring at the latest so they can establish properly before summer.

- Pick strawberries forced under cloches.
- Put slug control and then straw around outdoor strawberries.
- Plant out alpine strawberry seedlings sown in early spring.
- Get bird protection in place for all soft fruit.
- Thin out raspberry shoots.
- Deal with raspberry leaf and bud mite and raspberry rust from now on.
- Thin gooseberries if you want large fruits.
- Deblossom strawberry runners planted this spring.
- Water blueberries, cranberries, and lingonberries with rainwater regularly.

Vine fruits
- Take softwood cuttings of kiwifruits.
- Tie in leading and sideshoots of kiwifruits.
- Remove any winter protection from figs and carry out pruning.
- Move growing bags into greenhouses to warm up two weeks before planting indoor melons, and water well two days before planting.
- Plant indoor melons into growing bags in heated greenhouses.
- Sow outdoor melons individually in 7.5cm (3in) pots in a heated propagator.
- Gently run your hand over indoor grapevine flowers to pollinate them.

Early summer

General
- Make sure fruits aren't drought stressed at this time of year, especially those in pots, growing against a wall, or newly planted.

Tree fruits
- Change feed for pot-grown fruit trees to a high potash liquid one.
- Move citrus outside for the summer months.
- Thin out citrus fruits to leave the strongest dozen or so.
- Carry on training fan-trained trees.
- Net cherries against birds.
- Prevent the skin splitting on ripening cherries by erecting polythene covers over the trees (see page 57).
- Pick early cherries.
- Thin pears, plums, peaches, apricots, and nectarines.
- Deal with fruit tree red spider mite, codling moth, and plum moth.
- Thin apples at the end of the month.
- Look out for "shothole"(see page 61) – a sign of possible disease infection.

Soft fruits
- Pick outdoor strawberries, early raspberries, red and white currants, and gooseberries.
- Peg down runners of strawberries.
- Train in new shoots of black- and hybrid berries.
- Summer prune red and white currants and gooseberries.
- Remove cloches from outdoor strawberries once cropped.
- Shorten newly planted raspberry canes once new shoots are produced.
- Move forced strawberries outdoors.
- Deal with raspberry beetle, glasshouse red spider mite, and grey mould.
- Water cranberries, lingonberries, and blueberries with rainwater regularly.

Vine fruits
- Summer prune kiwifruits.
- Summer prune indoor grapes.
- Pinch prune figs.
- Water and feed indoor melons daily once they are established.

- Deal with glasshouse red spider mite and whitefly on indoor melons.
- Transplant outdoor melons under cloches, pinching out the growing point.
- Thin out fruits of indoor grapevines if large dessert grapes are required.

Midsummer

General
- Protect heavy fruit tree and bush branches against snapping.

Tree fruits
- Deal with woolly aphid, plum rust, pear leaf blister mite, and pear rust.
- Liquid feed fruit trees in containers with a high potash feed.
- Pick cherries, peaches, apricots, and nectarines.
- Hang wasp traps around the branches of peaches, nectarines, and apricots.

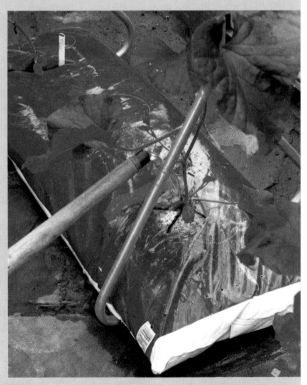

NEWLY PLANTED INDOOR MELONS should be watered only lightly to keep the compost just moist. Once a healthy root system has established you can give plants much more water.

JUST BEFORE CHERRIES START TO RIPEN, erect some netting over the fruits to protect against birds. A frame is best as netting can be kept taut; this stops birds getting caught up in it, but you should still check it regularly.

- Check tree ties as tree trunk girth increases.
- Prune cherries straight after harvest.

Soft fruits
- Pick strawberries, gooseberries, currants, blueberries, lingonberries, and raspberries.
- Complete summer pruning of gooseberries and red/white currants.
- Tip-layer new black- and hybrid berry canes.
- Trim over lingonberries as soon as they have been harvested.
- Take semiripe cuttings of cranberries and lingonberries.
- Watch out for and remedy raspberry chlorosis.
- Water cranberries, lingonberries, and blueberries regularly with rainwater.

Vine fruits
- Summer prune outdoor grapes.
- Summer prune kiwifruits if not done last month.
- Remove the lower sideshoots of indoor melons up to a height of 30cm (12in).
- Fertilize female indoor melon flowers, then pinch out 2cm (¾in) beyond the flower.
- Pinch out the growing point of outdoor melons twice, at four-week intervals.

- Water and feed outdoor melons regularly once established.

Late summer

General
- Continue to provide support for heavy tree and bush fruit branches as fruits swell.

Tree fruits
- Summer prune sideshoots on restricted trees to 3–4 leaves to form fruiting spurs.
- Liquid feed fruit trees in pots with a high potash feed.
- Festoon young tree shoots while they are still flexible.
- Pick early apples and pears.
- Summer prune restricted apples and pears.
- Deal with apple leaf miner.
- Prune nectarines, apricots, and peaches after they have fruited.
- Prune plums, gages, and damsons immediately after harvest.
- Deal with brown rot on tree fruits.
- Pick plums, damsons, and gages.
- Hang wasp traps around apples, plums, damsons, and gages.

Soft fruits
- Loosely tie together new black- and hybrid berry canes.
- Remove straw and old leaves and tidy up strawberries after fruiting.
- Prune out fruited summer raspberry canes and tie in new ones.
- Plant out rooted strawberry runners.
- Water cranberries, lingonberries, and blueberries regularly with rainwater.
- Pick perpetual strawberries.
- Pick black- and hybrid berries, blueberries, raspberries, gooseberries, and currants.

Vine fruits
- Harvest figs and early grapes.
- Protect grapes from wasps.
- Thin out indoor melon fruits to four per plant and remove the main growing tip.
- Support indoor melon fruits as they swell with tights or netting.

- Hand pollinate female outdoor melon flowers, pinching out the shoot 2cm (¾in) beyond the flower, then thin to four fruits per plant once set.
- Deal with powdery mildew on indoor and on outdoor melons.

Nuts
- "Brut" new shoots on cobnuts and filberts (see page 213).

Early autumn

General
- Order new, certified nuts, fruit trees, canes, and bushes.

Tree fruits
- Prepare your fruit store (or fridge) for apples, pears, quinces, and medlars.
- Last chance to prune stone fruit immediately after harvest.
- Lay medlars in a tray and place in the fruit store to "blet".
- Remove sap drawers or secondary flushes of growth from restricted tree forms.
- Control against bacterial canker at the end of the month.
- Hang wasp traps around apples, plums, damsons, and gages.
- Finish tying in shoots on wall-trained fan trees.
- Pick apples, plums, damsons, gages, pears, quinces, and medlars.

Soft fruits
- Order cold stored strawberry runners for delivery in winter.
- Harvest cranberries.
- Continue planting new strawberry beds.
- Pick autumn raspberries from now until the first frosts.
- Cut out old canes of black- and hybrid berries after fruiting and tie in new ones, or bundle these together in very cold districts.
- Prune blackcurrants.
- Pick perpetual strawberries.

Vine fruits
- Harvest kiwifruits and figs.
- Spur prune kiwifruits after harvest.
- Harvest grapes.

- Protect grapes from wasps.
- Harvest indoor melons once fruits smell ripe.

Nuts
- Harvest almonds, cobnuts, and filberts and store in a dry, cool, rodent-free shed or garage.
- Prune almonds immediately after harvesting.

Midautumn

General
- Prepare the ground for new fruit trees, nuts, vines, canes, and bushes.
- Store only those fruits and nuts in that are in sound condition.

Tree fruits
- Don't store apples and pears together.
- Switch to citrus winter feed.
- Remove damaged stems from stone fruits and paint the wounds.
- Move citrus under frost-free glass for winter and reduce watering to keep almost dry.
- Go to apple tasting days and order stock from fruit nurseries.
- Check rootstocks and pollination groups before ordering fruit trees.
- Control winter moth with grease bands.
- Pick apples, pears, medlars, and quinces.

SUPPORT INDOOR MELONS as they swell because individual fruits are quite heavy. Once ripe, fruits will fall from the vine (unless you pick them first) so it also helps avoid disaster!

Soft fruits

- Trim over cranberry beds.
- Detach layered cranberries and replant.
- Order your new raspberry stock this month, making sure they're certified.
- Plant cranberries and lingonberries.
- Take cuttings of blueberries, currants, and gooseberries and dig up rooted layers of black- and hybrid berries.
- Cover perpetual strawberries with cloches to extend season.
- Pick autumn raspberries.

Vine fruits

- Harvest the last grapes.
- Harvest outdoor melons once the fruits smell ripe.

Late autumn

General

- Take delivery of and plant fruit trees, nuts, canes, vines, and bushes.
- Remove any rotten fruits and nuts in store.

AUTUMN IS A TIME when many fruits ripen, their high sugar levels attracting wasps. Pick up fruits rather than leaving them on the ground, and hang wasp traps near by.

Tree fruits

- Spray against peach leaf curl and bacterial canker.
- Complete picking of apples and pears.
- Renovate fruit trees.
- Watch out for apple and pear canker.
- Erect rabbit control around fruit trees.
- Check that tree ties and stakes are secure.
- Root prune overvigorous fruit trees.
- Prune apples, pears, medlars, and quinces.
- Put humming tape in plums if bullfinches are a problem.

Soft fruits

- Pick autumn raspberries and cover with fleece.
- Complete strawberry bed planting.
- Pack away netting and fruit cage protection.
- Erect supports for new raspberries.
- Tidy up beds of perpetual strawberries.
- Prune red/white currants and gooseberries.
- Put humming tape in gooseberries if bullfinches are a problem.

Vine fruits

- Erect winter protection for figs or bring under cover.
- Winter prune indoor and outdoor grapes.
- Carefully remove the old, loose bark of indoor vines to deter overwintering pests.
- Take hardwood cuttings of grapes and kiwifruit.

Early winter

General

- Heel in plants if the soil is too wet. If frozen put in pots in a frost-free place and ensure the roots don't dry out.
- Take delivery of and plant nuts, fruit trees, and bushes.
- Deal with rodent damage on any stored fruits and nuts.
- Remove any rotten stored fruit.

Tree fruits

- Harvest citrus fruits once mature.
- Deal with apple and pear canker.
- Deal with bitter pit on stored apples.
- Thin out congested spurs of restricted fruit trees.
- Tie in new tiers of espaliers.
- Prune apples, pears, quinces, and medlars.

Soft fruits
- Prune autumn raspberries.
- Prune red and white currants and gooseberries.

Midwinter

General
- Apply winter washes to fruit trees and bushes.
- Take delivery of and plant nuts, fruit trees, and bushes if the soil isn't frozen.
- Apply a top-dressing of sulphate of potash to all fruits and nuts.

Tree fruits
- Keep checking stored fruits and remove rotten ones.
- Erect a lean-to over peaches, almonds, apricots, and nectarines, or place pot-grown fruits in an unheated greenhouse.
- Ensure tree stakes and ties are firm and sound.
- Spray against peach leaf curl.
- Check apples and pears for canker and prune out.
- Harvest citrus fruits once mature.
- Prune apples, pears, quinces, and medlars if no harsh frosts are forecast.

Soft fruits
- Prune currants and gooseberries.
- Prune autumn raspberries if not done last month.
- Prune gooseberries and red/white currants if no harsh frosts are forecast.

Vine fruits
- Lower indoor grapevine stems for even bud-break.

Late winter

General
- Take delivery of and plant nuts, fruit trees, and bushes if the soil isn't frozen.
- Apply a top dressing of sulphate of potash to all fruits and nuts if not done last month.
- Clear ground under trees and bushes of weeds.

Tree fruits
- Remove any rotten stored fruit.
- Protect almond, peach, apricot, and nectarine blossom from frost, but make sure insects can access blooms.
- Spray against peach leaf curl for a second time.

ONCE FRUITED, AUTUMN RASPBERRY canes can be cut back to ground level with secateurs or loppers. New canes will appear in spring and these will fruit in late summer and autumn.

- Untie festooned fruit tree branches that have set into position.
- Prune citrus.
- Harvest citrus fruits once mature.
- Last chance to winter prune apples, pears, medlars, and quinces.

Soft fruits
- Move some pot-grown strawberries under heated glass for an early, forced crop.
- Cover soil-grown strawberries with cloches.
- Last chance to prune established autumn raspberries.
- Prune newly planted raspberries back to 30cm (12in) if not done already.
- Tip back summer raspberry canes to 15cm (6in) above their top support wire.
- Last chance to prune red/white currants and gooseberries.

Nuts
- Prune cobnuts and filberts once their catkins are fully open.

Preparing for planting

It's tempting to hastily plant up a fruit garden if you are eager to get plants established, but this can bring long-term disadvantages if the site isn't prepared properly beforehand. Problems such as weed control, poor soil structure, and low fertility are all much easier to remedy before your crops are planted, and this will help guarantee that your efforts are rewarded.

Tackling the weeds

The way to deal with weeds in a fruit garden depends on whether you are starting with a completely virgin plot of land or are inheriting a fruit garden with a new house or allotment.

Coping with a new plot

While weed growth can be dealt with as soon as vegetable crops are lifted, the more permanent nature of most fruit crops makes this opportunity rare. So if you are starting from scratch ensure your site is as free of weeds as possible before planting. Target perennial weeds such as ground elder, bindweed, and brambles first as these take the most time to eradicate. Brambles, nettles, dandelions, docks, and ground elder can successfully be dug out with a fork, but deep-rooted perennials such as bindweed, Japanese knotweed, and horsetail are best treated with a glyphosate-based herbicide between early and midsummer, when in full growth. Plastic sheet mulches are useful for clearing large areas if you prefer an organic approach, but these need to be in place for three or four years to clear the more persistent perennials. Only rotovate a new plot if it is free from perennial weeds, because most can quickly multiply from small root fragments.

Inheriting a fruit garden

The disadvantage of inherited weed problems should be weighed against the advantage of gaining a

---

REPLANT DISEASE

If you have inherited an established fruit garden and want to carry out some new plantings, or if you are taking on a cleared allotment that used to support fruit crops, you need to consider the possibility of replant problems. Many fruit crops are closely related, and if a new fruit is planted in a position that has recently grown a crop belonging to the same plant family (eg, a plum followed by a cherry) then the new plant may fail to develop a sufficiently strong root system in order to thrive. This is caused by a build-up in the soil of chronically harmful fungi, bacteria, and pests. If possible avoid planting new crops on sites where related ones once grew. If this is impossible the addition of plenty of organic matter, along with a root inoculant containing beneficial fungi, should limit the ill-effects. Ideally plant a pot-grown replacement specimen with a sturdy root system.

---

healthy, well-trained, mature fruiting plant. Again, target perennial weeds first, either digging them out or spot treating them with glyphosate. Annual weeds and weed seedlings can be scorched off with a contact herbicide or flame gun; hoeing these weeds is difficult because the shallow roots of established fruit plants can be damaged in the process.

WEIGHTED DOWN sheet mulches clear weeds without chemicals. Don't use old carpet as it can leach toxins into the soil.

USE A FORK to remove the roots of most perennial weeds from the ground.

A FLAME GUN easily kills off weed seedlings without disturbing the soil underneath them.

INCORPORATE A COMPOST HEAP into your kitchen garden if it is at all possible to make the space available. The woody prunings produced by fruit trees and bushes is an excellent companion to soft, sappy vegetable waste such as these pea stems.

IF YOUR SOIL HAS A GOOD STRUCTURE there's no need to add lots of organic matter to a planting hole.

Improving your soil

Because fruit gardens need less intensive cultivation than vegetable plots, the soil does not have to be quite so rigorously improved before planting, as long as issues such as poor drainage have been dealt with. The extensive addition of organic matter and the deconsolidating effect of double digging can cause these perennial plants long-term problems because the soil can slump over time, resulting in potential waterlogging, so should be avoided unless you inherit a plot with severely compacted soil. It is extremely unlikely that you will need to double dig a new site before planting it with fruit.

Single digging, where the ground is dug over to a spade's depth, is generally sufficient because the majority of fruit tree and bush roots are found in the top 20cm (8in) of soil. To single dig a new bed, start by digging a trench a spade's depth and moving the excavated soil to the far end of the bed. Then dig a second trench behind the first, placing its soil back in the first trench and breaking it up with a fork in the process. Repeat these steps until the whole bed has been dug. Finally, fill in the last trench with the soil excavated from the first one.

Any materials added to the soil should be of a pH preferred by the crop to be planted; for example, mushroom compost, which contains a certain amount of lime, can be incorporated into beds destined to support most fruit crops, such as apples, pears, cherries, and peaches. However, it shouldn't be added to beds for acid-lovers such as blueberries, lingonberries, cranberries, and raspberries.

Once compacted zones of soil have been remedied by single digging, you can then incorporate small quantities of organic matter into the soil. However, ample bulky organic matter should be dug into the soil prior to planting in some instances: for example, where the ground is severely compacted, or on a very heavy clay, a very light sandy soil, or thin chalky one. This should take the form of something substantial, such as composted bark, rather than garden compost, which will rot down very quickly and so have limited positive effects on soil structure.

Understanding soil fertility

Soil fertility refers not only to the amount of nutrients a soil contains but also to the ground's general health. Just one teaspoon of healthy soil will contain thousands of fungi, bacteria, and other microorganisms, all of which are essential in maintaining a balanced plot able to support plant growth. Provided your soil isn't compacted, extremely acid, or very alkaline its fertility should be perfectly adequate for a fruit garden.

Most soils tend to be naturally fertile so don't need any additional materials, but sandy and shallow chalky soils will benefit more from the addition of organic matter to enable them to hold onto nutrients. Also, a heavily cultivated piece of land could be devoid of certain nutrients so it's useful to research its history. An allotment bed previously supporting blackcurrants would be low in nitrogen for example, because these plants have a heavy demand for this nutrient. The addition of specific nutrients is something that should be addressed when you begin planting particular crops – each having its own requirement. These are dealt with under individual crop headings.

USE OF FERTILIZERS

Gardeners can use organic (plant- or animal-derived) fertilizers, such as farmyard manure or garden compost, or artificial (man-made) fertilizers. In the fruit garden, these are important resources that shouldn't be wasted. Once your fruit garden has become established it can be tempting to routinely apply fertilizers on an annual basis. While there's a need to replace nutrients lost by intensive cropping, surplus nutrients can cause root scorching and ground water pollution.

Crops that are heavily pruned, such as autumn raspberries or those with heavy yields like cooking apples, may require additional feeding, but provided growth is healthy and yields adequate for your needs don't automatically reach for the fertilizer packet each year.

WAIT UNTIL YOU HAVE DECIDED what crops to grow before applying fertilizers – if at all.

Growing your own

- How to plant fruit
- Basic pruning
- Coping with problems

Carol's fruit notebook

" Caring for your fruit trees and bushes can become a truly engrossing activity. The amount of care and attention you lavish on them can be much more than you would give to any perennial or even to the most prized ornamental shrub or tree in the garden. The promise of fruit seems to justify the lengths you are willing to go to obtain a crop. It also seems to focus the will to help the tree, bush or vine reach its full productive and aesthetic potential.

To start on the right foot, plant your fruit plant with lots of care and thoroughness, indulge it even, because this could be the start of a long and fulfilling relationship. If the planting situation is favourable and the plant is naturally vigorous, you could just leave it. Yet, if you can, you should actively guide it through its life. Pruning will not only shape it decoratively but will also harness and encourage its vigour. Such intervention will be rewarded with better cropping as well as contribute greatly to overall health, and a strong, healthy plant is much better able to resist viruses, infections, wounds, and the depredations of insects. Prevention is much better than the cure.

I garden organically and would only want to eat fruit that has had no toxic poisons in or around it. Successful organic gardening, however, depends on a system of natural checks and balances being established and operational – the opportunist attentions of one organism being limited by the attentions of another one. Everything is interlinked and nothing can really be sorted in isolation. Sometimes you have to be tolerant if the "wrong sort" of insects take up residence. I rely on protecting crops by physical means, such as netting to deter birds, fleece to cover blossom, and picking off insects by hand, but you have to be vigilant and regular, frequent even, in doing this. Once you have done all you can, the rest is up to the weather and the bees. **"**

How to plant fruit

It is essential to give fruit trees a good start in life. Planting is the most important stage of successful fruit growing. Get it right and a tree, shrub, or vine should provide you with abundant, tasty crops and stunning blossom displays for years to come. But if a plant is placed badly or in the wrong soil or conditions it will struggle to survive.

Planting tree fruit

The best type of trees for planting are bare-root fruit trees, as they have healthier root systems. Bare-root trees should be kept well watered until ready for planting, which should occur as soon as they reach your home. The ideal time to plant is in autumn when the soil is still warm from summer. Containerized plants, however, are available to buy and plant year-round. These will need extra watering if planted in summer.

Planting a cordon tree

Growing apples and pears as a cordon is a great way of training a range of different fruit varieties that can be packed into a tiny space. All that is required is a sheltered wall or fence with a system of three horizontal, galvanized wires spaced 60cm (24in) apart and attached to vine eyes with straining bolts.

Fruit trees always do best if they are planted at an angle – when they are known as oblique cordons. This slows up the vigour of a tree, encouraging it to form fruit spurs and buds spread equally along the trunk. If planted as a vertical cordon, it is tricky to prevent most of the growth appearing towards the top of the plant, and the wall or fence needs to be much higher in order to support such extra growth.

Cordons need to be on dwarfing rootstocks, which restrict the size of the tree. It also forces the tree to crop a year or two earlier than normal, and keeps it compact. The rootstock for apples is usually 'M26' or

for pears 'Quince C'. Also for cordons, choose varieties that develop spurs readily, such as the apple 'Spartan', and avoid those that are prone to producing lots of tip-bearing shoots.

Oblique cordons

Cordons to be grown at an angle should be planted 70cm (28in) apart. Dig a hole to accommodate the root system – in a spot 10–15cm (4–6in) away from the fence or wall. If there is any compacted soil beneath the ground, break this up using a fork or mattock. Incorporate organic matter such as well-rotted manure with the spoil from the hole and mix it together with controlled-release fertilizer.

Angle the tree's trunk at 30–45 degrees to the ground, making sure that the graft union is above ground level and the scion part of the union is not in contact with the soil so it cannot take root. The union joint is also stronger this way with less chance of the tree snapping.

As you are planting at an angle, some of the roots may be above ground. Cut these back and spread the rest out in the hole, ensuring that the soil will cover all the roots when planted. Firm the soil in around the plant using finger tips. Water in the tree and mulch around it with well-rotted manure.

Attach the tree to a cane using chain-lock ties and then fix this to the wires at 30–45 degrees. On long, spindly trees, lightly prune back the leader to encourage laterals or fruiting spurs along the trunk.

PLANTING A BARE-ROOT TREE

1 DIG OUT A HOLE wide and deep enough to accommodate the root system. Hammer in a strong stake.

2 PLACE A STICK across the hole to ensure that the tree is at the depth at which it was previously planted.

3 BACKFILL THE HOLE, firming the soil around the roots using the tips of your fingers. Water in well.

Planting soft fruits

There is a huge range of soft fruit that can be grown in the garden. If your garden has poor soil, don't despair as most fruit can be grown in pots. Blackberries and raspberries share similar soil requirements, but blackberries are usually planted on their own rather than in rows because of their vigour.

Gooseberry and red and white currants

There are many different methods of training gooseberries, and red and white currants; vertical cordons, standards, fans, and step-overs are all suitable for a north-facing wall. However, the most popular way is to grow them as open-centred bushes on top of a short leg. Varieties vary in vigour and therefore size, but each bush will need about 1.5m (5ft) between each plant. Before planting, water the plants well and dig over the soil if it is compacted.

Check over the plant and rub out any buds that are appearing on the leg. Dig out a hole that is about twice the width of the rootball and the same depth. Mix the soil from the hole into well-rotted organic matter and controlled-release fertilizer at the rate that is recommended on the label.

Plant at the same depth as the bush was grown previously in the nursery. Use a planting stick placed across the hole to check the level. When correct, backfill the hole, firming down the soil around the roots as you go.

MULCHING

After planting, a fruit tree should be mulched with a generous amount of well-rotted manure around the base of the plant, but do make sure that the mulch is kept away from the trunk to prevent it rotting. Mulching helps to retain moisture and should suppress some weeds. Its gradual breakdown into the soil is a useful soil conditioner. Most fruit trees benefit from regular mulching each year in early spring. If applied any earlier in the season it can be washed away before it has any chance to be effective.

Prune the plant immediately after planting, removing branches crossing into the centre of the bush and cutting back leaders by about two-thirds and laterals back to two buds. Water the plant in well and mulch with well-rotted garden compost or bark chippings.

Planting raspberries and blackberries

Prepare raspberry beds, which should be well drained, a month or two before planting. On heavy, compacted soils plant raspberries in raised beds. Alternatively, create planting ridges in which good topsoil mixed with organic matter is raked into a ridge along where the canes are to be planted.

Dig over the soil, incorporating organic matter into the soil before raking it level and leaving it to settle. Summer-fruiting raspberries will need posts and

PLANTING A CONTAINER-GROWN BUSH FRUIT

1 DIG OUT A HOLE about twice the width of the rootball and to the depth of the pot. Loosen soil at the bottom.

2 TEASE OUT THE ROOTS. Then, using a planting stick, ensure the top of the rootball is level with the ground.

3 FIRM DOWN the soil with the ball of your foot and water in well so the soil can settle around the rootball.

wires to support the canes, and these should be in place prior to planting (see page 145).

Allow about 1.8m (6ft) between rows of summer-fruiting raspberries, which should ideally be planted in late autumn (see page 54). Raspberries benefit from shallow planting at approximately 5cm (2in) depth, because deep planting reduces the production of new canes. Place the individual canes 30–40cm (12–16in) apart within the rows. Spread the roots over the planting hole to encourage the plants to send out suckers that will become next year's crop.

After planting, prune each cane back to about 30cm (12in) above ground level, to encourage it to send up suckers. Finally water in the plant and mulch over the planting area with well-rotted manure.

ADD PLENTY OF ORGANIC MATTER one to two months prior to planting raspberries. Plant canes 30–40cm (12–16in) apart and at a depth of only about 5cm (2in).

STAKING

Any fruit tree that is to be planted in the open ground, as opposed to against a wall or fence, will require staking to ensure that it stays upright and is able to carry a crop of heavy fruit. Use treated, round stakes – it is harder to tie a tree tightly to a square stake and the corners can damage the tree.

Although there is a fashion among ornamental gardeners for stakes angled at 45 degrees, they can look cumbersome and untidy if planting a row of fruit trees. They can also be a trip hazard if hidden among flower beds. Upright stakes are far easier to get close to the root system, and as most trees are planted bare-root it is easier to get the stake into the right position. A 45-degree stake is always needed for containerized plants so the rootball is not damaged. Such an angled stake is usually driven into the ground after planting, while an upright one should be inserted in the ground prior to planting. Both types of stake should be positioned on the side from which the prevailing wind comes. This is to prevent the tree from being blown onto the stake and so damaged.

On a spindle tree it is essential that the upright stake is as tall as the eventual height of the tree, which may eventually reach 2.5m (8ft). Such a tree requires two tree ties – one placed about half way

up the tree and another about two-thirds from the top of the tree.

Bush and standard trees require a shorter stake, usually reaching to just below the crown (or top four or five buds on a maiden whip). It should be tied close to the top of the stake.

Use tree ties with padding to prevent the tree from rubbing against the stake. A pair of tights can be a useful, cheaper alternative because they are flexible and will also cushion the tree from the stake. String or stretchy elastic should only be used for tying in new growth and should be removed each year. Tree ties should never be overtight. Check them each winter and loosen if necessary.

A FIGURE-OF-EIGHT TIE allows the tree trunk to expand without being strangled.

Planting strawberries

This popular fruit can easily be cultivated in tiny spaces by using containers and planters. The trailing habit of a strawberry plant makes it a wonderful subject for a hanging basket outside a kitchen window. Planting in a container saves the need for weeding a strawberry bed, and placing straw down each year between the plants. Slugs find the fruits harder to reach, and it is far easier to throw a net over a container to stop birds from eating the fruit than it is to put a cage over a large strawberry bed. Growing strawberries in a container is also a good idea for people with poor soil conditions.

Towers and barrels with holes in them are a wonderful space-saving device for a small garden. They vary in size, but 25–60 strawberry plants can be packed into these vertical spaces. Such towers and barrels are usually made from plastic or wood, although strawberries can be grown in any container so long as there is adequate drainage.

Strawberries grown in containers will need frequent watering. They should also be given a liquid feed with high potash content once a week .

Hanging baskets
Place the hanging basket on a old bucket or similar container, so it is stable while being planted up. Prepare the basket for strawberries by first punching a few drainage holes in its polythene liner. Then make up a special potting compost by combining two-thirds general-purpose potting compost and one-third John Innes No 3. Use this mixture to fill the hanging basket almost to the top of the basket.

Insert five strawberry plants into the compost close to the edges of the basket, spacing them out evenly and firming the roots in well. Water in the plants thoroughly and then hang the finished basket up in a sheltered, warm position well above head height.

Growing bags
Cultivating strawberries in purpose-made bags filled with specialized compost not only gives them the correct soil but also cuts out back-breaking weeding and hoeing because the bags can be placed on a strong table. Each growing bag can accommodate up to eight strawberry plants.

Strawberries in a planter
The traditional method of growing strawberries is in a terracotta planter with cupped planting pockets.

Fill the bottom of the planter with broken crocks, rubble, or bricks. Using the same special potting compost mix as for hanging baskets (see left), fill the planter with compost up to the lowest tier of cupped pockets. From the outside, push the strawberries through each lower hole and firm the roots into the compost. Then add more compost up to the next tier of pockets. Continue this planting process until the compost is near the top of the planter. Depending on the size of the planter, plant three to five strawberry plants in the top and firm in. Place the container on bricks so it drains freely and water the plants in well.

PLANTING STRAWBERRIES IN A GROWING BAG

1 MAKE SIX PLANTING HOLES in the surface of the bag. Use a knife to cut a cross and then fold back the flaps.

2 REDUCE A LARGE ROOT SYSTEM by about half, using a pair of sharp secateurs. This won't damage the plants.

3 DIG OUT A HOLE large enough to fit each plant, ensuring the crown is just above the surface. Water in well.

ALL FRUIT TREES can successfully be grown in containers. However, they will need watering each day during the growing season.

Trees in pots

Any fruit tree can be grown in a pot, so no matter how small your garden is you can be dazzled by a spectacular display of blossom in spring and later tasty home-produce direct from your garden. Containerizing plants is also a particularly useful method for people with poor soil (or even no soil). The pot will restrict the size of the tree, making it suitable for a small garden or courtyard.

Apples are usually the most popular choice for container-grown fruit trees, but for these you will need two trees that flower at the same time to help with pollination (see page 16). The most suitable apple rootstock for pot culture is 'M26'.

Planting in a container
Because it will be very heavy once filled, move the pot to its final position before potting up the plant. This should be sunny and sheltered, and the pot should be set on bricks to aid drainage. Also place crocks in the bottom of the pot, for drainage.

CARING FOR CONTAINER-GROWN TREES

Plant the tree up in a larger pot each year for the first three or four years as it increases in height. The eventual size of the container can be as large as you want.

A fruit tree in a pot will need daily watering during dry periods in the growing season.

Once the tree starts to flower, it will also require a liquid feed each week with high potash (such as tomato food) until the fruit begins to ripen.

Some trees may require staking or another form of support to help them carry the fruit crop. Don't let the tree overcrop because this will stress it owing to its restricted root system.

Repotting
Once established, a fruit tree will need to be repotted every two years.

Lie the pot down on its side and gently ease out the tree. Scrape away any excess soil from the rootball and use a knife to cut through any roots that appear to be restricting growth. Over the crocks at the bottom of the container, put fresh potting compost comprising John Innes No 3 mixed with slow-release fertilizer.

Place the tree back in the container, working fresh compost down the sides and around the roots. Finally apply a light top-dressing of well-rotted manure, keeping it away from the trunk, and water the plant in well.

Mix a loam-based potting compost such as John Innes No 3 with some controlled-release fertilizer in a large bucket or wheelbarrow and place some of the mix in the pot. Then set the tree in the pot; if the roots are too long for the pot, trim them with secateurs. Making sure that the graft union is level with the top of the pot, start to backfill with the compost mix, firming the soil around the roots and into the sides of the container. Leave about 2cm (¾in) between the rim and the top of the compost.

Insert a stake at a 45-degree angle, and tie it to the tree trunk. Mulch, then water the plant in well.

Basic pruning

Most fruit trees will benefit from an annual removal of branches to encourage vigour and healthy fruit, even though such pruning can appear brutal to the uninitiated. Always make sure that your pruning equipment is sharp to ensure clean, smooth cuts. Once the few basic rules have been mastered, pruning should be a pleasure.

Aims of pruning

Regular pruning is an essential part of fruit care if your trees are to be productive and look good all year round. There are four main reasons for pruning:

Firstly, it removes dead, dying, and diseased parts of the tree or shrub, which could spread if left alone.

Secondly, by removing some of the branches, pruning allows air and sunlight into a plant, and this is essential for the development of fruit and to avoid dense canopies in which fungal diseases thrive. Pruning branches growing close together also prevents them rubbing against each other, causing open wounds, which can become infected.

Furthermore, pruning improves the physical look of a tree or shrub, making it appear cared for. This is particularly important during the early, formative stages of a fruit tree's life.

Finally, suckers or double leaders need to be removed so that the tree grows into the shape that you want.

Effects of pruning

Because pruning stimulates growth, vigorous trees should only be given a light trim to avoid an excessive reaction. Alternatively instead of pruning, the branches can be festooned, that is, trained downwards towards a horizontal position to encourage fruiting instead of vigorous growth (see page 78). Trees lacking in vigour should be pruned back hard to stimulate more growth.

Traditionally pruning cuts were always sealed over with wound paint. However, research shows that trees recover better when wounds are left unpainted. The paint can sometimes seal in infections and can also inhibit the tree's natural ability to callus over the pruning cuts.

When to prune

Apple and pear trees were traditionally pruned during winter, a convenient time when it was otherwise quiet on the fruit farm. It is also easier to see the shape of the tree when it is leafless, and free standing trees are still pruned in winter for this reason. However, pruning restricted forms of apples and pears in late summer is becoming popular. Not

only is the weather more pleasant but vigorous trees put on less growth when pruned at this time of year. It can also help to prevent biennial fruiting (fruiting every two years).

Stone fruits such as cherries, peaches, plums, and apricots should always be pruned when the plant is in growth. This is to avoid disease problems that enter pruning cuts made in the dormant season.

Tools

Secateurs
These should be used for thinning out fruit spurs and cutting branches no thicker than 2cm (¾in) in diameter, or about the width of your little finger. A good, sharp pair is essential for making clean cuts. Bypass secateurs are the best type as they make a clean cut rather like a pair of scissors. Avoid anvil secateurs as these tend to crush the branch.

Pruning saws
On branches that are too thick for secateurs, use a pruning saw. This is long and narrow so its blade will fit between the narrow angles made by branches. Bow and panel saws should be used only to cut up large pieces of wood once they have been removed from the tree.

THE TOOLS OF THE TRADE: you need loppers, a pruning saw, a knife, a pair of secateurs, and a pair of thick gloves for effective and safe pruning.

Extended saw

Sometimes called a pole saw or long-armed saw, the extended saw is useful for cutting branches above head height. It is far safer to prune from the ground and therefore an extended saw is a better option than climbing a ladder and using a shorter saw. Always wear a hard hat and goggles when using this tool.

Loppers

These are useful for chopping up prunings once they have been removed from the tree and can occasionally be helpful when actually pruning. However, they don't make as clean a cut as a pruning saw. Loppers should never be used from a ladder as they require two hands to operate them, meaning that it is not possible to hold onto something else while pruning.

Ladders

Sometimes ladders are needed to reach high branches. Three-legged stepladders (tripods) are best because they are easiest to get in close to the tree and among the branches. Only use ladders on level ground and make sure that the legs are fully extended. Never overstretch or lean out too far over the sides. Very large fruit trees will need to be pruned by a professional tree surgeon. Don't risk it yourself.

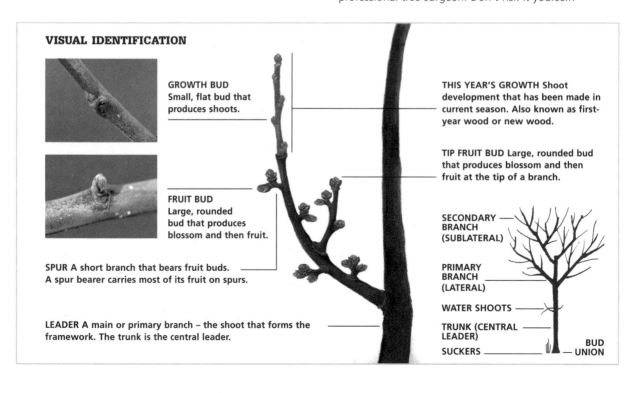

VISUAL IDENTIFICATION

GROWTH BUD Small, flat bud that produces shoots.

THIS YEAR'S GROWTH Shoot development that has been made in current season. Also known as first-year wood or new wood.

TIP FRUIT BUD Large, rounded bud that produces blossom and then fruit at the tip of a branch.

FRUIT BUD Large, rounded bud that produces blossom and then fruit.

SECONDARY BRANCH (SUBLATERAL)

SPUR A short branch that bears fruit buds. A spur bearer carries most of its fruit on spurs.

PRIMARY BRANCH (LATERAL)

WATER SHOOTS

LEADER A main or primary branch – the shoot that forms the framework. The trunk is the central leader.

TRUNK (CENTRAL LEADER)

SUCKERS

BUD UNION

Basic safety

Protection using a pair of thick gloves is particularly important when pruning thorny plants such as gooseberries and blackberries. Gloves will also reduce the risk of cutting your hand with secateurs or a pruning saw. Eye protection should be worn to prevent sawdust blowing into the eyes or a sharp branch scratching them.

Pruning cuts

Each tree should be treated individually when it comes to pruning, but there are some general guidelines that should be followed.

Remove long, heavy branches in stages to avoid tearing the bark with their weight. If pruning a branch back to the trunk, leave a small collar as this will help the tree to callus over the wound.

Make pruning cuts with secateurs at an angle just above a bud – never through a bud. Slant the cut downwards from 5mm (⅛in) above the bud. Where there are opposite buds, make a flat cut at a similar distance above the buds. A long stub left erroneously between the cut and the bud may cause the branch to die back, increasing the risk of disease.

Always cut back to a branch further down the tree or shrub. This branch needs to be at least one-third the width of the branch that has been removed.

Fruiting spurs or fruiting tips?

Successful fruit pruning depends on having a basic understanding of a plant's physiology. Fruit trees – particularly apples – fall into two categories as to

CORRECT PRUNING: a clean and smooth, correct pruning cut is made close to the adjacent branch or trunk. Avoid cutting the branch flush with the trunk and possibly damaging it.

how they produce their flowers and therefore, after pollination, their fruit: these are spur bearers and tip bearers. Most fruit trees form both types of growth but are usually prone to producing more of one type than the other. Spur bearers, which are the most common, bear their fruit on short, stumpy shoots (the spurs), which are usually more than two years old. The fruit of the tip bearers develops on shoots that were formed during the previous season.

If a tree is mainly a tip bearer and you cut back all the new shoots to one or two buds to form short spurs (as for a spur bearer) then you won't get much fruit that year because most of the fruit buds will have been removed. This is one reason why trees that are mainly tip bearing in habit such as a 'Bramley's Seedling' are unsuitable for growing as restricted forms. Not only are they vigorous but also by pruning

INCORRECT PRUNING: to prevent the branch tearing from the weight of the branch, it should first have been undercut before the main cut is done from above.

INCORRECT PRUNING: not only has this branch torn because there was no undercut made first but also the cut should have been made much closer to the trunk (see top).

new growth back to two buds any potential fruit is lost. It is therefore important to distinguish between the two habits of fruiting.

Once you understand how your tree produces its fruit, you can then prune it to maximize potential high yields. Peaches and acid cherries, for example, bear fruit mainly on wood from the preceding year, so on such tip bearers you must ensure that plenty of new shoots are tied in for next year's crop. Sweet cherries, however, develop their fruit on a series of spurs built up over the last two or three years, so a system of spur pruning is necessary. Summer-fruiting raspberries bear fruit on canes produced the previous year whereas autumn-fruiting ones form fruit on the current season's growth.

Grapevines bear fruit on shoots produced in the current year. Prune annually in winter to encourage new, healthy canes, and avoid using water shoots (canes coming directly off the central trunk) as they will contain far less clusters of grapes. Instead, try to select canes coming off the spurs of the trunk.

The climbing habit of grapevines makes them ideal for training over arches, pergolas, and trellis systems. Because their tendrils wrap around wires and posts they require less hands-on support in terms of tying in and pruning.

THIS OUTDOOR WINE GRAPEVINE has been trained using the guyot system on a set of wires. Training fruit horizontally like this encourages fruit bud formation.

Training methods

A plant's fruiting habit dictates not only how it is to be pruned but also what sort of training system is needed both initially and when established.

Trellis training
Wooden trellis can be used to create quick impromptu screens, whether this is to prevent neighbours overlooking your back garden or to create smaller, intimate spaces within the garden. Trellis is also useful for dividing up long, narrow gardens. It comes in all shapes and sizes and is readily available. Alternatively, it can simply be made by nailing wooden battens together and attaching them to posts driven into the ground.

Pergola training
Pergolas have a system of wires or wooden structures overhead, and create relaxing shady havens from which to shelter from the midday sun. Use a system of vine eyes and straining bolts to keep wires tight across the overheads.

Arches and tunnels
Apples, pears, and grapevines are suitable for training up and over arches. By placing a series of arches in rows to form tunnels you can provide depth to any garden. Train these fruits initially as upright cordons, pruning new growth back to a couple of buds in late summer. Eventually they can be bent over at the top. Hybrid berries can also be trained up arches but it is best to use thornless types (such as 'Oregon Thornless') because they will otherwise snag clothing when people walk past.

For a really authentic and rustic look, use hazel rods to form structures for growing. Embed thick, strong, upright supports into the ground and then nail or weave cross supports onto them. Weave young, whippy growth in among the main structure to provide additional support. Alternatively, secure trellis or wires to the uprights and cross supports.

Training against wires
Restricted tree and bush forms, as well as cane and vine fruit, usually need to be tied to a series of galvanized wires for support. These wires are typically attached to a wall or fence, or to wooden posts.

As a general rule, fans require horizontal wires to be trained about 15cm (6in) apart with a gap of about

USE A SYSTEM OF WIRES for supporting restricted fruit trees and bushes such as fans, espaliers, and cordons as well as vine fruit. Vine eyes with straining bolts such as seen here on this cherry fan means that the wires can be tightened easily each year.

10cm (4in) between the wall and vine eyes to allow for good air circulation. As the branches are usually equally distributed over a wide area a 14-gauge, galvanized fencing wire has sufficient strength to carry the weight.

Espaliers and cordons are based on developing tight spur systems and therefore require wires to be further apart (45–60cm/18–24in). However, they need a heavier gauge wire such as gauge 12, because they will take more weight.

Secure wires firmly in place using vine eyes driven into a fence post or wall. Wooden batons can be attached to brick walls to make it easier to attach the vine eyes. It is important to be able to tighten the wire if it goes slack, and so a straining bolt should be slotted through the vine eye. Place straining bolts at both ends of the wire. For long lengths of wire that are stretched over a number of fence panels, space vine eyes at frequent intervals along the wall.

TRAIN VINE FRUIT, such as these kiwifruit, to scramble and climb over arches, trellis, and tunnels to create attractive, eye-catching structures in the garden.

Coping with problems

One of the problems of growing an abundance of delicious fruits is that you're not the only one wanting to devour them. Pests such as birds and wasps are notoriously fond of such delights. Diseases too can be problematic, not least because many fruits are closely related and so can succumb to the same fungal and bacterial infections. However, there are many ways to limit the damage.

Many gardeners want to adopt organic principles wherever possible, encouraging a natural balance in their garden between beneficial creatures such as pollinating insects, and problematic organisms, or introducing naturally occurring parasites or predators (termed biological control) rather than relying on chemical methods of pest and disease control. Indeed, the vast majority of pesticides available to gardeners aren't legally allowed to be used on edible crops, and recent legislation in some countries has revoked a number of well-known products. This leaves fruit gardeners with less choice when it comes to selecting a suitable and, more importantly, effective pesticide. Many of us therefore rely on organic management of pests, diseases, and disorders. However, some pesticides are still available for use on fruit crops and, when applied correctly, and at the right time, can work very effectively. Consequently, when such chemicals are available, they have been listed under the appropriate problem in this chapter. Always read and follow the manufacturer's instructions carefully.

Cultural problems

Providing the wrong growing conditions for plants can cause them to exhibit signs of stress, which can affect plant health and productivity. It is not always easy on a less suitable plot to give your fruit crops the conditions they need. Factors such as frost pockets, pollination, and soil pH can be difficult to accommodate or adjust, and these incorrect elements can present gardeners with cultural problems.

Flower frost damage Most fruits are vulnerable, especially at flowering stage. Symptoms include poor fruit set and fruit scarring. On frosty nights, cover small plants with a double layer of horticultural fleece or temporarily move potted specimens to a frost-free location. Gently mist frozen flowers on larger trees to slow thawing.

Iron deficiency/lime-induced chlorosis Most fruits can show symptoms if grown on shallow chalky soils, but acid-loving crops such as raspberries, blueberries, cranberries, and lingonberries often suffer on soils with a neutral to alkaline pH. To alleviate symptoms, which are revealed by interveinal yellowing on the lower, older, leaves, add sulphur chips to the soil to reduce its pH and feed plants with sequestered iron.

Magnesium deficiency Crops grown on soil with a pH lower than pH6 can show symptoms of magnesium deficiency – interveinal yellowing on the lower leaves – unless they prefer an acidic soil. Overapplication of high potash fertilizers can also cause magnesium deficiency, and it also occurs on chalky soils at high pH. Correct the problem by raising acid soils to a neutral pH (7) using garden lime.

IRON DEFICIENCY can occur when acid-loving plants, like this citrus, are grown at the wrong pH.

Poor fruit set This can be caused by flower frost damage (see left), poor flowering, or inadequate pollination. The appearance of only a few flowers might be as a result of heavy pruning, inadequate nutrition, or the build-up of old, unproductive wood. Many fruit crops require cross-pollination by another variety to set a crop (see individual crops for details).

Splitting Grapes, cherries, currants, and melons are particularly prone to fruit splitting, which can be caused by any of the following four circumstances: fluctuating moisture; powdery mildew; the fruit skin absorbing too much water (cherries only); or fruits becoming over-ripe. To avoid this, irrigate regularly, control diseases, pick ripe fruits promptly and cover ripening cherry trees with polythene covers.

Weedkiller damage All fruits can suffer but those with a suckering habit such as raspberries, blackberries, and hybrid berries are particularly vulnerable. Symptoms include twisted, distorted foliage (hormone weedkillers) or irregular, brown scorch marks (contact weedkillers). Apply weedkiller with a dedicated sprayer and avoid using on windy days. Prune out affected growth and feed well.

Pests

A variety of pests commonly attack fruiting plants by spoiling fruits, damaging stems and foliage, or transmitting viruses. There are also many pests specific to a particular fruit host, and these are dealt with under the individual fruit entries. Insecticides must never be applied when pollinating insects are visiting open blooms, because the beneficial insects may be killed as well as the pest. A number of natural fruit pest predators and traps can be applied as biological controls – these are particularly effective on crops grown under glass.

Aphids Most fruits suffer from aphids. Damage is particularly noticeable in early summer on shoot tips. Many fruit aphids migrate to other hosts in midsummer so their damage can be tolerated. However, aphids can transmit harmful viruses for which there is no control. Squash colonies between finger and thumb or spray with pyrethrum, bifenthrin, or thiacloprid.

Birds Most fruits can be damaged by birds, although cherries, blueberries, raspberries, strawberries, and red currants are most prone to attack. Erect taut netting over vulnerable crops as soon as the fruits begin to show some colour, using a fruit cage or cloche hoops as a frame. Check the netting often.

Brown scale insects The woody stems of many fruit trees and bushes can be colonized by brown scale, which are small (up to 5mm/⅕in long), convex, brown insects attached to the bark. They are static and feed on the plant's sap, so the foliage below is often covered with honeydew that attracts sooty moulds. In midsummer, spray affected plants with fatty acids or plant oils.

Bullfinches These birds will eat fruit buds, especially of plum, cherry, and pear, in late winter, when their normal diet of seeds becomes scarce. Netting is the most reliable method of control (see birds, left). Deterrents such as humming tape or reflective scarers only offer temporary relief because birds soon realize that they aren't a threat.

Codling moth Both apples and pears can be affected, the main damage being caused by the larva, which tunnels into the centre of the fruit to feed on the core. This in itself can spoil the fruit but the tunnel also encourages secondary rotting so damaged fruits won't store. Erect codling moth traps in late spring to catch male moths, and spray in early and midsummer with bifenthrin before larvae tunnel into the fruits.

Fruit tree red spider mite The main crops affected are apples and plums, especially in hot, dry summers, which allow the mites to breed rapidly. Leaves appear flecked and mottled, and on the undersides dozens of tiny (1mm (½in) long) mites can be seen. Heavy attacks can cause premature leaf loss. Spray affected plants with bifenthrin or plant oils.

Glasshouse red spider mite Glasshouse crops and those growing outdoors but in a sheltered spot (eg against a wall) are most at risk from this pest. Foliage develops yellow flecking and mottling, and fine webbing appears between the leaves. Tiny (1mm (½in) long) mites can be seen on the leaves. The biological control *Phytoseiulus persimilis* is effective if introduced early on; alternatively spray with bifenthrin, fatty acids, or plant oils.

Gooseberry sawfly Gooseberries and red and white currants are vulnerable to sawfly attack. In early summer shoots suddenly appear defoliated and, on closer inspection, green, caterpillar-like larvae, to 2cm (¾in) long, can be found on the leaves. Persistent attacks will weaken plants considerably. Pick off light infestations by hand and spray plants with pyrethrum as soon as damage is seen.

RABBITS (left) can quickly cause a lot of damage if allowed to access young trees, while winter moth caterpillars devour newly emerging leaves (right).

Mealybugs Crops such as citrus, figs, and grapes are most at risk. White, fluffy insects, 5mm (⅛in) long, can be seen in and around leaf axils and along leaf midribs. Leaves become covered in a clear, sticky residue, which often attracts black, sooty moulds. Treat greenhouse infestations with the biological control *Cryptolaemus montrouzieri*. Alternatively, spray plants with fatty acids or plant oils.

Rabbits The main damage rabbits cause is to fruit trees, especially newly planted ones. The outer layer of bark is eaten away and this can severely weaken the tree's growth. In the worst cases the bark is removed around the whole trunk's circumference, so the tree dies. To deter rabbits, erect rabbit-proof fencing around multiple fruit trees, or place spiral guards or grills around individual trees.

Shothole borers Tree fruit branches become peppered with holes 2mm (¹⁄₁₆in) in diameter, where larvae have tunnelled into and fed on the wood. They then emerge as adult beetles. The problem is more likely to affect trees that are already weak, so address problems that could be causing this, such as lack of pruning or inadequate nutrition. Prune out affected growth if possible.

Wasps All tree fruits and grapes are prone to wasp damage. As fruits ripen, their high sugar content and odour attracts this pest, which not only damages the fruit but also poses a threat to gardeners because of its painful sting. Hang wasp traps in trees, and harvest crops as soon as they ripen. Avoid leaving windfalls or over-ripe fruits on the ground.

BLACK CHERRY APHIDS (left) attack growing points in large numbers, while aphids on strawberry leaves (right) pose more of a risk via the viruses they transmit.

Winter moth Most fruit trees are vulnerable to attack, with newly emerging leaves being damaged by the winter moth caterpillar. Individuals are up to 2.5cm (1in) long, pale green, and walk with a looping action. Prevent the flightless female from laying eggs on the branches by placing grease bands around tree trunks in midautumn. Spray newly hatched caterpillars with bifenthrin as leaves emerge.

Woolly vine scale Bush and vine fruits can be affected, particularly grapes and currants. Flat, dark brown insects, 6mm (¼in) long, can be seen on the bark. In mid- and late spring the females lay masses of white, woolly eggs bound in cotton-like threads. Because the scale insects feed on the sap, honeydew is also visible. Spray affected plants with plant oils or fatty acids in early and midsummer.

Diseases

Fruit diseases can be destructive, with cankers and shoot dieback destroying growth in a matter of weeks that took years to train. Early diagnosis and remedial action are essential. It is also important to buy certified stock of virus-prone plants such as raspberries and blackcurrants, as there is no cure for such problems, which are easily transferred from plant to plant. Resistant varieties offer gardeners a chemical-free method, whereas fungicides, while effective, can be difficult to apply to large plants.

Bacterial canker Stone fruits can succumb to this canker, the first signs of infection often appearing as clear, brown gum oozing from various points on the main limbs or trunk. These coincide with flattened areas of bark. Prune out affected areas, limiting pruning times to the summer months to deter re-infection. Consider resistant varieties such as cherry 'Merton Glory' or plum 'Marjorie's Seedling'.

BROWN ROT (left) causes fruits to turn brown and rot very quickly, while apple canker (right) will eventually girdle plant stems over many months.

GRAPE POWDERY MILDEW (left) can cause fruit skins to split and rot. American gooseberry mildew (right) is less of a problem on varieties with resistance, such as 'Invicta'.

Blossom wilt Apples, pears, and stone fruits are vulnerable. Blossom withers and rots soon after emerging, then remains hanging on the tree. The fungus then travels through the flowers into the foliage behind, causing this to brown. Prune out affected stems well into healthy tissue. Just before flowering, spray Bordeaux mixture for apples, cherries, and plums, or copper oxychloride for peaches.

Botrytis (grey mould) This fungal problem is most prevalent on soft fruits. Encouraged by high humidity it causes fruits and other soft tissues to develop a fuzzy, grey covering and eventually decay. Deter by ventilating covered crops well to decrease humidity and by irrigating from below rather than overhead. Remove affected plant parts promptly.

Bracket fungi All tree fruits can suffer from bracket fungi, which appear all-year-round as flattened, single or overlapping, horizontal fungal bodies on a tree's trunk or main limbs. Some may cause wood decay, weakness of limbs, and eventual death of the tree, although this can take many years. The main concern is that the tree can become unstable and so cause a safety risk; therefore check it regularly.

Brown rot Many fruits can suffer from brown rot near harvest time. Fruits turn brown and become covered in grey, raised, circular spots. The fungus enters the fruit via skin wounds, so identify the source of these (eg, wasps, birds, codling moth) and take action to reduce its occurrence. Remove affected fruits from the tree to stop the fungus overwintering on fruit spurs.

Coral spot Currants are especially prone, though all woody plants can suffer. Orange-pink, raised dots appear on dead stems, and, if left unchecked, dieback can continue down the stem and become extensive. The fungus is encouraged by wet conditions and enters through untidy pruning wounds. Using sharp secateurs, cut out all affected growth well into healthy tissue, then burn it.

Crown gall Most fruits can suffer from crown gall, which appears as oversized, woody swellings on or around the base of plants or on roots, especially on wet soils. Except when on roots, galls rarely affect the vigour of the host but they can encourage secondary infection when they disintegrate. Remove affected plants promptly to deter their spread.

Downy mildews Grapes and melons can succumb to downy mildews, which appear as irregular, yellow patches on upper leaf surfaces with corresponding, downy, grey growth on the undersides. Remove affected leaves and ventilate covered plants well to improve air flow and reduce excess humidity. Water from below, rather than overhead. Spray plants with Dithane 945 (mancozeb).

Fireblight Apple, pear, and quince trees are susceptible. Flowers wilt, and subsequent dieback then progresses down the stems. Bacterial ooze can sometimes be seen, along with discolouration under affected bark. Prune out growth well back into healthy tissue, burning prunings and sterilizing pruning tools after use. Check with agricultural authorities whether fireblight is a notifiable disease in your area.

Fungal leaf spot Irregular, brown/purple spots surrounded by a yellow ring can appear on many fruits, including black- and hybrid berries, currants, cherries, figs, and strawberries. The spotting spreads throughout the foliage and is extremely rapid during warm, humid weather. Severe infections can weaken plants. Remove affected leaves as soon as possible, and ventilate covered crops freely to improve air flow and reduce humidity.

Honey fungus Most fruit plants can be infected by honey fungus, which causes progressive weakness and eventual death. In autumn, clumps of midbrown toadstools appear around the base of infected plants. A white fungal layer smelling strongly of mushrooms can be found under the bark of larger infected roots. Remove infected plants promptly and avoid replanting in that site.

Phytophthora All woody fruits are at risk, especially if on waterlogged soils. Plants weaken and eventually die. If dug up, the root cores are often stained orange and emit a sour smell. There is no control for this fungus, so affected plants must be disposed of. Improve drainage to deter the problem in the future and avoid replanting on affected soils.

Powdery mildew Many fruit crops are susceptible to powdery mildew fungi. They cause leaves to develop a milky white covering, which eventually yellows and dries out the foliage. The skin of affected fruits often cracks. Plants suffering from drought stress are more vulnerable to attack, so keep plants well mulched and watered. Spray with mancozeb or choose resistant varieties.

Replant problems Most tree fruits are vulnerable to replant problems when they are planted on a site that has previously supported the same or a similar crop, especially for prolonged periods of time. Trees appear weak and fail to put on new growth. Various soil factors are to blame, including fungi and nematodes. Avoid planting on old sites, or change the soil to a depth of at least 45cm (18in).

Rusts Rust fungi can attack most cane and some tree (plum and pear) fruits. Encouraged by high humidity, symptoms appear as bright orange pustules on the leaf upperside in early summer. These gradually turn to dark brown as the season progresses. Leaves fall early and so vigour is reduced. Remove and burn affected leaves promptly, and spray with mancozeb.

Shothole Stone fruits are at risk of developing small, roughly circular patches on the leaves during early summer. By the end of the season the now-brown patches have fallen out, leaving the foliage peppered with holes. The problem is often a sign that the tree is suffering from bacterial canker or powdery mildew (see relevant entries) so these diseases should be treated thoroughly.

Silver leaf All stone fruits, almonds, and apples are vulnerable to infection, which appears as a silver sheen on the foliage of some or all branches. The fungus enters via pruning wounds. Because spores are most prevalent in the air during winter, pruning of stone fruits should be carried out immediately after harvest in summer. Mild cases can be suppressed with feeding, otherwise remove the tree.

Viruses Most if not all fruits can suffer from viruses. The symptoms vary from crop to crop but stunting, distortion, blistering, or irregular yellowing of the foliage often occurs. Crop yield is often drastically reduced. There is no cure for viruses so affected plants must be disposed of. To reduce vulnerability to viruses, control pests such as aphids, leafhoppers, and whitefly, because they are virus vectors. Also, always purchase certified virus-free stock.

BOTRYTIS CAN BE A PROBLEM on soft fruit crops such as raspberries, particularly in wet or humid weather.

Tree fruit

- Apples and pears
- Quinces
- Medlars
- Plums, damsons, and gages
- Peaches and nectarines
- Apricots
- Cherries
- Citrus fruit
- Figs

Carol's fruit notebook

" It might seem like a big moment to move from growing vegetables or soft fruit to growing your own tree fruit, like a step up into the world of the serious gardener. But as anyone who has inherited a mature fruit tree in a new garden will tell you, the tree just carries on with producing good harvests or bad harvests with complete indifference to you. If you have the room, you plant the tree and let it get on with it. It's when you want to prune or rejuvenate the tree that people get worried, but here this book will help you, for example, on how to open out the branches to better ripen fruit. If you are tight on space or fancy a decorative structure to your fruit garden, more advanced techniques become relevant, but again this book will guide you, for example, on how to espalier or create a step-over apple tree. There's nothing like learning for yourself, with guidance, to see what works well and what was a mistake; as with all gardening, patience and observation are rewarded.

Trees are pretty vigorous and have a will to thrive and grow; you just have to select the best variety for you and your garden and provide the optimum conditions of space, aspect, drainage, moisture, and shelter you are able to. Plant your tree with love and do what you can to help it settle in, because your kindness will be returned – eventually – with the gift of wonderful fruit for many years to come. In cool-temperate areas, tree harvests are usually won or lost at blossom time. Here is an opportunity for you to intervene for the better by protecting the blossoms from overnight frosts (and careless handling) with fleece, hessian, or plastic. Above all, encourage bees into your garden by providing shelter and food plants right through the year. They will be the ones who will pollinate the flowers that will grow on to give you the fruit you will relish. "

Pollination

For almost all fruit trees to successfully produce fruit, their flowers need pollinating. This involves pollen grains from the male anthers of a flower being transferred to the female stigma. This process is usually carried out by flying insects like honey bees and bumble bees, and flies, beetles, and wasps. Nuts such as cobnuts and filberts, however, are pollinated by the wind.

MOST TREE FRUIT – even self-fertile varieties – rely on insects to transfer pollen from one flower to the next. If it is wet, windy, and cold during flowering, poor fruit set may result.

Some fruit trees such as 'Victoria' plums and 'Stella' cherries are self-fertile, meaning that they pollinate their own flowers. This is ideal in a small garden because only this one tree is required to produce fruit. However, even self-fertile varieties tend to crop better when another tree is nearby for pollination.

Most fruit trees, however, have self-incompatible flowers, meaning that they require another variety of tree growing nearby to pollinate their flowers. When a tree receives pollen from another tree for fertilization it is known as cross-pollination.

Successful cross-pollination generally requires trees that are of the same fruit type: for example, an apple will pollinate another apple tree while a pear tree cannot pollinate an apple, and vice versa. Also, the trees may need to be two different varieties of the same fruit: for example, two 'Golden Delicious' apple trees will not cross-pollinate each other. A 'Golden Delicious' requires another apple variety that is flowering at the same time, such as 'Ellison's Orange'.

If you live in a built-up area, there are likely to be lots of other apple trees growing in close proximity, so there may be adequate pollination nearby and just the one tree will suffice in your own garden. Although pollinating bees can travel 3–4km (1–2 miles), the general rule of thumb is that trees for cross-pollination should be within 18m (55ft) of each other to be really effective.

Timing is everything

For cross-pollination to take place, the fruit trees must produce flowers at the same time so that bees and other pollinating insects can pass the pollen grains from one tree to another. For this reason, nurseries have classified trees into various flowering groups, so that it is easy to choose two varieties that will flower at the same time (see page 218). If all this sounds too confusing, ask the advice of a specialist nursery.

Just to complicate things, however, a few apple and pear varieties (known as triploids) such as 'Bramley's Seedling', 'Holstein', 'Ribston Pippin', 'Blenheim Orange', and 'Catillac' produce mainly sterile pollen. These trees won't be any use for cross-pollinating other trees, yet they still require other trees to set their fruit. Therefore if you wish to grow a triploid variety you will also need two other trees that will pollinate each other as well as the triploid, and these three varieties must all flower at the same time.

Crab apples are particularly useful for pollinating dessert and cooking apples as they produce an abundance of flowers over a long period. This is why they are often grown in commercial apple orchards.

Attracting pollinators

The majority of pollination is carried out by insects and, among these, honey bees are one of the most effective pollinators because while travelling from flower to flower they inadvertently transfer pollen.

Successful flower pollination depends on creating favourable flying conditions for insects. Bees prefer warm, sunny positions and despise the wet and cold. They need shelter from the wind. This can be provided by deciduous and mixed native hedging creates ideal, semipermeable screens that protect the fruits and filter out the wind. Ensure that hedging is far enough away from fruit trees so they do not compete for water, nutrients and sunlight.

To create a habitat that will attract bees and other pollinating insects, keep grass longer than normal and tolerate some weeds. Cultivate a diverse range of plants that will flower over a long period to provide the bees with pollen and nectar. As well as the blossom from fruit trees, bees are attracted by many other plants including borage, clover, honeysuckle, ivy, and heather.

Beekeeping is not only an absorbing hobby but it could also benefit your fruit trees. Honey bees, based in a hive at the end of the garden, will greatly increase yields because they will feed from the

IN URBAN OR SUBURBAN AREAS there are likely to be other sources of pollen nearby, such as these crab apple flowers.

BEEKEEPING AND FRUIT GROWING are very compatible hobbies. Bees are an overlooked resource in the garden and should always be encouraged, especially in the fruit garden.

flowers in your garden. One bee hive can contain as much as 60,000–80,000 bees – that is quite a labour force for the pollination of fruit trees.

Solitary bees, such as the red mason bee, are also invaluable pollinators. They tend to fly in cooler and less favourable conditions than honey bees, making them particularly useful for early flowering plants in early spring. Make a winter refuge for them with hollow plant stems bundled together, pushed into a cut-off piece of plastic drainpipe, and hung outside in a sheltered position. Alternatively, holes can be drilled into pieces of wood or logs, which the bees will quickly nest in if a source of blossom is nearby. Ready-made "hotels" for mason bees are also available from shops and via the internet.

Apples and pears

England and France have been blessed with a climate that favours growing apples and pears, so historically they have a long tradition in their cultivation. Growers in the cool-temperate regions have access to a wealth of distinctive cultivars. The apple, however, is the prime example of an all-year-round fruit sold nowadays without any regard to its seasonal growth. And the flavour when it reaches you? An insipid pay-off between sweetness and sourness with a watery crunch.

When you grow your own apples and pears you can select from the huge repository of named varieties that embody every conceivable balance of subtle flavours and textures. It's not élitist to make a choice based on refinement of taste and discernment because the exalted varieties are no more difficult to grow than ordinary ones. The choice is made on the fruit within, not on the appearance of the skin. An organically grown apple or pear may or may not have an unblemished appearance because it depends on some factors beyond the grower's control. Even if you have to peel your own produce and operate on it before you can eat it, you will come to love it because it is yours.

I always remember the rector who used to live next door to our cottage, dissecting an apple from his garden with a special sharp knife, in a ritualized climax to his meal. The apple trees at the top of his old walled garden had been planted long ago, and this was one tradition worth honouring, preserving the continuity through time of the leisurely and considered selection of the noblest apple varieties.

My mum loved 'James Grieve' apples, and when they were finally ready their appearance constituted for her an occasion almost as valued as Christmas or Easter. And, for me, to catch a pear in a perfect state of ripeness is worth any amount of trouble.

WHEN APPLES AND PEARS begin to swell and colour, you know that harvest time has finally arrived.

Apples and pears
Malus domestica and *Pyrus communis*

Both of these fruits have a wonderful versatility to them, enabling them to be trained into decorative and elaborate shapes, creating stunning focal points in even the smallest of gardens. It is generally the same pruning regime for both apples and pears and so for this reason they have been categorized here together.

The best sites and soils

Apples and pears are good cool-climate fruit because they tolerate low winter temperatures, and there are varieties that suit most sites and soils. In fact, the choice is so great that it is sensible to consult a local specialist nursery or grower who can recommend varieties that suit your local conditions and that will be able to pollinate each other (see page 218). The ideal position for an apple or pear tree is a sunny, sheltered site, well away from any frost pockets. The perfect soil pH is 6.5. Poorly drained or shallow soils should be improved or avoided.

APPLES AND PEARS make beautiful trees, with their lovely blossom in spring to their colourful fruit in autumn.

Buying tips

Like most tree fruit, you should only buy named varieties of apple and pear trees from a reputable specialist nursery. They are supplied as young trees ready for planting. Sowing apples or pears from their seed, or pips, would just take too long, and just as children are not identical to their parents, fruit trees are not true to type when reproduced from seed.

To retain consistency of variety, a young branch (scion) of the parent tree is grafted onto specially developed rootstocks that restrict the size of the tree. The most important decision you can make when buying an apple or pear tree is to select a variety on a rootstock that is appropriate to your needs.

A WAY TO CHOOSE YOUR VARIETY

Most pears produce spurs readily and are therefore suitable for training in a restricted tree form such as a cordon or espalier (see page 74), but not all apples develop spurs. Good spur-bearing apple varieties include 'Arthur Turner', 'Cox's Orange Pippin', 'Charles Ross', 'Howgate Wonder', 'James Grieve', 'Ribston Pippin', and 'Sturmer Pippin'.

Other apple and pear varieties are tip bearers, meaning they produce fruit at the end of short sideshoots. If grown in a restricted tree form, these would be pruned off in late summer, resulting in no fruit. Most apple trees mainly produce spurs, which include varieties such as 'Worcester Pearmain', 'Bramley's Seedling', and the pear 'Jargonelle'. Grow in an unrestricted form such as a bush or standard (see page 74).

Apple rootstocks

Rootstocks have unmemorable names and unfortunately their numbers do not denote or relate to any size or order. With regards to apples, the M (Malling) or MM (Malling Merton) refer to the trials ground from where they were developed.

'M27' A tree grafted onto this rootstock will reach only 1.5m (5ft). 'M27' struggles in poor soils, but it is useful for growing as a step-over, as a bush in a tiny space, and for vigorous triploid varieties.

'M9' Slightly more vigorous than 'M27', this is still a very dwarfing tree, reaching 1.8–2.1m (6–7ft), depending on the soil. It can be grown as a step-over, small tree, or as a cordon on good, fertile soil.

'M26' Probably the best overall dwarfing rootstock suitable for cordons, espaliers, growing in a container, or as a spindle or bush tree. 'M26' reaches 2.5m (8ft) depending on soil conditions and the vigour of the variety.

'MM106' This moderately vigorous rootstock is suitable for larger espaliers and for growing reasonably sized bush and spindle trees up to about 4m (13ft) high.

'MM111' Reasonably vigorous 'MM111' is suitable for small standards and half-standards, reaching heights of approximately 6m (20ft) high.

'M25' Suitable for small standards and half-standards, 'M25' matures to 7m (23ft) high. It does well on most types of soil, and needs a large garden or orchard to grow in.

Rootstock for a pot 'M26' is the most popular choice, although 'MM106' and even 'M25' can be used successfully. Avoid 'M27' and 'M9' because these extremely dwarfing rootstocks struggle in poor soil conditions such as those found in a pot.

Pears

Pears are generally grafted onto quince roots. The two most popular rootstocks are:

Quince A The most commonly found rootstock in garden centres, 'Quince A' can be used for espaliers or bush trees.

Quince C Being slightly less vigorous than 'Quince A', 'Quince C' is more suitable for cordons, but can also be used for an espalier or bush tree.

SPACING FOR APPLE AND PEAR TREES

RESTRICTED FORMS

- **Oblique cordons** – 70cm (28in) apart
- **Step-over** – 1.5m (5ft) apart
- **Pyramid** – 1.8m (6ft) apart
- **Spindle tree** – 1.8m (6ft) apart
- **Espalier** – 4m (13ft) apart, or two standard fence panels
- **Fan** – 4m (13ft) apart, or two standard fence panels

FREE-STANDING TREES

- **Bush** on 'M27'
  between plants in a row – 1.5m (5ft)
  space between rows – 1.5m (5ft)
- **Bush** on 'M9'
  between plants in a row – 1.8m (6ft)
  space between rows – 1.8m (6ft)
- **Bush** on 'M26'/'Quince C'
  between plants in a row – 2–2.5m (6½–8ft)
  space between rows – 2–2.5m (6½–8ft)
- **Bush** on 'MM106'/'Quince A'
  between plants in a row – 2.5–3m (8–10ft)
  space between rows – 2.5–3m (8–10ft)
- **Half-standard**
  between plants in a row – 6m (20ft)
  space between rows – 6m (20ft)
- **Standard**
  between plants in a row – 9m (30ft)
  space between rows – 9m (30ft)

THE BUD OR GRAFT UNION is a slightly swollen scar on the trunk where the rootstock and scion were grafted together.

Recommended apple varieties (dessert)

There are hundreds of apple varieties to choose from. In the UK alone, there are about 2,000 varieties held in the national collection of the Brogdale Horticultural Trust, in Kent. Listed below are some of the most popular ones, but it is worth searching for local varieties to help retain local and cultural distinctiveness. By growing such a variety you are helping to preserve your local history and heritage. Regional fruit trees should thrive in their own areas because they would have been selected to suit the climate and growing conditions of the surrounding landscape. Local recipes would have been based on the varieties grown close to home.

'Barnack Beauty'
(pollination group 3, pick midautumn, store until early winter) This old variety has a sharp flavour and a crisp texture, so it can also be useful as a cooker. It has a good reputation for reliable crops.

'Ellison's Orange'
(pollination group 4, pick early autumn, store until midautumn) A first-class Cox-style apple with a strong, aromatic flavour that crops early in the season and bears lovely spring blossom. It has some disease resistance.

'Cox's Orange Pippin'
(pollination group 3, pick early autumn, store until midwinter) The fruit has flushed-orange skin and the finest flavour in the apple world. But 'Cox's Orange Pippin' isn't easy to grow due to its susceptibility to disease.

'Elstar'
(pollination group 3, pick midautumn, store until early winter) This Dutch variety is descended from 'Golden Delicious' and produces heavy yields of intensely flavoured, cloyingly sweet, juicy apples.

'Discovery'
(pollination group 3, pick and eat late summer) This flushed-red apple is probably the tastiest and juiciest of all the earlies with good, firm flesh. It is a partial tip bearer and has good resistance to disease.

'Falstaff'
(pollination group 3, pick midautumn, store until late autumn) A crisp, juicy, pleasantly sharp tasting apple, which also cooks well. 'Falstaff' is a good variety for making apple juice and its yields are good.

'Egremont Russet'
(pollination group 2, pick midautumn, store until late autumn) Its intriguing flavour combines honey and nuts. The fruit is small and golden with large patches of russeting and a rough skin.

'Fiesta'
(pollination group 3, pick midautumn, store until midwinter) This is a Cox-like apple in terms of its flavour and fruit size. 'Fiesta' is more reliable and a heavier cropper than its parent 'Cox's Orange Pippin'.

'Greensleeves'
(pollination group 3, pick midautumn, store until late autumn) A cross between 'James Grieve' and 'Golden Delicious'. The fruit starts to ripen from early autumn but tastes best if it mellows on the tree a little.

'Pixie'
(pollination group 4, pick midautumn, store until late winter) The juicy, delicious, small apples are ideal for children. 'Pixie' produces high yields of yellow apples, with orange-red flushes, which store well.

'James Grieve'
(pollination group 3, pick early autumn, store until late autumn) A classic early apple with excellent flavour and well-balanced acidity, making it suitable for cooking as well as eating straight off the tree.

'Ribston Pippin'
(pollination group 2 – triploid, pick midautumn, store until midwinter) One of the parents of 'Cox's Orange Pippin' this was considered to be the finest apple of its day before its famous prodigy appeared.

'Jonagold'
(pollination group 3 – triploid, pick midautumn, store until early spring) 'Jonagold' produces high yields of large, greenish yellow fruit with light red flushes. Apples have a good, crisp flavour.

'Spartan'
(pollination group 3, pick midautumn, store until midwinter) This popular variety has dark maroon fruit with crisp, white flesh. It possesses delicious elderflower aromas and has a slightly vinous flavour.

'Kidd's Orange Red'
(pollination group 3, pick midautumn, store until late winter) A good cropper bearing yellow-skinned fruit with orange-red flushes and patches of pale russeting. Has a superb Cox-like flavour.

'Sunset'
(pollination group 3, pick early autumn, store until late autumn) A tidy, compact, disease-resistant tree producing high yields of smallish fruits coloured yellow-orange. Thin out heavily to obtain larger fruits.

'Lord Lambourne'
(pollination group 2, pick midautumn, store until late autumn) This early to midseason variety has a good compact habit, so is ideal for a small garden. The apples possess an excellent, aromatic flavour.

'Worcester Pearmain'
(pollination group 3, pick early autumn, store until midautumn) An early to midseason, partial tip bearer with small to medium, red-flushed fruits and superb strawberry aromas. It is prone to scab.

Recommended apple varieties (cookers)

With such a heritage of apple growing and a plethora of varieties to choose from, it is a luxury and privilege that apples in cool-temperate regions can be distinguished as being either a cooker or a dessert. Cooking apples have a sharp, acidic quality to them, and it is this that makes them suitable for cooking or breaking down into a purée. Some varieties mellow with storage and are thereby transformed into good eating apples later in the year. When you choose a cooking apple, consider how it will break down on cooking. Some purée well, while others tend to keep their shape – different properties that suit different kitchen needs.

'Blenheim Orange'
(pollination group 3 - triploid, pick midautumn, store until midwinter) Dual-purpose apple requiring dwarfing rootstocks to control its vigour. It has heavy yields but is prone to biennial cropping.

'Golden Noble'
(pollination group 4, pick midautumn, store until late winter) One of the best cooking apples with creamy white, nicely textured, juicy flesh and a good fruity flavour. Produces pale pink flowers in spring.

'Bountiful'
(pollination group 3, pick early autumn, store until early winter) Compact tree with good disease resistance and heavy crops. Suitable for a cordon or espalier. Mellows in store to make a good dessert apple.

'Grenadier'
(pollination group 3, pick late summer, store until early autumn) Greenish yellow fruit breaks down into a sharp, whitish purée when cooked. Has a compact habit and some scab resistance.

'Bramley's Seedling'
(pollination group 3 - triploid, pick midautumn, store until early spring) It is a very popular, vigorous tree requiring a lot of space. The apple breaks down to a creamy purée after cooking.

'Howgate Wonder'
(pollination group 4, pick early autumn, store until midautumn) Produces enormous apples that cook down into a light purée, but they lack the intense flavour of a 'Bramley's Seedling'.

'Edward VII'
(pollination group 6, pick midautumn, store until early spring) Good disease resistance. Is suitable for a cordon or espalier. Late flowering so find a suitable partner. Cooks down to a pale purée.

'Reverend W. Wilks'
(pollination group 2, pick early autumn, store until midautumn) Huge fruits are borne on this small, compact tree. Cooks down to a light, sweet purée. Can be prone to biennial cropping. Good disease resistance.

Recommended pear varieties

Despite their delicate aromas and their buttery-rich flavours, pears are less popular than apples. Therefore, pollination considerations are important when choosing a tree because there are less likely to be other pear trees growing nearby. Fortunately, a wide choice of pear varieties is available. Bear in mind that pears frequently give lower yields than apples, and that the blossom is more sensitive to frost because it opens earlier in the season. With the exception of a few cooking varieties such as 'Catillac', pears also do not store nearly so well as apples. All but one listed below are dessert varieties.

'Beth'
(pollination group late, pick late summer, store until early autumn) Pale yellow skin and delicious, white flesh. The fruits are small, but the crops are heavy and regular. Has an upright growth habit.

'Doyenné du Comice'
(pollination group late, pick midautumn, store until early winter) Pick this one for its outstanding flavour and perfumed aroma. Needs a good warm, sheltered site, so train against a south-facing wall.

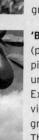

'Beurré Hardy'
(pollination group mid, pick early autumn, store until midautumn) Excellently flavoured, vigorous pear with no graininess in the flesh. The large, yellowish green fruit has reddish russeting on the skin.

'Louise Bonne of Jersey'
(pollination group early, pick early autumn, store until midautumn) It has good flavour and produces heavy yields. It is partially self-fertile but is better grown with another variety in the same pollination group.

'Concorde'
(pollination group mid, pick early autumn, store until late autumn) A fine, compact hybrid (of 'Conference' and 'Doyenné du Comice') bearing heavy yields of medium to large fruits.

'Onward'
(pollination group late, pick early to midautumn, store until midautumn) A delicious, juicy pear with reliable crops. The fruit do not store well at all so needs to be eaten almost straight away.

'Conference'
(pollination group mid, pick early autumn, store until late autumn) It is a popular commercial variety due to its reliable, heavy crops. The greenish fruit is distinctive due to its elongated shape.

'Catillac' (cooker)
(pollination group late – triploid, pick midautumn, store until midspring) Reduces down to an attractive, pink colour after a couple of hours' cooking. 'Catillac' is heavy cropping and has a vigorous habit.

RESTRICTED TREE FORMS Only spur-bearing varieties can be used to form restricted trees.

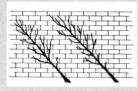

Cordon
This simple form is popular in a small garden as several varieties can be crammed into a small space. The tree is usually planted as an oblique cordon (shown) at an angle of 30–45 degrees, and has fruiting spurs along the stem. Can also be grown as a double-stemmed (or U-shaped) cordon. Use 'M9', 'M26', or 'MM106' rootstock for apples and 'Quince A' or 'Quince C' for pears.

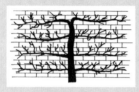

Espalier
Probably the most intricate way to grow a fruit tree against a wall or fence. A central stem is trained upwards with pairs of opposite branches trained horizontally along a system of wires. There are usually three or four tiers. Fruit spurs are encouraged along these horizonal branches. Use 'M26' or 'MM106' rootstock for apples and 'Quince A' or 'Quince C' for pears.

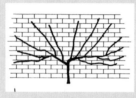

Fan
Perhaps one of the most attractive and popular tree form shapes, a fan has a short trunk in the centre of the plant and then branches radiating out on either side into a fan shape, usually to cover a wall or fence. Use 'M26' or 'MM106' rootstock for apples and 'Quince A' or 'Quince C' for pears.

Spindle
This form is becoming popular because its tapering shape allows sunlight to reach most parts of the tree, unlike a bush where the centre can be shaded. For apples use 'M26' or 'MM106' rootstock; 'Quince A' or 'Quince C' for pears. **Pyramid** Like the spindle tree, a pyramid has a central leader enabling better distribution of sunlight. It requires a little more pruning than a spindle, but has a neater growing habit that appeals to some people. The height usually is 2m–2.5m (6½–8ft). Use 'M26' or 'MM106' rootstock for apples and 'Quince A' or 'Quince C' for pears.

Step-over
These are perfect for edging paths and borders. Step-overs are best grown on 'M27' or 'M9' rootstock. They are supported by one wire pulled tightly between two posts. Pears are generally too vigorous for this type of training.

UNRESTRICTED TREE FORMS Both tip- and spur-bearing varieties (see page 53) can be used as free-standing trees.

Bush
The traditional choice for the small garden, an open-centred tree is trained on a trunk 60–75cm (24–30in) long. It is sometimes called an open-centre goblet. Use 'M27', 'M9', 'M26', or 'MM106' apple rootstock and 'Quince A' or 'Quince C' for pears.

Half-standard
Just a larger version of the bush tree, a half-standard has a taller, clear trunk of about 1.5m (5ft). It is a smaller alternative to a standard tree. For a half-standard, use 'MM106' or 'MM111' rootstock.

Standard

The largest fruit tree form, which usually has a clear stem of 2m (6½ft) and an open-centred crown, so requires a big garden. The tree could reach 7m (23ft), so consider also how the fruit will be picked. For a standard, use 'MM111' or 'M25' apple rootstock and *Quince* for pears.

Tree forms

Restricted tree forms such as cordons, fans, and espaliers (see box, opposite) are usually pruned annually in late summer as their growth slows down for dormancy during winter. Pruning in summer allows sunlight to get into what would otherwise be a crowded and congested canopy. This helps the wood to ripen and to initiate the development of fruit buds for the following year. This system of late summer pruning is known as the Modified Lorette system.

Unrestricted trees such as bushes and standards have more open branches, meaning sunlight can enter the canopy allowing the fruit buds to develop without summer pruning. They are pruned in winter.

Creating a cordon

Apples and pear trees are well suited to training as cordons as they can be kept compact and react well to hard pruning. Plant an oblique cordon angled at 30–45 degrees (see page 45) to encourage a system of fruiting spurs to develop along its trunk, and tie the leader to a cane, fixed to the support wire.

An apple or pear tree can also be trained to grow over an arch. The technique is similar to oblique cordon pruning except that the leader is trained upwards towards the centre of the arch. In late summer, prune sideshoots back to one or two buds past the basal cluster, (the group of leaves at the base of the stem).

Formative pruning
A feathered maiden is the best tree to use, because it will start cropping earlier than a maiden whip (a one-year-old tree). If a maiden whip has been bought, shorten the leader by about two-thirds to an upward-facing bud after planting to encourage sideshoots to develop. Thereafter, follow the same procedure as for a two-year-old feathered maiden.

If the feathered maiden is wispy with poor branching, lightly prune the leader to encourage more sideshoots and fruiting spurs below; otherwise the leader should be left untouched. Cut shoots of more than 10cm (4in) in length back to two or three buds above the basal cluster.

In spring, remove the blossom for the first two years after planting a maiden whip, or the first year after planting a feathered maiden.

WHEN A SPUR SYSTEM becomes overcrowded, thin it out to leave the spurs with plenty of fruit buds.

SPUR THINNING

Mature cordons benefit from a thinning of spurs every two or three years in winter when their shape can be seen better because the leaves have fallen. The swollen, short sideshoots can become crowded, so remove the older spurs in favour of the younger wood, to encourage new growth to replace the old spurs.

Regularly check that the ties between the developing leader and its cane aren't strangling the plant, and loosen them where necessary. Also ensure the cane remains attached to the wires at the correct angle. When the leader reaches the desired height, prune it back in late summer.

Established pruning of an apple or pear cordon
In late summer, prune most of the new growth back to one or two buds past the basal cluster, using a pair of sharp secateurs. Ensure that the wood has ripened and is no longer green. If growth is less than 20cm (8in) long, leave it to develop further; then prune it in autumn or winter. Also in late summer, shorten any shoot that has developed directly from the main stem, cutting it back to three or four buds above the basal cluster, to encourage a system of fruiting spurs to develop. This is known as the Full

Lorette system. Prune any weak or wispy growth to just one leaf past the basal cluster.

Occasionally wispy growth develops after summer pruning. This is usually because the pruning has been carried out too early before the plant has started to slow down for dormancy. If this happens prune back the growth to one bud in late autumn.

In addition to summer pruning, every two to three years also prune the cordon in winter by thinning out any congested spurs (see box, page 75). This stimulates growth and helps to rejuvenate the tree.

Creating an espalier

Choose a warm, sunny wall or fence on which to transform a young tree into a superb decorative feature, using a method that was a firm favourite in the 19th century. Although the training process takes a few years, for a little bit more money, ready-grown espaliers are available. Establish a framework of horizontal wires 45cm (18in) apart, starting from 45cm (18in) above ground level, prepare the ground, and then plant the tree (see page 45).

Formative pruning
After planting a maiden whip, cut it back to 45cm (18in) above the ground, to encourage buds to break just beneath the cut. Attach the central trunk to a vertical cane tied to the wires.

AN ESPALIER NEEDS to have its tiers of horizontal branches trained along supporting wires. Patience is required to create an espalier, but it is very effective once established.

In spring, two of the shoots that develop just below the initial cut will become the first horizontal tier. Train the top shoot up the vertical cane attached to the wire, so the stem grows upwards. Then select a vigorous shoot from either side of the main trunk and tie each to a cane placed at 45 degrees to the main stem. Remove other shoots growing from the main stem.

In late summer, lower the 45-degree canes to a horizontal position. Prune the tip only if the shoot has reached the end of the wire.

In winter, cut back the central stem to 45cm (18in) above the lower tier (at the height of the second-tier wire) to a healthy bud. This will encourage buds to break below the cut; these will form the second tier.

MATURE ESPALIERS make excellent ornamental screens and can be used to partition a garden in an eye-catching way.

Repeat this process each year until the desired amount of tiers have been created. When the final tier is reached, remove the central leader only after the sideshoots have developed and been tied in. Keep fruiting to a minimum during these early years.

Established pruning of an apple or pear espalier

In late summer, prune sideshoots of more than 25cm (10in) that have formed from existing spurs back to one bud past the basal cluster. Shorten new growth directly from the horizontal branch tiers to three or four buds above the basal cluster. Remove spurs or shoots on the central trunk. Leave shoots that are short or still unripened until winter, when they should be pruned back to one bud past the basal cluster. Also thin the spurs in winter (see box, page 75).

Creating a fan

Suitable for a fence or wall, a fan has a central, short stem with branches or ribs radiating out on each side. If buying a feathered maiden, make sure that it has a good pair of sideshoots growing at 35–45cm (14–18in) above the ground, because these will be used to form the first ribs of the fan. Prepare the ground, then plant the tree (see page 45).

Formative pruning

In winter, prune a maiden whip back to a healthy bud about 45cm (18in) above ground level. In summer train in two of these branches – one in each direction – and tie them into canes attached securely to the wires at 45 degrees. The following winter, tip-prune the branches by removing about one-third of the new growth, ideally to an upward-facing bud. Thereafter, follow the same procedure as for a two-year-old feathered maiden after its initial winter of formative pruning (see right).

If you have planted a feathered maiden, in winter cut the leader back to the height of the first branches, which should hopefully be at about the height of the lowest wire, that is, 35–45cm (14–18in) above ground level, one branch on each side of the stem parallel with the fence or wall. Shorten the branches by removing about one-third of the top-growth, ideally to an upward-facing bud.

In summer, the branches should have developed sideshoots of their own. Select two or three of these sideshoots and spread them equally on the wire

A FAN HAS A SHORT TRUNK with branches or "ribs" radiating from it on either side to create a fan shape.

system and tie them with string – ideally two above the branch and one to train downwards. In winter cut these branches back by about one-third. Remove any shoots growing towards the wall or fence.

The following year, continue to tie in two or three sideshoots coming off the branches, thereby extending the fan shape. If there isn't room for all the sideshoots, prune some of them back to two or three buds to form fruiting spurs. Remove other sideshoots completely.

Established pruning of an apple or pear fan

In winter, prune the main branches when they are the desired length and thin the spur system (see box, page 75). Then in late summer, prune new growth back to a couple of buds above the basal cluster. Remove any dominant shoots that are attempting to take over as the central leader.

If the tree is predominantly a spur bearer, shorten some sideshoots to one or two buds past the basal cluster in late summer. Fill in empty spaces by tying in other sideshoots and pruning back the tips.

If the fan is predominantly a tip bearer, then a form of replacement pruning can be used whereby some of the older fruiting branches are removed to create space for younger shoots. Tie in sideshoots as they develop in summer.

Creating a spindle or pyramid

Spindle trees make attractive features in the garden with their Christmas tree shape – with green or red apples hanging like baubles before harvesting. This central-leader tree consists of three or four tiers evenly spaced along the trunk. It requires a permanent, upright stake, 2.5m (8ft) long, driven 60cm (2ft) into the ground, before planting in well-prepared ground (see page 45). An alternative method is to grow trees as pyramids. Yields and size of tree are similar but the pyramid is a more attractive shape, though it requires intensive pruning.

Formative pruning

After planting a maiden whip, prune it back to 75cm (30in) above ground and tie the leader to the stake as it begins to grow during summer. After planting a feathered tree, select three or four branches at 60–70cm (24–28in) above the ground to form the first tier of the spindle and remove all others. Ideally the chosen branches should have a wide angle between the branches and the trunk, because it will be easier to set them in a horizontal position. Leave the branches unpruned unless they are spindly, in which case cut each tip at a downward-facing bud. Shorten the leader to 12cm (5in) (about five buds)

WHEN FORMING A SPINDLE, cut overly long branches back to a downward-facing bud in winter; otherwise leave them unpruned. Tie down the branches as they grow.

above the chosen branches. Tie down the branches as they grow (see box, left).

In summer, remove any sideshoots that are making vigorous, upright growth from the first tier of branches. Encourage weaker stems because these will be more fruitful. Each winter, prune back the leader by about one-third and tie it to the stake. Choose a second tier of branches 30–45cm (12–18in) above the lower tier and treat as for the first tier. Continue in this way until you have set up the required number of tiers.

For a pyramid, start with a feathered maiden and in late summer shorten the leader and lateral branches by two-thirds to downward-facing buds. In spring, shorten the leader by two-thirds, each time cutting back to a bud on the opposite side to the previous year. Remove any branches lower than 45cm (18in). Continue until the pyramid reaches its intended height.

Established pruning of a spindle or pyramid

The aim of pruning an established spindle is to keep the upper branches cut shorter to maintain the cone shape and allow sunlight to reach the lower tiers. It should be done in winter.

On the top tiers cut back the older branches every two or three years to ensure shorter branches and a regular supply of cropping wood each year. Cut out any vigorous leader that exceeds the height of the

TYING DOWN ("FESTOONING")

Trees bear fruit much better when the branches are laid horizontally because it slows up the vegetative growth and allows fruit buds to develop along it. Spindle trees are trained around this principle by developing a series of almost horizontal branches create the tiers. In spring or late summer, loop string gently over the ends of the branches and tie them downwards to nails banged into the base of the stake. Alternatively, attach small weights to the ends of the branches. Remove the strings or weights a few weeks later, after the branches have set in their new positions.

WHEN PRUNING BACK LARGE BRANCHES leave an angular cut and try not to damage surrounding bark. Clean cuts using sharp tools should heal quickly.

TO MAINTAIN THE VIGOUR of a mature spindle, renew the cropping wood from time to time by removing older branches and training new growth in their place.

For a pyramid, maintain the shape in late summer by removing vertical growth and keeping growth at the apex short. On lateral branches, cut back new growth to 20cm (8in) or less, to a downward-facing bud.

Creating a step-over

Apples can be trained as low-growing step-over hedges, creating intriguing and elaborate edges to a pathway, flower border, or vegetable patch. Secure a single horizontal wire at 45–60cm (18–24in) high pulled tight between two posts. Pears are generally too vigorous for this method of training. There are two ways to train a step-over.

STEP-OVER FRUIT TREES make an unusual, productive edging to a garden bed or an allotment plot.

stake and replace it with a more spindly, weaker leader. On the lower tiers, remove some of the older branches to make space for new ones and tie them down if there is space. Remove completely or cut back other branches to three or four buds to encourage fruiting spurs to form. In spring or late summer, tie down any sideshoots using string (see box, opposite), gently looping the string between the branches.

Formative method one

Plant maiden whip apple trees 1.5m (5ft) apart (see page 45). Gently bend each tree over until it is lying horizontally along the wires. Attach the tree securely to the wire using a tree tie. Gently tip-prune the leader to encourage fruiting spurs along the trunk.

Formative method two

Step-overs can be trained as a single-tiered espalier (see page 76), so rather than arching the tree over, it is instead pruned at 45cm (18in) – or the height of the wire – and the two topmost shoots trained along the wire in opposite directions. All other shoots are removed. Step-overs trained by this method will occupy more space (2.1–2.5m/7–8ft) than method one, because the tree has branches going in both directions. Fewer trees are therefore required, saving you money. However, method-two trees will be slower to crop, and furthermore, it does not allow you to pack in lots more varieties of apples into a small garden.

Established pruning of a step-over

Prune step-overs in the same way as established cordons (see page 75) and espaliers (see page 77).

Creating a bush form

An apple or pear tree trained as a bush with a short stem and open centre is the traditional method of growing apples and pears. Not only do they look attractive but their open structure also allows for good air circulation. Prepare the ground thoroughly, then plant the tree (see page 45).

Formative pruning

Create a basic structure of about four strong branches that will form the open shape and regularly bear fruiting sideshoots and spurs. As with any formative pruning, keep cropping to a minimum during the first three years by removing flowers so that the tree's energy is directed to new branches.

In the winter after planting a maiden whip, prune back an apple tree on 'M26' or 'MM106' rootstock and all pear trees to 75cm (30in); shorten trees on 'M27' and 'M9' rootstock to 65cm (26in). Thereafter, follow the same procedure as for a two-year-old feathered maiden.

In the winter, after planting a feathered maiden, remove the leader, cutting back to three or four good strong branches above ground level. These branches should ideally form a wide angle with the trunk. They will become the primary branches of the tree and will form part of its permanent structure. Remove any other branches from the trunk. Cut back any vigorous branches by one-half to an outward-facing bud and shorten less vigorous ones by two-thirds.

By the following winter, the three or four branches chosen the previous winter should have developed a few sideshoots of their own. Select two or three equally spaced sideshoots from each of these branches; you should avoid those growing into the centre of the bush. Cut back the selected sideshoots by one-third and shorten any other shoots to three or four buds, to encourage them to develop as

BUSH TREES, like this 'Cox's Orange Pippin', are a very popular way of training apple and pear trees and bear a lot of fruit. But they do take up a lot more space.

REMOVE CROWDED BRANCHES on established bushes and standard trees, each year in winter. Aim to keep the centre of the tree open.

NEW SHOOTS can also become quite congested. These will need thinning in winter until they are well spaced and all the weaker growth has been removed.

fruiting spurs. Prune back the main branches by one-third, and remove any new shoots that have formed lower down the trunk.

By the next winter, the tree should have a well-established framework of branches. Continue to extend the network of branches by tip-pruning new, well-spaced sideshoots by one-third. Reduce other sideshoots to short spurs of three or four buds or remove them completely. Also cut out branches that are crossing or growing into the centre.

Established pruning of an apple or pear bush

Each winter continue to keep the centre of the tree open by removing branches growing into the centre, with a pruning saw. Lightly prune vigorous trees. Those that are making poor growth can be pruned harder. Cut out all diseased or dead wood.

If the tree is predominantly a spur bearer, tip back one-third of the new sideshoots to 3–4 buds to encourage fruit buds and eventually spurs to develop along their length; leave shorter sideshoots unpruned. On predominantly tip-bearing trees, remove any dense or crossing branches; any remaining sideshoots or new growth should be left unpruned to avoid removing potential fruits that form in the tips.

Remove some of the older branch framework to make way for new, younger shoots. Also cut away all water shoots growing directly from the trunk flush with the trunk.

WATER SHOOTS growing from the main trunk, below the main network of branches, need to be removed at an early stage before they dominate and spoil the look of the tree.

Creating a standard

Standard and half-standard trees are essentially bushes but on taller stems so that the branches start at a different height. The pruning and training method is the same.

Plant care

Apples and pears are some of the easiest fruit trees to grow in temperate climates, although pears can suffer from frost damage in spring.

Weeding

Fruit trees grow better if they are kept free from competing weeds around the base of the tree. Hand weeding and hoeing are the most effective non-chemical method of controlling weeds, along with mulching around the trunk. Avoid strimming near the base of trees because it can rip the bark and in extreme cases kill the tree – in the commercial world strimmers are known as mechanical rabbits because of the damage they can cause. Weedkillers are also effective methods of weed control provided they are used safely (see page 57).

Thinning

Fruit trees naturally drop excess fruit in early summer. This is sometimes referred to as the "June drop". However, nature sometimes needs a helping hand if fruit is going to fully ripen, and biennial cropping and broken branches from heavy yields are to be avoided. Therefore thin apples and pears in midsummer, unless fruit yields have already been seriously reduced by early frosts. Do this for apples by removing the king apple, which is the fruit at the centre of the cluster of fruit and is generally misshapen. Thin dessert apples to leave one or two fruits every 10–12cm (4–5in), and cooking apples to leave one fruit every 15–20cm (6–8in).

On free-standing pear trees, thin fruits out to two fruits every 10–12cm (4–5in), and on restricted forms such as cordons and espaliers to one fruit every 10–12cm (4–5in).

Watering

Water apples and pears during dry spells and from when the fruit starts to swell, particularly if they are newly planted or on restricted rootstocks. The most effective method of doing this for rows of fruit trees is to place a drip line or seep hose under the trees. Large, established trees will be more resistant to periods of drought.

APPLES AND PEARS can set a lot of fruit in good years. Although they drop excessive fruit naturally in early summer, thinning may be needed by hand in midsummer.

FRUIT BUDS ARE FAT because they contain not only next year's leaves but also the flower buds. It is important to recognize these when pruning.

BEFORE RENOVATION, study a neglected apple tree while it is dormant and you can see the branch structure. Usually, this is a tangle of twiggy branches.

CUT OUT NO MORE THAN A QUARTER of the branches in one growing season. Thin out the crown and remove dead, diseased, and crossing branches.

Feeding

In early spring, sprinkle a balanced general fertilizer in early spring around the root zone, following the manufacturer's instructions.

Maypoling

Trees heavily laden with fruit may require support as the fruits swell and develop. Maypoling is a popular method with spindle trees (see page 78), whereby strings are looped around the centre of the branches and tied upwards to the top of the posts. Alternatively, stake individual branches if they look as though they may break.

Summer pruning

To stimulate fruit bud initiation, cut back any overvigorous trees in late summer. (Winter pruning encourages vegetative growth.) Restricted forms such as cordons, fans, and espaliers should also be pruned in late summer.

Rejuvenating a neglected tree

There are a number of reasons why apple and pear trees benefit from rejuvenation. It is important because congested canopies cause poor air

circulation, which can potentially create a build-up of pests and diseases within the canopy. Congestion also creates shade, which reduces the light levels necessary for fruit bud initiation and ripening and therefore causes low yields of apples and pears. Furthermore, whatever fruit there is is usually undersized, has poor colour, and rarely tastes good because the tree hasn't been able to produce adequate sugars.

Oversized, congested apple trees often dominate older gardens, and the question of whether it is worth restoring is often an issue confronting the owner. An oversized tree in a small garden can certainly be a problem with it casting too much shade or its roots absorbing too much moisture and nutrients from the rest of the garden. Mature trees will never be as fruitful as young trees – most apple and pear trees are most productive for their first 8–20 years, although they can still continue to give large, healthy crops for considerably longer if looked after properly. Old trees can also create an invaluable habitat for wildlife, and they can also make attractive features with their old gnarled trunks. Climbing

CUT DYING BRANCHES close to the base where they join the main framework. Use a sharp and clean pruning saw.

THIN OVERCROWDED STEMS growing into the centre of the tree and those that are rubbing against other stems.

TIDY UP AROUND THE BASE of the tree by removing suckers and water shoots as well as competing weeds.

plants such as roses and clematis can be trained up into them to compensate for any lack of blossom.

If the decision is made to completely remove an apple tree it is worth consulting a fruit expert to discover whether the variety is rare – many old varieties have been lost and it would be tragic to lose yet another one. One method of preserving the variety would be to save a few branches and send them off to a fruit nursery to be propagated (either by grafting or budding) onto dwarf rootstocks, which can then be replanted in the garden at a more manageable size.

However, any tree that is worth saving should be renovated in winter, when the leaves aren't on the tree. Just as a surgeon wouldn't operate on a fully clothed person, a tree needs to be seen as a whole, with its bare limbs exposed, so that clinical decisions can be made as to which parts of the tree should be removed and which should be saved.

Basic approach In addition to the basic pruning instructions on pages 50–53, bear in mind when removing large limbs from a tree that it should be restored gradually to its former glory and in stages over a few years. Making lots of large cuts and removing all the large limbs will stress the tree, causing it to overcompensate the following year by sending out an excess of vigorous branches.

That said, apple and pear trees are resilient and can deal with far more pruning than other trees. Dispense with secateurs and only use a pruning saw. Tree restoration requires big decisions and usually

big cuts. Snipping away with secateurs will just encourage more vigorous growth to develop.

Assess the tree from the ground, looking at the overall shape of the tree. Identify the original shape of the tree. Was it supposed to be open centred or have a central leader? Which branches are making the tree look unbalanced or lose its shape? If the tree is too high for picking the fruit or for spraying, decide how to cut branches back to lower limbs.

Renovation Once main branches have been identified, use a tripod stepladder to get in close to the tree and begin to saw out selected branches. Always cut back to another branch. Don't leave large stubs because these will die back and can cause problems with diseases (see page 53). When in the canopy of the tree it will also be easier to identify crossing branches that have been rubbing against each other and therefore causing damage to the bark. Remove these initially, as well as dead and diseased branches such as those riddled with canker. Cut out large branches in any sections, making undercuts to prevent the bark from tearing (see page 53).

Over a period of several years, prune most branches lower down close to the crown of the tree. A useful rule of thumb is to remove no more than a quarter of the branches in one pruning session. Don't make the mistake of cutting back all the tips on the growth – a bit like hedge trimming – because the tree will regenerate from the cuts making it top-heavy, which will cause shading and poor fruiting.

Keep getting down from the ladder to reassess the tree, which will look very different from the ground than from up close on a ladder.

At harvest time

Apples With most fruit, the obvious method of testing if it is ready for picking is to taste it. This is certainly possible with some of the early apples such as 'Discovery', which can be eaten fresh off the tree. However, some of the later-maturing apples require a period of storage before being ready for eating – a bit like a fine wine – and therefore other methods of identifying when a fruit is ready for harvesting are required.

The telltale sign of an apple being ready for picking is a few windfalls lying beneath the tree. The fruit should have swelled up to a good size and have started to colour up. Cut the apple in half and look at the pips – if they have changed from white to brown then the apple is close to harvest time.

To pick an apple, cup it lightly in your hand, lift gently, and give it a slight twist. The fruit should come away in your hand with the stalk intact. If it doesn't, then it isn't ready for picking. Never pull at the fruit, because this can break the fruiting spurs.

Place the apples gently into a box or bucket, being careful not to drop them or bruise them. Specially

STORAGE

Apples Early apples need to be eaten within one or two days after picking, while some of the later fruits can last for months, if kept properly. Store in a dark, cool place – a cellar is ideal; a shed or garage is the next best option. A slight humidity in the atmosphere also helps to preserve the fruit. Ideal temperatures are 2–5°C (35–41°F). Good ventilation is important, so store apples in slatted wooden or plastic crates or boxes, spreading the fruit out evenly and ensuring they do not touch each other. The fruit can also be wrapped in paper to help prevent contact. Check over the fruits frequently removing any ones showing signs of rot.

Pears These fruits benefit from storage or period of ripening before eating: early varieties usually need a week or so until they become softer, while later ones can require months before being ready for eating. Press the pear for softness, particularly around the stalk, for indications of the fruit being ready for eating. Pears tend to rot very quickly so regular inspections are imperative. Store pears in the same way as apples (see above).

A LINED FRUIT BUCKET is the ideal tool for collecting an apple and pear harvest. Discard rotting and damaged fruit.

WRAP AN APPLE in paper or a perforated freezer bag, or lie unwrapped on a tray away from others. Keep the stalks intact.

STORE APPLES AND PEARS in a cool, dark place. Inspect the fruit regularly and remove any rotting fruit immediately.

PEARS BENEFIT from a period of ripening before eating while they turn soft and juicy. Most pears do not store well; those that do are treated as for apples.

designed buckets that hang from the shoulders are useful if lots of apples are to be harvested.

Pears Harvest pears just before they are fully ripened. They should be firm and swollen, with a subtle colour change to their skin. Test early varieties by tasting one of the fruit for sweetness, yet firmness. Later varieties should part easily from the tree when lifted and gently twisted.

Pests and diseases

Be vigilant for pests and diseases that can drastically reduce your fruit crop or in the worse case kill your apple or pear tree. Codling moth (see page 58), winter moth (see page 59), blossom wilt (see page 60), brown rot (see page 60), fireblight (see page 60), powdery mildew (see page 61), and replant problems (see page 61) can also cause problems, as can the following more specific pests and diseases.

Apple and pear scab Dark green patches appear on leaves followed by raised, brown or black corky scabs on the surface of the fruit. This can cause the fruit to split, which in turn can be an entry point for brown rot (see page 60). The spores are spread by rain and wind. Removing and burning fallen leaves will partially help to reduce the spread of spores. Alternatively, spray with mancozeb or myclobutanil at regular intervals from bud-burst until midsummer.

Apple sawfly The sawfly lays its eggs in apple blossom. When the larvae hatch they create scar-like markings are created on the skin of the forming fruits. The fruitlets will either drop in June or if the larva dies before reaching the core it will leave unsightly scarring on the outside of the fruit. Frass can usually be seen at the exit hole. Remove damaged fruitlets as soon as the symptoms are seen and destroy damaged fruit lying on the ground. Alternatively, spray with bifenthrin at petal-fall.

Bitter pit Sunken holes appear on the surface of apples. Underneath the flesh is discoloured. Particularly susceptible varieties include 'Bramley's Seedling', 'Egremont Russet', and 'Newton Wonder'. This disorder is caused by poor distribution of calcium around the plant, combined with erratic watering. A foliage spray with calcium nitrate, applied at regular intervals from midsummer to early autumn, will help to alleviate the problem.

Capsid bug This sap-sucking insect attacks leaves developing at the shoot tips during spring and summer. Its toxic saliva kills off cells, and the damage distorts leaves that tear into many small holes. It also causes small, corky scabs to appear on the fruit. Spray with bifenthrin at the first signs of damage.

Fungal canker Apples and pears are frequently affected by canker, which can eventually kill the tree. It causes depression and cracks within the branches, often near pruning cuts or wounds. The infection prevents nutrients and water being distributed around the plant, so dieback can frequently be seen above the wound. Remove affected branches as soon as the symptoms occur. Spraying with a copper-based fungicide may help to slow up the spread of the fungus.

Pear and cherry slugworm The slugworm is a sawfly larva covered in a slimy, black mucus. It grazes the upper leaf surfaces of apples and pears, causing

APPLE POWDERY MILDEW is typified by a dry, whitish powder coating the leaves and shoot tips. Deter it by keeping plants well grown, well watered, and ventilated.

APPLE SCAB causes dark green patches on the leaves and then discoloured areas on the fruits themselves. Scab can result in splitting of the fruit.

damaged parts to dry up. The slugworm rarely affects the fruits, but you can spray it with bifenthrin if the larvae are numerous.

Pear leaf blister mite This mite is a common problem on pear foliage, causing yellow or red blisters that eventually turn black; foliage also appears blistered. The damage is unsightly, but does not tend to affect the crop, although it may cause premature leaf fall. There is no control other than removing the damaged leaves on lightly infested trees.

Pear midge This pest causes fruitlets to turn black and fall prematurely. When cut open, the fruit may reveal lots of white grubs. Remove infected fruitlets as soon as the damage is discovered. Placing carpet or ground-cover fabric under the tree may reduce the number larvae that succeed in pupating in the soil after dropping from the fruitlets. Also spray with bifenthrin just before the blossom opens.

Rosy apple aphid The rosy apple aphid causes curling leaves and sometimes stunted fruits. The aphid overwinters as eggs in crevices on the trunk, branches, and twigs. They hatch at bud-burst and remain until midsummer, when they migrate to plantains. Rosy apple aphid can be controlled with a plant oil wash. Alternatively, spray with bifenthrin or thiacloprid at bud burst. These are of short

persistence, so thorough treatment, especially of the underside of leaves, is necessary.

Woolly aphid The woolly aphid secretes a whitish, woolly-like substance that can clearly be seen on the stems and branches in spring and summer. Brush the affected area with soapy water. Alternatively, spray with bifenthrin or thiacloprid at the first sign of wooliness.

THE APPLE SAWFLY lays its eggs in the blossom and causes either premature dropping of the fruit or unsightly scarring. Remove damaged fruit as soon as problems are noticed.

Carol's fruit notebook

Quinces

" The quince is a delicious and useful fruit that historically has been valued all over the western world, both in its own right and as an improver of other cooked fruit. It is full of pectin, and its subtle flavour made it indispensable for the setting of jams and fruit jellies; but the advent of cheap sugar and the commercial marketing of a narrow range of fruit types has left it on the margins. However, quince is delicious cooked – with stewed apples, for example – although its tough skin makes it much harder to peel than apples or pears. The toughness of its skin is one reason quinces rot slowly, lasting well into the new year following harvest. This was a particular advantage quinces had before the introduction of cold storage for apples and pears. Its spring blossom can be very attractive, too, and it sustains several species of British moths.

For the fruits to ripen fully the quince needs a sheltered position and a long, hot summer, so unsurprisingly it is especially popular in the Mediterranean and the Middle East. *Dulce de membrillo* (quince paste) is imported as a speciality from Spain, though easy enough to make in more northerly climes. In fact, there is a long history of quince jelly-making in England, and because it will hold detailed shapes very well there was an entertaining tradition of creative mould-making. The Portuguese word for quince is *marmelo*, hence the English word "marmalade". Wherever there is a surfeit of quinces, man's idle ingenuity has found numerous uses for them, notably quince ratafia (the equivalent of sloe gin), in which grated quince is added to brandy to infuse over several months. Just like sloes, quinces can be made into an alcoholic liqueur – but you do need to be very patient because it does take a long time to mature. "

THE HEADY PERFUME OF A RIPE QUINCE is quite delicious to drink in and, in my opinion, something every gardener should experience.

Quinces

Cydonia oblonga

The quince tree makes an unusual addition to the fruit garden, but one that is well worthwhile because the trees are easy to look after and are not prone to many of the more common fruit problems. The hard, pear-shaped fruits emit a heady perfume and flavour. These are a wonderful addition to fruit pies and jellies – their unique taste being hard to match.

QUINCES ARE ORNAMENTAL as well as productive. Their single, large, bowl-shaped flowers are borne in abundance in spring and are followed by colourful fruits.

The best sites and soils

Quinces are happy in most soils, but particularly those that are relatively moist throughout the summer yet well drained to avoid waterlogging in winter. Light or shallow chalky soils should have plenty of organic matter added prior to planting, and be well mulched afterwards. Avoid frost pockets for these early-flowering trees. Quinces need a long growing season to ripen well and so are best trained as a fan against a south- or west-facing wall in more exposed or northerly gardens. Gardeners in warmer climates or in sheltered, urban, or coastal sites, however, can train their quinces as free-standing trees provided they position them in a sunny location. Free-standing specimens will attain a height and spread of 3.75–5m (12–16ft) at maturity, depending on the rootstock, position, and soil type.

Buying tips

There are a dozen or so varieties of quince to choose from, of which 'Vranja' and 'Champion' are two of the most popular (see box, below). Quinces can be purchased as grafted plants, either onto a 'Quince A' (semidwarfing) or 'Quince C' (dwarfing) rootstock. Being self-fertile only one tree is needed to obtain fruits, although you often find that yield per tree is increased with two or more different varieties.

Recommended varieties

'Champion'
This variety bears large, pear-shaped fruits that ripen relatively early compared to other quinces. The tree crops regularly and heavily. When cooked, the flesh of 'Champion' turns blush pink.

'Vranja'
The numerous pale green to golden, pear-shaped fruit of 'Vranja' are larger than normal among quinces. Its fruit has exceptional flavour and perfume, making this a very popular choice to cultivate.

ONCE A BASIC FRAMEWORK of stems has been established quince pruning can be kept to a minimum, and consists mainly of removing unproductive, damaged, or dead wood.

When buying a feathered maiden, look for one with a uniform framework of branches because quinces can occasionally produce rather unbalanced growth. Alternatively, buy a maiden whip and prune it back to the height that you wish the branches to start on planting to encourage multiple side branching.

Plant care

Quinces are a relatively low-maintenance crop compared to other fruits, the most important consideration being watering. Because they prefer relatively moist soils, the trees need supplementary irrigation during periods of drought, even once established. Apply an organic mulch, 7.5cm (3in) thick, in midspring to help keep roots cool and

STORAGE

One of the quince's assets is that the fruits can be stored up until mid- or late winter before they will spoil, so their season of use is much extended. The fruits emit a strong perfume once ripe and this can taint less aromatic produce that may be nearby. It is therefore essential that they are stored separately, ideally on slatted trays or in cardboard boxes in a cool, dark but frost-free location.

moist, and a top-dressing of a high potash fertilizer, such as sulphate of potash, in late winter to boost yields and ripen fruits. A similar application of sulphate of ammonia or other high nitrogen fertilizer every three or four years will also be beneficial, especially on light, sandy soils.

A quince tree in full bloom is quite a feature in a garden, but the flowers should be protected if a late frost is forecast. The fruits can take a long time to develop in cooler summers, and no thinning should be necessary.

At harvest time

Although quinces ripen well in hot, sunny summers they are very unlikely to produce fruits that are edible straight off the tree. Leave the fruits to hang on the tree as long as possible, but harvest them before the first frosts. Then cook the quinces before consuming them. Store in isolation in a dry, frost-free site (see box, below left) until required.

Training and pruning

Quinces bear their flowers singly at the tips of one-year-old stems and to a lesser extent on short fruiting spurs.

Carry out formative pruning in winter – aim to create a system of well-spaced branches on a clear stem, as for apples and pears (see page 80). The erratic growth of quinces means that you'll occasionally have to remove wayward stems as they're produced, but it is better to sacrifice an inappropriate shoot in the initial stages of training rather than trying to remedy the situation once the tree's framework is otherwise well established.

Established pruning simply consists of removing dead, diseased, and damaged growth every winter, along with thinning out congested or unproductive stems. Pull off any suckers as soon as they develop.

Pests and diseases

Quince leaf blight (small brown spots on the foliage) can be a problem in moist summers, so rake up and burn any affected leaves. Quinces can also suffer from powdery mildews (see page 61), brown rot (see page 60), rusts, and fireblight (see page 60).

Medlars *Mespilus germanica*

The medlar makes an attractive tree with good autumn colour and single flowers sometimes tinged with pink. Due to its spreading nature it is better suited to medium or large gardens. The fruits are unusual in that they need to be stored for an appreciable amount of time before they become palatable.

MEDLARS ARE CLOSELY RELATED to apples, but their distinctive fruits can't be eaten until they have been stored for many weeks.

The best sites and soils

Medlar trees are fully hardy and crop best if they are positioned in an open, sunny site. Although they will tolerate a position in dappled shade, their flowering, cropping, and golden-yellow autumn leaf colours will all be reduced. Avoid frost pockets if at all possible, because medlars flower in late spring. Position them in moisture-retentive yet free-draining soil. Although medlars are more tolerant of moist soils than other tree fruits, you should add bulky organic matter on heavy clay soils prior to planting to aid drainage.

Buying tips

Medlars can develop into very spreading trees – up to 8m (25ft) wide and 6m (20ft) tall at maturity – so are most suitable for medium-sized or large gardens. To appreciate their unusual habit, site them as specimen trees rather than in a mixed border.

Trees are occasionally sold on their own roots, but more often are grafted onto hawthorn (*Crataegus*, semidwarfing), 'Quince A' (semidwarfing), or 'Quince C' (dwarfing) rootstocks. This can limit the tree's size slightly, as can choosing naturally compact varieties such as 'Nottingham'.

Medlars are self-fertile so only one variety needs to be grown to obtain fruit. Their branches tend to droop to the ground. Avoid this by choosing a tree with high branches or tip back the leader of a tall maiden whip to a strong bud on planting.

STORAGE

To make medlars more palatable lay fruits that are unblemished in a wooden or cardboard box and place this in a dark, cool but frost-free shed or garage for a few weeks. The fruits will gradually turn from light to dark brown (a process called "bletting"), and their texture will become much softer. Medlars can then be eaten raw; they are often used to make a perfumed, amber jelly for game and other meats.

MEDLARS ARE OFTEN GRAFTED onto rootstocks, so any suckers need to be removed. Ideally pull them off at the base, but if this proves impractical cut them off at ground level with secateurs.

Plant care

Once established a medlar tree can be left to its own devices and will still produce a respectable crop. Because free-standing trees can become quite sizeable, however, you may need to restrict the tree's size by pruning and training, if your growing area is relatively small.

At harvest time

Medlar fruits are hard and extremely astringent when they are picked, which should be as late as possible

but before the first frosts. The fruits are best stored before being eaten (see box, opposite).

Training and pruning

The large, single flowers are borne on the tips of sideshoots and naturally forming spurs after 3–4 years, and these give rise to the spherical, squat fruits. The spreading nature of medlars means that the first few years of training consists of removing the lower branches to form a single, clear stem (called a "standard").

Thereafter, the tree will require a certain amount of pruning to keep it within bounds. In winter, remove congested wood and shorten overlong branches. Older specimens may need lower limbs propped up if they haven't been shortened sufficiently. Renovation isn't recommended because it spoils the natural shape of the tree.

A medlar that has been grafted onto a quince or hawthorn rootstock may occasionally produce suckers during summer. Remove these from the parent plant while they are still small by pulling, rather than cutting them, if possible, which removes dormant buds at the sucker's base. If the suckers are numerous they can, as a second choice, be cut out.

Pests and diseases

These fruit trees are relatively trouble-free but may suffer from hawthorn leaf spot (*Diplocarpon mespili*), which appears as multiple brown spots, 1–2mm (1/32–1/16in) across, on the foliage. Rake up and burn the affected leaves. There is no chemical control for this fungal disease.

Recommended varieties

'Dutch'
This variety bears very large fruit, with each being up to 8cm (3½in) in diameter. The tree is quite vigorous and so should be given plenty of room to spread.

'Nottingham'
A more compact variety than 'Dutch' so suitable for smaller gardens. The fruits are also slightly smaller (up to 5cm/2in in diameter) and are produced even on relatively young trees.

Plums, damsons, and gages

" There are many, many varieties of plums and gages – from tiny, sour bullaces and small, tart damsons to stickily sweet dessert plums and gages, with a wealth of cookable plums in between. If you are lucky enough to have the space for a plum tree or two

you will be initiated into a world of new flavours. There are wide variations in the wild versions with much intermixing between sloes, bullaces, and damsons with distinctly individual fruits, sometimes particular to one tree in one locality. Indeed, you might be able to find yourself a "local" variety. Mirabelle plums from France are a culinary bridge between the wild versions and the cultivated plums, being not too sweet for cooking yet perfect for jam-making. A note of sourness often accompanies a good, full-flavoured cooking variety.

An easier choice is between plums for cooking and dessert plums for eating raw. It can be a disappointment to bit into a sour cooking plum expecting the yielding flesh, loose stone, and gentle sweetness of a ripe dessert plum. So try to grow a choice dessert plum for yourself: a "honey sweet" 'Cambridge Gage', a temperamental but superb 'Coe's Golden Drop', a 'Transparent Gage', or a blue-bloomed, dark-purple 'Kirke's' gage – just the names are quaint, the fruit is luscious. "

I DON'T KNOW MANY gardeners who could resist the sugary temptations of a perfectly ripe plum.

Plums, damsons, and gages
Prunus domestica and *P. insititia*

These trees have to be some of the least demanding in the fruit garden; they require little established pruning and most varieties crop heavily and reliably. Modern rootstocks, training methods, and increasing availability of self-fertile varieties now allow gardeners to grow a single tree in even the smallest gardens.

The best sites and soils

Because these fruits have quite high moisture demands they are best planted on clay or loamy soils. All sites need to be well drained as plums and gages in particular hate waterlogged soils. Add bulky organic matter to sandy or shallow chalky soils prior to planting. When container-grown, make sure pots are of sufficient size to prevent the potting compost drying out in summer, otherwise flower development and therefore yield will be very much reduced.

These stone fruits are some of the earliest crops to flower in the fruit garden. While the plants themselves are often extremely hardy, the flowers can easily be killed by frosts. It's therefore essential to position your trees out of frost pockets or windy sites. A sheltered, sunny spot will encourage insects emerging from hibernation to visit and pollinate the flowers, and also provide some shelter from extremes of cold. Gages in particular are best sited against a south- or west-facing wall to ensure the fruits are exposed to sufficient sunshine and warmth to develop their sweet, rich flavour and to ripen wood.

Buying tips

Thanks to modern rootstocks and restrictive training techniques any garden whether large or small can accommodate a plum, gage, damson, or bullace tree, which used to be too vigorous for most gardens. Standard, pyramid, fan, and festooned tree forms are all possibilities. These stone fruits don't make productive cordons or espaliers, because they crop well along the length of young shoots and therefore don't need to form fruiting spurs. Possible rootstocks include 'Pixy' (semidwarfing, ideal for pyramids and fans), 'Ferlenain' (semidwarfing, again ideal for pyramids and fans, gives fruit of better size than 'Pixy' but more prone to suckering), 'St Julien A' (semivigorous, useful for larger pyramids and fans), and 'Brompton' (vigorous, use for standards; generally produces a tree up to 6m/20ft tall).

There are hundreds of varieties to choose from for both cooking and dessert use – those with limited outdoor space can opt for a dual-purpose variety to get maximum use from the crop. Many of these are self-fertile so a single tree can be planted, while some plums and gages, and to a lesser extent bullaces and damsons, are self-infertile (that is, require another compatible variety to pollinate the flowers in order to set a crop). Some incompatibility exists with certain self-infertile varieties (for example, 'Coe's Golden Drop' won't be pollinated by 'Allgroves Superb' and vice versa) so check with the supplier before buying. Plums are divided into five separate flowering groups so ensure self-infertile varieties are in the same or adjacent groups for cross-pollination purposes (see page 218).

When buying a plum, gage, damson, or bullace look for a system of well-balanced branches with a strong central leader. You can then train and prune the

PLUMS, GAGES, DAMSONS, AND BULLACES are some of the first fruit trees to flower, so it's essential to site them in a sheltered spot where insects can access the blooms and exposure to frosts can be minimized.

Fruit types

Although there are hundreds of varieties of plum, gage, bullace, and damson (the National Fruit Collection in Kent, UK, holds more than 300 varieties of plum alone), their cultivation needs are much the same. However, to get the most from this diverse group it's useful to understand the different fruit types.

Plums
By far the largest group, all plums are varieties of *Prunus domestica*, and can be dessert, culinary, or dual purpose. Fruit size can vary greatly between varieties, but their shapes tend to be ovoid.

Gages
All are varieties of *P. domestica*, and can be dual purpose, culinary, or dessert. The main characteristic of gages is their sweet, often extremely good flavour. Fruit shape tends to be spherical.

Damsons
These are varieties of *P. insititia*, and generally produce smaller fruits than plums or gages. The skin is much more tart, making damsons excellent for culinary use, but not for eating raw off the tree.

Bullaces
These *P. insititia* varieties bear even smaller fruits than damsons. They tend to crop heavily and are very hardy. The fruit is extremely hard and tart, even when fully ripe, so is only used for cooking.

plant to accommodate any of the popular tree forms (see pages 75–81).

Pyramid-trained trees are ideal for gardens where free-standing space is limited because the spread of a pyramid is less than a standard form. A pyramid tree retains its central leader and then has its sideshoots tipped back to encourage branching. The tipping is done in such a way that the tree develops

ONE OF THE BEST WAYS to train a plum, damson, gage, or bullace tree is as a fan, so the sunlight can develop the full flavour of these sugary fruits as they ripen.

a cone shape, allowing sunlight to access and ripen all the fruits (see page 78). This is a useful method to develop the full flavour of sun-loving gages, especially for those gardeners who don't have the space for a fan.

Recommended varieties (plums)

'Blue Tit'
This dual-purpose, very hardy, self-fertile plum variety produces regular, heavy crops on compact, bushy plants. Ready in late summer, the medium-sized fruits have a deep blue skin and an excellent flavour.

'Czar'
This self-fertile variety is best used as a culinary plum, although some find its acidic fruits palatable when raw. The heavy crops are reliably produced. The purple fruits are ready to harvest in late summer.

'Laxton's Delight'
The main merit of this dessert plum is the delicious flavour of its plentiful, large, yellow fruits. These are ready to eat in late summer. Is partly self-fertile so best planted with another variety.

'Marjorie's Seedling'
A self-fertile, very hardy tree with very good disease resistance. In a hot summer the fruits, which are ready in early autumn, have a good flavour when raw; in poorer summers use them for cooking.

Plant care

Cover fan-trained trees temporarily in a tent of double-thickness horticultural fleece on frosty nights when plants are in flower, holding the fleece away from the flowers with canes. Fruit set is generally finished by early summer, after which the fruits start to swell significantly. Once fruits have set, they may well require thinning to ease congestion and weight in the canopy, as well as to boost fruit size. It is often essential to prop up branches in mid- and late summer, as fruit weight can otherwise snap them.

While a tree may well bear fruit without a gardener's intervention, yields can be greatly increased by appropriate and timely feeding and watering. Because they can set such heavy crops, plums and gages, and to a lesser extent damsons and bullaces, respond well to fertilizer application, especially nitrogen. On established trees apply a mulch of well-rotted farmyard manure in midspring to help retain soil moisture, keep down weeds, and provide nitrogen. This can be supplemented with a top-dressing of dried poultry pellets or non-organic nitrogen fertilizer such as sulphate of ammonia. Add a top-dressing of sulphate of potash in late winter.

VARIETIES THAT CROP very heavily benefit from having their fruit thinned out in midsummer. This will boost fruit size, reduce biennial bearing, and avoid snapped branches.

At harvest time

Harvest fruits carefully so as not to bruise them, then eat fresh, destone and freeze, or make the fruits into preserves. Damsons and bullaces can also be steeped in alcohol to make a sloe gin-like liquor.

'Opal'
This self-fertile Swedish dessert variety is very hardy and produces heavy crops on vigorous, upright trees. The small, purple fruits have a good flavour and are ready to harvest in late summer.

'Pershore'
The large, yellow fruits of this culinary plum are ready to harvest in late summer. The tree crops heavily and reliably, and has excellent disease resistance. One of the best cooking plums, and a self-fertile variety.

'Sanctus Hubertus'
This is a reliable, early plum with large, purple fruits that are ready to eat in late summer. The fruits can be used both for cooking and dessert, the flavour being good and not overly sweet. Only partly self-fertile.

'Victoria'
A popular, self-fertile, dual-purpose variety bearing heavy, regular crops. The pink, medium-sized fruits are ready in late summer. Their flavour raw is average but when cooked they make an excellent jam.

Training and pruning

Plums, gages, damsons, and bullaces flower predominantly on the base of one-year-old shoots and along the length of two-year-old shoots. They also flower on any fruiting spurs that form.

Always prune these stone fruits in spring or summer. If pruned in winter they are much more prone to bacterial canker and silver leaf infection. Remove the central leader from a tree to be fan-trained in its first summer; tie canes to the horizontal wire supports and the remaining sideshoots to the canes. Tie in new shoots that develop from these stems to fill any gaps. Standard trees are trained as for standard apples and pears (see page 81). Due to their spread they are only really suitable for a large garden.

Festooning (see page 78) is a useful technique to encourage plums and gages to fruit more heavily and to restrict the size of your tree. It is ideal for young standard or pyramid trees. Tie the main branches (not the pyramid's central leader) over in an arch using soft foam ties or tights – this encourages better flowering. At the same time pinch back sideshoots,

TO KEEP YOUR TREES COMPACT it's essential to regularly pinch back shoots on established fans and festooned trees in early and midsummer.

to encourage fruiting spurs. Untie the stems once they are set in place (generally after one year).

Once the initial shape is obtained subsequent pruning consists of removing congested growth as well as dead, diseased, or damaged stems, and it should be done immediately after fruit harvest. Restricted tree forms such as pyramids also require additional pruning to help retain their shape (see pages 75–80). On established fans remove badly placed or congested shoots and tie in new ones. Pinch out their tips when they have produced six leaves, shortening them again to three leaves after harvest.

Pests and diseases

The most common disease problems on these stone fruits are brown rot (see page 60), silver leaf (see page 61), blossom wilt (see page 60), rust (see page 61), and bacterial canker (see pages 59). Common pests include wasps (see page 59) and bullfinches (see page 58). Mealy plum aphid (white insects on the growing points and undersides of leaves) and plum leaf-curling aphid (curling young leaves) can appear in early spring – either tolerate or spray with thiacloprid (not when trees are in flower). Plum sawfly attacks young fruits that fall prematurely – pick these up. Plum moth larvae attack ripening fruits – hang pheromone traps in trees in mid-May to trap the male moths.

SILVER LEAF IS A FUNGAL DISEASE that can cause lack of vigour, and even dieback, in plums, damsons, and gages. It can be avoided by pruning your trees at the right time of year, that is in spring or summer.

Recommended varieties (bullaces)

'White Bullace', syn. 'Golden Bullace'
This variety bears very small, spherical fruits with a pale yellow skin and flesh. The fruits are ready to pick for cooking in midautumn, and are produced in abundance on self-fertile trees.

'Black Bullace'
This self-fertile variety has been in cultivation since the early 16th century, producing regular, heavy crops of small, deep purple fruits. These are ready for harvest in early autumn and make excellent jams.

Recommended varieties (damsons)

'Farleigh Damson'
This culinary variety produces regular, heavy crops with an excellent flavour. Ready to pick in late summer, the small black fruits are borne on compact, partly self-fertile, very hardy trees.

'Prune Damson', syn. 'Shropshire Damson'
Another self-fertile culinary variety, it bears deep purple fruits with an excellent flavour that are ready to pick in early autumn. The compact, hardy tree is tolerant of moister soils than most.

Recommended varieties (gages)

'Cambridge Gage'
The fruits on these compact, partly self-fertile trees have an excellent flavour and are produced very regularly if not too heavily. Use both as a dessert and culinary variety, picking in late summer.

'Golden Transparent'
The flavour of this dessert gage is sweet and excellent, and the yellow fruits are borne regularly and heavily. The trees are self-fertile and the fruit is ready to pick in early autumn.

'Jefferson'
This dessert variety has extremely good disease resistance but is self-infertile so must be planted with other varieties. The fruits are ready in late summer and are borne regularly and moderately.

'Oullins Gage'
This dual-purpose gage has a good flavour and crops regularly and heavily. The yellow, medium fruits are ready in late summer and are borne on vigorous, self-fertile trees, which make good pollinators.

Carol's fruit notebook

Peaches and nectarines

" A ripe nectarine always evokes the Mediterranean to me – fragrant air, concentrated sunshine, summer heat, warm balmy evenings. Fortunately, it is perfectly possible to grow nectarines in the cool-temperate areas; you just need the right conditions and a little bit of luck. The blossom in early spring cannot be allowed to get at all frosted, the roots must be kept moist, and the tree must live in a sheltered suntrap to collect all the sun going. Peaches are a little bit more robust than nectarines and have a longer track record in cool climates. There is also a greater choice of peach varieties than nectarine ones, either as trees to plant or as fruit to buy, but it is still certainly worth identifying and seeking out the nectarine variety you want to grow.

Both peaches and nectarines can have white or yellow flesh. The yellow flesh tends to be a little more tart and acidic, and this helps in any cooked or preserved dishes. White flesh is probably derived from the Asian branch of the genus and is milder, and, without the sour contrast, often tastes sweeter. To some people a nectarine is just a peach without the furry skin, due to a recessive gene. To me, they are both fabulous fruits.

Peaches and nectarines must be allowed to fully ripen on the tree to develop their full flavour. In the fruit bowl the acidity weakens over time, leaving only a blander sweetness. A peach ripened in its own time on the tree, warmed by the sun, and picked by gently cupping your hand around its full delectable contours is a sensual delight and a privilege to enjoy.

Usually the ripe fruits have gloriously splashed, two-tone coloured skins; the pale shade on the skin of both peaches and nectarines can indicate the flesh colour inside. They won't be ripe if there is any touch of green on the skin, unless it is a 'Nectar' variety, bred under patent to be ripe early but stay a whiter shade of pale. Enjoy them all! "

WHAT A TREAT TO DISCOVER that you can grow peaches and nectarines in your own garden. If you have a warm, sunny wall, there should be nothing to stop you trying.

Peaches and nectarines

Prunus persica

A ripe peach picked straight from the tree is one of the juiciest fruits that can be grown in the garden, rewarding you with a drink as much as an edible feast. The closely related, smooth-skinned nectarine is slightly harder to cultivate, but its sensational taste makes this a must for any gourmet gardener.

The best sites and soils

Peaches and nectarines are best grown as a fan on a sunny, south- or south-west-facing wall if the fruits are going to successfully ripen in temperate climates. Peaches can also be grown as free-standing bushes in very favourable sites, but nectarines will struggle. A sheltered position will help prevent the leaves and fruit becoming damaged, while exposure to rain will create problems with peach leaf curl. Early spring blossom can easily become damaged, so avoid placing in a frost pocket.

Plant in well-drained soil that contains plenty of well-rotted humus to help retain moisture. Peach trees will struggle in light, shallow soils, meaning that any underlying compacted soil should be broken up prior to planting and plenty of organic matter incorporated into the soil the month before planting.

Due to their slightly tender nature, both peaches and nectarines can successfully be grown in glasshouses, too, but will require diligent watering. Both these fruit trees need a period of dormancy, so do not use a heated greenhouse.

Buying tips

Peaches and nectarines are ideal for small spaces. Firstly because they are self-fertile, meaning they don't require another tree for pollination. Secondly, there are compact forms of peaches that can successfully be grown in pots, making them suitable for a sunny patio, courtyard, or balcony. These varieties rarely reach more than 1m (3ft) tall when grown in a pot, and require minimal pruning.

Most peaches are supplied on a 'St Julien A' rootstock. This restrains the vigour and restricts the size of the tree, making it better suited to the average-sized garden.

Training a peach or nectarine as a fan on a south- or south-west-facing wall will be the most successful method of producing fruit. Expect a fan to grow to the height of a fence panel (1.8m/6ft) and about 3.5m (11ft) across.

It is best to buy a partially trained, two- or three-year-old fan from a garden centre or nursery as this will save both time and money. There should be at least eight branches on the partially trained fan.

IN A GOOD YEAR peach and nectarine trees will yield upwards of 9kg (20lb) of fruit. The fruit are ripe when the flesh around the stalk begins to soften.

ON A DEVELOPING FAN select three or four new shoots that are growing from each rib, in summer. Cut the others back to just above the first leaf. One of these shoots can be tied downwards and the rest can be trained upwards.

TIE IN THE SHOOTS that are growing at the tip of each rib to extend their length and fill in the wall space. Use soft twine tied in a figure of eight to cushion the young growth.

Spread these out evenly over the wall space, with four branches on each side tied to canes already attached to wires on the wall.

If you have got space for only one fan and cannot decide between a peach or nectarine, it is possible to grow both on the same plant. Ask a specialist fruit nursery to bud a nectarine onto a young peach tree. One side will eventually produce peaches and the other side nectarines. Almonds are very closely related, and have a similar growth habit, meaning that they too can share the same rootstock.

The best time to plant is late autumn when the soil is still warm and there is more chance of the tree establishing itself before the big push in early spring. Although a container-grown peach tree can be planted at any time of year, it is better not to do so during summer when the newly planted tree will require copious water. Bare-root trees are usually healthier plants as they are not rootbound.

Plant care

Generally it is not the cold of winter that harms peach and nectarine trees, which will quite happily survive outside. Instead it is their early flowering habit in early spring that makes them susceptible to frosts. Keep compact peaches grown in containers in a greenhouse until the risk of frosts are over, and cover fan-trained or bush-shaped trees with hessian or fleece. Alternatively, erect temporary polythene structures similar to the ones used to prevent peach leaf curl to provide extra protection against early spring frosts (see page 106).

Watering and feeding

In early spring, sprinkle a general granular fertilizer around the root zone. At the same time, mulch around the base of the plant with well-rotted manure to help retain moisture. Afterwards, tomato fertilizer can be given to the plants occasionally as they start to grow. Keep the area around the root zone free of weeds.

As the fruits start to swell, regularly water both peaches and nectarines. This is particularly important for trees planted near walls as the soil here tends to be very dry, especially in spring and summer.

Water container-grown trees almost every day during the growing season and give them a high potash

A FRAME AROUND A PEACH or nectarine tree is a vital requirement as it protects the blossom from frost in spring, and it also prevents infection from peach leaf curl if left in place from early winter to late spring.

THE PRETTY BLOSSOM of peaches and nectarines is a welcome sight in spring, but occurs at a time when there are few pollinating insects around, so use a rabbit's tail or soft brush to transfer pollen from one flower to another.

feed every couple of weeks. They don't require much, if any, pruning and should be moved into an unheated greenhouse from early winter until late spring. Repot compact peaches in containers every couple of years, using John Innes No 3 soil-based potting compost.

Hand pollination

Despite being self-fertile, peaches and nectarines benefit from assistance with the pollination of their flowers. They flower early in the year, when there's a lack of pollinating insects around. Traditionally hand pollination is carried out with a rabbit's tail, gently pushing it into the flower and transferring its pollen to the surrounding blossom. These days it is more common to use a soft brush or even cotton wool. This should ideally be carried out each day throughout the flowering season.

Thinning fruit

As the fruits develop, thin them to allow the remaining fruits to mature to their full size and to obtain maximum sugar levels. A commonly used rule-of-thumb is to thin the fruitlets out to 10cm

Recommended varieties (nectarines)

'Lord Napier'
Although an old variety 'Lord Napier' is still the most popular nectarine that is grown in many temperate areas. It requires a very good site to produce heavy crops of its white-fleshed, aromatic fruit.

'Pineapple'
A large, self-fertile variety with red skin and golden-yellow flesh. It is suitable for greenhouse culture or for training as a fan on a very warm south-facing wall.

(4in) apart when they are hazelnut size, and to 20cm (8in) when they reach walnut size. Aim to have the fruits spaced equally over the plant, removing ones that will become trapped and bruised against the wall or fence when fully ripened.

At harvest time

Expect 9–12kg (20–27lb) of fruit from a mature, healthy fan that hasn't been affected by frosts or peach leaf curl. A free-standing bush will produce as much as 20kg (44lb). Peaches and nectarines are best eaten directly after being picked from the tree. Alternatively, they can be stored in a cool place for a few days after picking. Fruits picked just before ripening will last longer and can be left to mature in the fruit bowl, but they are unlikely to achieve their full potential in terms of juiciness and flavour.

Harvest time is dependent on individual varieties and weather conditions. However, most peaches and nectarines grown outside will be ready in mid- or late summer. The fruit is suitable for harvesting when it has fully coloured and the flesh near the stalk feels soft. To pick the fruit, cup it in the palm of the hand and gently lift. It should easily come away from the tree. The tree will require regular visits for picking as the fruit will not ripen all at once.

Training and pruning

In terms of pruning, both peaches and nectarines can be treated in the same way because their flowering and fruiting habits are the same. Both form fruits on the wood produced in the previous year. The pruning technique is sometimes referred to as "replacement" pruning because it consists of replacing older branches with new growth from the current year. Pruning involves looking towards the future – one year in advance of the current year.

As with all stone fruits, always prune peaches and nectarines in spring and summer in fine weather. This task should never be done when these trees are dormant (during winter) due to their susceptibility to canker and silver leaf. Nor should the trees be pruned when it is raining because this can spread the spores. If pruning more than one peach or nectarine tree, disinfect secateurs to prevent passing on potential infections.

PEACHES AND NECTARINES are thinned twice a year. If it is difficult to remove them without damaging neighbouring ones, slice the unwanted fruit in half; it will soon wither.

FRUIT THINNING IS ESSENTIAL to get good-sized peaches such as these, and it also keeps the tree in good condition. Mature fruit should be approximately 15cm (6in) apart.

Initial training as a fan

The cheapest way of obtaining a fan-trained peach is to train it yourself, but as it will establish quickly it is important to train the fan when young in order to set a good branch framework. Select a feathered maiden and remove the central leader in spring, cutting back to the lowest of two side branches, one on either side of the plant. They should ideally be about 40cm (16in) above the ground. If upright shoots are not removed, they will tend to hinder the development of the fan. Train the side branches onto canes attached to wires, angling the branches to about 45 degrees. These two branches are sometimes referred to as ribs. Remove any other sideshoots.

Prune the ribs back by about one-third to an upward-facing bud. This will stimulate buds to break along the pruned branch. In summer, tie in the shoots that are growing at the tip of each rib to extend their length. Select about three or four new shoots that have branched out along the ribs and cut the others back to one bud/leaf. One shoot can be tied downwards and a couple upwards.

The following early spring, cut back this new growth by about two-thirds to stimulate new growth. The basic structure of the fan is now complete, with about eight ribs/branches.

Pruning an established fan
In early spring when the plant is in growth, remove any undesirable shoots, such as ones coming off the trunk and where they are going to cause congestion. Leave all the swollen, fat buds, which will become this year's flowers and subsequently the fruit. Identify the vegetative buds or shoots as they will bear next year's crop. Leave one new shoot towards the base of the branch and another one half way up the branch. The shoot at the base will be used for next year's replacement, while the second one can be a back-up in case the basal shoot fails. The terminal bud (in the tip of the branch) can also be left.

Tie in the new shoots as they grow. In early summer, pinch back all secondary shoots to one leaf. Pinch back to about six leaves the shoots that were left in early spring. Leave the terminal bud alone.

After harvesting, in late summer, prune out some of the older wood and some of the shoots that fruited last year. Tie in some of the new growth from the current year as replacements, because these will be the branches that produce your crop the following year. Remove any shoots that are overcrowding the fan and also any diseased wood.

Pests and diseases

As with most fruit, birds can damage the ripening fruits. Watch out for glasshouse red spider mite and brown scale on the stems (see page 58).

Recommended varieties (peaches)

'Doctor Hogg'
Grown for its enormous size rather than flavour or reliability, this variety of peach requires a warm site to ripen to its fullest. Fruits in mid-August.

'Duke of York'
This popular, yellow-fleshed variety produces high yields of well-flavoured fruit, which is ready for harvesting in early summer.

'Hale's Early'
Ripening in midsummer, this attractive variety has red streaks overlying its white skin. The flesh is pale yellow.

'Peregrine'
A very popular peach in the temperate areas due to its reliability, good yields, and excellent flavour. It bears large, white, juicy flesh with superb flavour, ready for eating in late summer.

Peach leaf curl Another main problem when growing peaches and nectarines is this fungal disease – *Taphrina deformans* – which also affects almonds and apricots. It is easily recognizable during early spring when the leaves become covered in reddish or whitish blisters and begin to curl up. Eventually the leaves drop to the ground. Although it will send out a second flush of leaves, the tree is placed under considerable stress; in severe cases, the crop yield is affected.

Covering the tree with a polythene or glass cover should help to keep the buds dry and reduce the spread of infection, because plants protected from the rain as the buds start to swell are less likely to suffer from peach leaf curl.

Alternatively, fit a cover over fan-trained trees against a wall or fence (see page 106). Ensure that the sides are left open to allow air circulation and to enable pollinating insects to reach the flowers. Set the covers in place by early winter and leave there until late spring.

The spread of infection can also be reduced by removing infected, fallen leaves and burning them. This prevents the spread of spores that will affect the following year's growth. Apply a copper fungicide, such as Bordeaux mixture, before the flowers open in mid- or late winter, spraying them again two weeks later. One more spray at leaf-fall during the autumn should help to reduce the incidences of peach leaf curl.

PEACH LEAF CURL is likely to be a problem for peaches, nectarines, and almonds if they are not given adequate protection from wind and rain, which spreads the spores.

'Red Haven'
Dark pink flowers are borne in spring, followed by red-flushed fruits with yellow flesh and excellent flavour. The fruit is ready for picking in late summer.

'Redwing'
Said to have some resistance to peach leaf curl, 'Redwing' flowers late and produces heavy yields of dark red fruit.

'Rochester'
Another popular peach in temperate areas, 'Rochester' has yellow flesh, is probably more reliable than 'Peregrine' due to its later flowering, and its heavy crop ripens by late summer.

'Garden Lady'
This dwarf variety bears pink flowers in spring. The fruit has yellow flesh and a good flavour that ripens in late summer.

Apricots _Prunus armeniaca_

Early, pure white apricot blossom makes a superb feature while the golden-orange fruit outshines anything that can be achieved with flowers in the garden. The succulent, fleshy fruits possess delicate and juicy flavours and aromas. Many modern varieties are worth trying, and the rewards are well worth the effort.

The best sites and soils

If you can grow a peach in your garden, then you should definitely be able to succeed with an apricot as they require similar growing conditions (see page 104) – a warm, sheltered site in full sun. Although tolerant of a wide range of soils, they prefer well-drained soils and will struggle in shallow conditions. Always dig in plenty of well-rotted organic manure into poor soils, well before planting.

A SHELTERED, SUNNY SITE is vital for a good crop of apricots, and even then the yield is often dependent on weather conditions at the time of fruit set.

Buying tips

Apricots are self-fertile, so just the one tree is required for pollination to take place. Apricots are vigorous trees and should therefore be grafted onto rootstocks. The most popular rootstocks are 'St Julien A' and 'Torinel' – both of which are semivigorous. Fan-train on a south- or south-west-facing wall or fence, 4m (13ft) wide and 2m (6½ft) high. Apricots can also be grown as free-standing trees, either as open-centred bushes or as pyramids (see page 74).

Plant care

Although the trees are fully hardy and will survive cold winters, the main priority is protection from the frost to avoid damage to the blossom, which appears in early to midspring.

When frosts are predicted, cover fan-trained trees with fleece at night to protect the blossom. Roll the fleece up during the day to allow sunlight and pollinating insects to reach the plant. Some people light their chimeneas or barbecues during frosty evenings and place them near the trees.

Hand pollination helps increase yields as not many pollinating insects are around when apricots are in flower (see page 106).

If there is a heavy crop thin the fruit to about 8cm (3½in) apart when the fruits are the size of hazelnuts.

Water newly planted trees frequently as they establish in their first spring and summer. More settled trees only need to be watered during dry spells. Apricots benefit from a granular feed using a general compound fertilizer in late winter, followed

A PERMANENT FRAME around a wall-trained apricot makes the job of protecting the vulnerable early flowers and embryo fruit from frost much easier. In summer, netting can be draped over the frame to deter birds.

by mulching around the rooting area with well-rotted farmyard manure.

At harvest time

The fruit is ready when it feels soft and parts easily from the tree, which is likely to be from mid- to late summer. Apricots can only be stored for a few days so are best consumed right away. Alternatively, they can be dried or made into preserves.

Training and pruning

Apricots bear fruit on one- and two-year-old wood. As with all stone fruit, prune apricots when the sap is rising in spring or summer and only in warm weather. Never prune them when they are dormant (in winter) because the open wounds leave them susceptible to disease. Pruning in the rain also increases the chances of infection.

Apricots have a similar fruiting habit to plums (see page 100) and so are managed in much the same way. To form an apricot fan, cut back the central leader of a feathered tree to two side branches low down on the main stem; these will form the ribs of the fan. Tie in new shoots as they develop. Once the initial shape is formed, subsequent pruning consists of helping the fan retain its shape.

Pests and diseases

Apricots are fairly problem-free. However, they are vulnerable to silver leaf (see page 61) and bacterial canker (see page 59). Birds (see page 58) are fond of pecking at the ripening fruit, which can be devastating if you have nurtured your crop through the year. Therefore, remember to net it securely.

Recommended varieties

'Alfred'
This traditional variety has orange flesh and a reputation for some resistance to dieback. The fruit is medium sized. 'Alfred' requires good soil and a sunny, sheltered site.

'Tomcot'
One of the more modern varieties available, 'Tomcot' is early cropping - midsummer - and produces large, orange fruits with crimson flushes.

'Moorpark'
A late variety with orange-red fruits. It is prone to dieback, but is one of the most reliable varieties on the market. The fruit is golden-orange with a very attractive, crimson flush.

'Flavorcot', syn. 'Bayoto'
This Canadian variety is known for its reliability and its frost tolerance. It produces juicy, orange-red fruit, which ripens in late summer.

Carol's fruit notebook

Cherries

" It is probably just as well that "life isn't a bowl of cherries" – a promise of luscious indulgence, a mouthful of juicy fun, the wanton disregard of rational thought in pursuit of more, followed remorselessly by a wistful pile of spat-out stones and old stalks. The smoothness and glossiness of their skins, associated in the memory with intense flavour, yielding but chewable flesh, and an abundance of flowing juice, all make cherries irresistible. They are a seasonal treat worth waiting for.

Cherries have always been difficult to harvest but are worth the effort. "Cherry-picking" used to mean a tedious, laborious, and precarious job for a seasonal worker up a long, wobbly ladder. Up high on the branches of old cherry trees, the best fruits were the only ones worth picking because, by the time of harvest, the crop was already decimated by birds and rain damage. Nowadays, a "cherry-picker" is a motorized machine with a platform on a set of scissor lifts – but you won't need one in your own garden. Modern rootstocks for cherries are short and manageable, so in order to protect your crop you can actually put fleece or netting over it to keep out frost, rain, and raiding birds.

There have been many generations of cherry selection and breeding, and most commercial types now conform to the supermarket model – good travellers and storers, with big, fleshy, juicy fruits. What has been sacrificed to achieve this ideal can be recovered by you, in your own garden by your choice of varieties. Small yields of exquisitely flavoured fruits are viable in the garden because here cherries are a much-anticipated but short-lived feast from a truly beautiful, ornamental tree. Antique sweet varieties such as 'Black Tartarian', 'Early Rivers', and 'Waterloo' are still available for the garden; they are really delicious when picked straight off the tree. "

MODERN DWARFING ROOTSTOCKS now mean that all gardeners can savour the brief but delicious cherry season with ease.

Cherries
Prunus avium and *P. cerasus*

One of the earliest tree fruits to ripen in the fruit garden are cherries, and their flavour is delicious, as the birds will try and testify! Once the privilege of larger gardens, the availability of dwarfing cherry rootstocks and self-fertile varieties now mean that any garden, big or small, can accommodate a productive tree.

CHERRIES FLOWER EARLY in the year so it's important that trees are positioned in a sheltered site away from frost pockets if a good crop is to be expected.

The best sites and soils

A fruiting cherry tree is a real jewel in the fruit garden. Not only does it provide delicious fruits but an established tree also bears beautiful spring blossom and provides great autumn colour, making it ornamental as well as fruitful.

Sweet cherries (*Prunus avium*) are most productive in a site in full sun, whereas acid cherries (*P. cerasus*) such as 'Morello' are happy to be positioned against a shady wall, making them a very useful crop in north- or east-facing gardens. Because they flower very early in the year, however, all cherries are best planted in a sheltered position so that pollinating insects (mainly bees) are encouraged to access the

HARDWORKING TREES

There is no doubt that an orchard of cherries in full bloom is an awe-inspiring sight, but only very few gardeners are lucky enough to have the space for such a treasure. Fortunately, an individual tree in full flower still makes an extremely strong feature in any garden when many other garden plants are only just stirring into growth. Fruiting cherries (which in themselves are a good enough reason to grow them) also display gorgeous autumnal hues ranging in shades of red, orange, and golden-yellow. Thus cherry trees provide value in the garden for three seasons of the year: spring blooms, summer fruits, and autumn colours.

BEAUTIFUL AS WELL AS PRODUCTIVE, many cherries will end the season with a flourish of stunning leaf colours.

A FAN-SHAPED CHERRY is ideal for a sunny wall, and allows the fruits to be protected more conveniently from birds and also for frost protection to be erected. Such a trained tree also looks a picture when in full flower in spring.

flowers. While cherries are tolerant of both acid and alkaline soils they do need good drainage. Cherry tree roots are naturally very shallow, and so any waterlogging will cause them to rot or to succumb to water-borne root diseases such as phytophthora (see page 61).

Buying tips

As with other fruit trees, cherries have been divided into groups depending on the time at which they flower (see page 218). Older cherry varieties tend to be self-infertile and so require an additional, compatible tree for pollination to occur, while modern self-fertile varieties and more dwarfing rootstocks now allow gardeners to grow a single tree. Consequently spacing of trees depends a lot on the variety, rootstock, and training method chosen.

Some self-infertile varieties, such as 'Summer Sun', 'Colney', 'Hertford', and 'Merchant', are still worth growing, but if choosing such varieties it is essential to check with your supplier so you understand their pollination needs. For a self-infertile cherry to set

fruit it must be in the same or adjacent flowering group as its pollinator. Self-infertile cherries not only need another variety to cross-pollinate their flowers, but also these two varieties must be compatible with each other, which many aren't even though they flower at the same time.

Self-fertile varieties, which don't need another cherry variety nearby, are more suitable for a small garden. Many of these self-fertile cherries are also universal donors, meaning that they exhibit no incompatibility and will pollinate any cherry in the same or adjacent flowering group.

In times past the available rootstocks for cherries were very limited. 'Colt' was the main one used, and this had a semivigorous effect on the variety, making trees too large for most modern gardens: for example, a fan-trained tree on 'Colt' roots would grow 5.5m (18ft) tall and 2.5m (8ft) wide. However, in recent years two rootstocks, 'Gisela 5' and 'Tabel', which are both semidwarfing, have been introduced, allowing gardeners to restrict the growth of their trees. A fan-trained cherry on either of these two

CHERRIES ARE VULNERABLE to silver leaf and bacterial canker infections, so to minimize the risk prune in the summer months when cuts heal quickly.

BEING ONE OF THE MOST LIKELY FRUITS to be eaten by birds, it is essential that cherries are covered with some taut netting just before they begin to colour up.

rootstocks would only attain 1.8m (6ft) in height and grow 3.75m (12ft) wide.

When buying a cherry look for a tree that mirrors the initial shape that you want, because young cherry plants don't respond as well to hard pruning as apples or pears so are more difficult to retrain if growing incorrectly. Cherries can be trained as free-standing trees or fans; a tree selected for a fan should have two equally vigorous sideshoots emanating from roughly the same point on the main stem, whereas a bush should have three or four strong sideshoots arising from the main stem, with a clear trunk to a height of at least 38cm (15in). In both cases the sideshoots should appear at a wide angle, because narrow ones tend to make weak unions and can also collect rainwater, which can lead to decay and bacterial canker infection.

Plant care

Protect cherry flowers, which are susceptible to frost damage, from late frosts. If possible, cover free-standing trees with double-thickness horticultural

fleece on frosty nights. Hold the fleece away from the flowers with bamboo canes or similar. Drape a similar insulating material over fan-trained cherries. The cover can be left in place during the day as long as access is left for pollinating insects. As well as providing frost protection, ensure trees are kept well watered during the early stages of fruit development, to avoid excessive "run-off", when some fruits turn yellow and fall off. Run-off occurs in three main stages: when unpollinated flowers and blooms with immature embryos are shed; when pollination is incomplete; and when fruits swell but are then aborted because they have suffered a growth check through lack of moisture, inadequate food reserves, or excessively cool temperatures.

Neither sweet nor acid cherries require fruit thinning. Before fruits start to show some colour, erect netting to deter birds. Ripe fruits are prone to skin splitting during wet weather so try to keep fruits dry and pick over trees regularly.

Cherry growth is quite vigorous and so they benefit from an annual top-dressing of a general-purpose

fertilizer in midspring, and, if fruiting is poor, a top-dressing of a slow-release high potash fertilizer such as sulphate of potash in late winter.

At harvest time

Once pollinated in spring the fruits set, thin naturally, and then ripen during mid- and late summer. Pick fruits during dry weather, doing so by the stalks, not the body of the fruits, which bruise easily; this will increase their shelf life. Eat sweet cherries fresh or store them in the fridge in a sealed, plastic bag for a week. Acid cherries are too tart to be eaten raw, but these are excellent cooked and make delicious pies, puddings, liquors, and preserves.

Training and pruning

Cherry blossom, then fruit, develops on sweet cherries at the base of one-year-old stems and on older wood. Acid cherries crop instead along the length of one-year-old wood. Although cherries can be planted in autumn and winter, undertake formative pruning only in late spring and carry out established pruning immediately after harvest.

To form a fan train a feathered maiden to strong horizontal wires spaced 38cm (15in) apart. At bud-burst in spring, cut out the central leader. On each side of the leader, secure a sturdy bamboo cane tightly to the wire supports at an angle, then tie a strong sideshoot loosely to each cane. To avoid snapping the stems, untie and lower the canes as the season progresses until the desired angle is reached. As the tree's framework develops tie new main stems onto canes already secured to the wires, the aim being to develop a framework of well-spaced branches radiating from the centre of the tree. Rub off or prune unwanted shoots as they appear.

To train an open-centred, free-standing cherry tree, cut the central leader out just above the highest sideshoot to leave three or four of the sturdiest. Then tip back these sideshoots to encourage further side branching. As the framework develops, prune or rub out unwanted stems.

MOST CHERRY TREE PRUNING should be carried out after harvest. To keep their restricted shape, pinch out wayward growth regularly on fans and tie in well-placed shoots.

CHERRY TREES NATURALLY SHED some of their immature fruits, but this can be overly excessive if there is a check in growth or inadequate pollination.

Once a basic framework is established, an open-centred sweet cherry tree needs simply to have dead, diseased, damaged, and congested growth, and crossing branches removed annually, immediately after harvest. Little other pruning is required.

Sweet cherry fans also need to have this wood removed, but to keep their restricted shape they require additional pruning. During early summer shorten all new growth to roughly 7.5cm (3in) long to encourage sunlight to ripen the developing fruits. Also remove shoots growing directly into or away from the wall or fence, and prune out a proportion of old or unproductive, twiggy growth, tying in well-placed replacement shoots.

Because of their different cropping habit acid cherries need heavier pruning than sweet cherries to keep them productive. Each summer prune out a proportion of the older stems of both fans and free-standing trees, training in new replacement growth, which will then bear the crop the following summer.

Pests and diseases

Cherries are prone to bacterial canker (see page 59), blossom wilt (see page 60), honey fungus, phytophthora and shothole (see page 61), and cherry blackfly (see aphids, page 58). Cherry "slugworms" are small, black, slug-like insects on the leaves – there is no control and damage is rarely significant.

Recommended varieties

'Lapins'
A self-fertile, upright sweet cherry bearing heavy crops of large fruits in dark red when fully ripe. Harvest in midsummer. This universal donor tree shows some resistance to bacterial canker.

'Morello'
This self-fertile acid cherry for an east- or north-facing wall crops well in shade. Its large, dark red fruits are produced heavily and are perfect for jams and tarts. Pick fruits from mid- to late summer.

'Stella'
One of the oldest self-fertile varieties, this compact sweet cherry is still popular due to its abundant, large, dark crimson fruits that have a good flavour. Its skins can easily split. Pick in late summer.

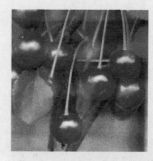

'Summer Sun'
A relatively compact, spreading sweet cherry bearing reliable and heavy crops of well-flavoured, dark red fruits. These mature by late summer. Has some resistance to bacterial canker. Self-fertile.

'Bigarreau Napoléon'
This self-infertile variety bears fruits late in the season. These have a sweet flavour and an orange skin flushed with red when fully ripe. This variety in particular needs a well-drained soil to deter bacterial canker.

'Sunburst'
This spreading, self-fertile sweet cherry bears moderate yields of large fruits with a sweet, rich flavour and dark red skin when ripe, in mid- to late summer. Skins of 'Sunburst' can be prone to splitting.

Citus fruit

❝ My husband Neil, on one occasion before we were married, presented me with a love offering of a flowering, miniature orange tree. It had half a dozen oranges, about 2.5cm (1in) in diameter, and two white flowers giving off the most exquisite, light scent. We kept the plant for months in the moist, tropical house-plant jungle our flat had become. We let the fruits stay on the tree as delightful, little, orange baubles until they went dry and wizened; we cut one in half warily and it was shockingly sour but definitely orange-flavoured. We were enormously impressed, and to this day I am still excited to think we were actually growing our own citrus fruit in our urban flat.

Recently our consumption of lemons has grown enormously, from very first thing in the morning in a cleansing drink with raw ginger in warm water to first thing in the evening with an apéritif. Lemon juice is one of those essentials of life it would be good to be generous with, and it is an ambition of mine to become self-sufficient in lemons – though I am still some way off.

Citrus x *meyeri* has a lovely, easy-going flavour, but growing the lemon 'Garey's Eureka' may be more realistic as, being very intense, a little goes a longer way. Very few of us will ever have the good fortune to have our own "Classical" orangery but a modern conservatory can serve plants better than it can serve people – its origins were after all glazed protection for year-round cultivation. The beautifully scented citrus family will make perfect inhabitants there, provided you supply high levels of humidity. Citrus fruits need a cold winter spell to fully change colour and ripen so they don't want to live in a hothouse – even if you do. **❞**

THERE'S SOMETHING immensely satisfying about harvesting home-grown, flavour-packed lemons that still thrills me to this day.

Citrus fruit

Citrus spp, x *Citrofortunella microcarpa* and *Fortunella japonica*

Although citrus always evoke thoughts of the Mediterranean, in cooler climates gardeners can still accommodate these fruits provided they have a frost-free porch, conservatory, or greenhouse available for winter. With increasingly mild winters and improved hardiness of new varieties this requirement may even become unnecessary.

The best sites and soils

A gardener has a fascinating range of citrus fruits from which to choose, including sweet oranges (*Citrus sinensis*), mandarins (*C. reticulata*), lemons (*C. limon* and *C. x meyeri*), limes (*C. aurantiifolia*), grapefruits (*C. x paradisi*), kumquats (*Fortunella japonica*), and calamondins (x *Citrofortunella microcarpa*). Any of them will make an attractive, compact addition to the garden. Their fragrant,

creamy white flowers appear in the leaf axils of one-year-old shoots in late winter, and the fruits then set and slowly swell, ripening 9–12 months later. Because their fruits take so long to mature they are often in flower and fruit at the same time.

Position citrus plants in as sunny a spot as possible, especially in a cool climate, as it's essential they receive sufficient sunlight to ripen their fruit. However, it is better in a cool climate to grow citrus

Fruit types

There are many different types of citrus, each varying in fruit size, colour, and shape. While the cultivation requirements of each is similar, factors such as hardiness can vary quite considerably. Consequently it's helpful to identify the different types so that you can meet your particular plant's needs.

Oranges, calamondins, and mandarins
All bear spherical, orange fruits. While sweet oranges and mandarins are tolerant of temperatures down to 7°C (45°F), calamondins require a temperature of at least 13°C (55°F).

Lemons and limes
Of the two lemon species, *C. limon* is much more cold sensitive than *C. x meyeri*, which survives down to 5°C (41°F). Limes and *C. limon* will only tolerate temperatures down to 10°C (50°F).

Grapefruits
While grapefruits (sometimes known as pomelos) become more hardy as they mature, a young plant mustn't be exposed to temperatures below 10°C (50°F). These trees can attain a height of 5m (16ft).

Kumquats
This is an unusual citrus in that the fruits are eaten whole – skins and all. The plants are naturally very bushy and can be highly productive. They can tolerate winter temperatures down to 7°C (45°F).

HEALTHY CITRUS PLANTS often produce lots of vigorous vertical growth. To control height and encourage side branching, remove the tips of these shoots.

WAYWARD SHOOTS should always be removed to keep your tree's appearance balanced. This is especially important if you want to grow your citrus plant as a standard.

in pots, so the plants can be moved around. For this, use a loam-based compost such as John Innes No 3.

While some species are comparatively more cold-tolerant, none is fully hardy and so they benefit from being brought into a frost-free environment for winter. Despite often being marketed as such, citrus generally don't make good house plants where there is a dry atmosphere caused by central heating.

Buying tips

Most citrus (except grapefruits) attain a height of only 1–1.5m (3–5ft) when grown in a pot so you may be able to accommodate quite a few plants. While most citrus are grafted onto rootstocks, this is to speed up propagation rather than to influence each plant's rate of growth. All varieties are self-fertile, so only one plant is needed to set a crop of fruit. These two factors make choosing which citrus to grow much easier than with other tree fruits.

When buying, select a plant that has a balanced framework of branches and a strong graft union; it can take citrus scions a few years to graft strongly to their rootstock.

Plant care

Citrus are hungry plants and respond well to regular feeding. The bulk of flowering and fruit ripening occurs in winter, when they need a balanced fertilizer; conversely summer is a period of leaf

OVERWINTER CITRUS under cover in a slightly humid atmosphere, preferably in a conservatory or greenhouse. You should always ensure that you can provide such conditions before purchasing a container-grown citrus tree.

growth so a high nitrogen fertilizer is preferred. Use specialist citrus feed for both summer and winter applications, switching from summer to winter feed in midautumn, then swapping back to a summer fertilizer in early spring.

CITRUS FRUITS SHOULD BE THINNED OUT to ensure that the remaining fruits are able to swell and ripen sufficiently, even though it is tempting to leave all the fruit on.

A HUMID ATMOSPHERE is needed by citrus plants, especially when in flower because this aids pollination and fruit set. Regular handmisting with tepid water will ensure this.

Keep citrus plants well watered except during winter, when the compost should be allowed to dry out slightly between waterings.

To ensure adequate pollination keep the atmosphere humid in winter when plants flower. Regular handmisting with water, standing plants on trays of moist gravel, and grouping plants together will all help raise humidity and ensure good fruit set.

The fruits may need to be thinned out – a plant 1m (3ft) tall should bear no more than 20 fruits. Kumquats, however, don't need thinning.

Pot up plants annually in early spring, or top-dress with fresh compost.

At harvest time

Once fully grown the fruits develop a rich skin colour, at which time they can be harvested. They can then be eaten fresh, made into preserves, dried, candied, or preserved in alcohol.

Training and pruning

Because most citrus are bought as established plants, often no formative pruning is required. However, regular pruning is required to maintain the shape of the many citrus trees that are trained as standards, with a clear single stem and a rounded canopy. When pruning, take care to avoid the vicious thorns that many citrus bear, and wear a pair of stout, thornproof gloves.

The main pruning period is late winter, just before plants come into growth. Thin out congested shoots and prune back leaders to maintain a balanced canopy, using a sharp pair of secateurs.

As well as winter pruning, citrus also require management of the new growth as it is produced. During summer, pinch out the tips of new shoots, to promote bushiness. Stop pinching out in late summer to give the new growth time to mature and harden up before winter.

Pests and diseases

The main problems of citrus are mealybugs (see page 59), aphids (see page 58), glasshouse red spider mite (see page 58), and soft scale. Soft scale insects are up to 4mm (⅙in) long, yellowish brown in colour, and flat with no recognizable head, antennae, or legs. Spray regularly with fatty acids or plant oils.

CITRUS FLOWERS appear in clusters in late winter. As well as developing into fruits, they also emit a deliciously sweet perfume, which hangs in the surrounding air.

Recommended variety (calamondin)

'Tiger'
The leaves on this calamondin variety have variegated stripes, hence the name. Bears masses of orange fruits, 4cm (1½in) wide, on vigorous plants, which are best pinch pruned regularly to keep them in shape.

Recommended variety (sweet orange)

'Washington'
This sweet orange variety is widely grown commercially, and its large, seedless fruits have an extremely good flavour and high juice content. The trees are vigorous and ripen their fruits in late autumn.

Recommended variety (lemon)

'Garey's Eureka'
A popular variety with commercial growers, this lemon produces extremely good and plentiful juice in fruits with few seeds. The very productive tree can be in flower and fruit for most of the year.

Recommended variety (lime)

'Tahiti'
The small fruits of this lime have an excellent flavour and no seeds. The plants are fairly vigorous, growing to 1.8m (6ft) tall, and extremely productive. The fruits ripen to a pale green.

Recommended variety (grapefruit)

'Star Ruby'
A good choice for the gardener because 'Star Ruby' is less vigorous than other grapefruit varieties. Its large fruits have deep red, extremely juicy flesh, thin skin, and a very sweet flavour.

Recommended variety (kumquat)

'Nagami'
This variety is extremely productive, bearing dozens of small, oval fruits on compact plants. The balance of flavours between the sour flesh and sweet rind makes this kumquat tasty whether cooked or fresh.

Carol's fruit notebook

Figs

" Figs exert an exotic fascination for me, and a ripe fig, moist fleshed but full of dry seeds, scented, and flavourful, and multitextured, is a wondrous thing. You can imagine the excitement of Cardinal Pole on receiving a gift of a 'White Marseilles' fig tree in 1555. When his gardeners planted it out in the garden of Lambeth Palace, no one expected its roots to bore under the foundations and come up at the other side of the palace centuries later.

I too have experienced the tremendous vigour of figs. About 25 years ago, a friend of mine gave me a sickly plant in a pot, knowing I was running "Carol's hospital for poorly plants". The

fig perked up so I planted it in a sandpit – abandoned by the children – at the front of a raised, south-facing patio. The sandpit was about 1m (3ft) square and 60cm (2ft) deep, and was lined with rubble. The fig grew enthusiastically to about 5m (16ft) tall and as much across. However, its huge, glossy, dark green, almost tropical leaves looked a bit incongruous in our naturalistic garden setting, so after 20 years I reluctantly dug mine out – it took two solid days of digging. I would still recommend anyone to grow a fig tree if they have a suitable situation and are prepared to make a careful selection of the variety.

If you can grow them yourself, you can have the privilege of eating fully ripe, fresh, sun-blessed, warm figs straight from the tree. Such figs have been revered by mankind for millennia, and the bountiful fig tree has an honoured place in every major religion. Commercially, figs don't store or travel well, neither will they continue ripening once they have been picked.

The latest science is discovering the mutual evolution of figs, the pollinating wasps that use the occasional fruit as a hatchery, and the parasitic wasps that keep the pollinating wasps from overrunning the tree. Truly amazing! "

FIGS FORM IN THE TIPS so to ensure a bumper crop the next year, pinch or cut back some of the other side shoots to a couple of buds in spring to encourage lots more tips.

Figs  *Ficus carica*

Originating from Asia, yet equally synonymous with Mediterranean planting schemes, figs can successfully be grown outside in cooler climates if given adequate protection in winter and by carefully selecting the hardier varieties. Their attractive, lobed leaves and delicious fruit make them an essential plant for a sunny, sheltered location.

The best sites and soils

Choose a warm, sunny site, such as a south- or south-west-facing wall, and train the fig as a fan. The soil should be well drained, although figs aren't too fussy about its quality, tending to thrive in chalky conditions. Alternatively, a sun-drenched patio is perfect for growing a fig in a container and adds a touch of the Mediterranean to any courtyard garden, particularly when the fig is combined with vines and olive trees. Figs can also be grown in a heated greenhouse, where you can expect a flush of two or

FIGS IN COOL CLIMATES usually bear two crops. Spring figs grow large but rarely ripen in time. Tiny summer embryo figs form at the branch tips and ripen the following summer.

even three crops during summer. However, due to the cost of heating and excessive watering it is not a practical or an environmentally friendly proposition for most people.

Figs are easy plants to grow and in the right location will produce vigorous, luxuriant growth and quickly establish a large root system. However, it is not so easy to get a regular crop of figs each year. To encourage a fig plant to bear crops of fruit it's advisable to restrict their root system. The theory is that by restricting the plant's vegetative growth, the plant will channel its energy into reproduction and therefore bear more fruit.

There are three ways to restrict fig roots: by creating a planting pit; by growing the plant in a container; and by plunging a container into the ground. The advantage of growing a fig in a pot is that it can be moved before winter arrives into an unheated greenhouse or even a shed or porch.

To prepare a planting pit, dig a hole 60 x 60 x 60cm (2 x 2 x 2ft). Line the sides of the holes with patio slabs, setting them 2.5cm (1in) proud of the ground to prevent the roots from spreading over the top of the soil. Leave the bottom unlined; instead fill the hole with rubble or broken bricks and crocks to 10–15cm (4–6in) deep, to prevent roots penetrating the soil underneath. Backfill the hole using ordinary garden soil or a loam-based potting compost.

Buying and planting

Plants are bought from garden centres in containers and are usually either single- or multistemmed.

As figs can become large, vigorous plants they can be used to cover large walls, even the sides of houses.

TIE WALL-TRAINED FIGS to a sturdy support to form a strong framework. New shoots may attempt to grow away from the support; tie these in or remove them.

However, most people should choose one that will eventually reach about 2m (6½ft) high and 3–3.5m (10–11ft) wide – the equivalent of two fence panels. Plant it 20cm (8in) away from the wall, in spring.

Spring is also the best time for potting up a fig plant. Start the plant off in a 25cm (10in) container, and as the plant grows pot it up each year, with it eventually ending up in a 45cm (18in) pot. Use a container with plenty of drainage holes and lots of broken crocks at the bottom. Standing the container on bricks helps excess water drain away. If you are wanting to plunge a containerized fig into open ground, fill a 30–40cm (12–16in) pot with John Innes No 3 soil mix and the young fig plant. Then position the pot well into the ground.

Plant care

In spring, apply a general-purpose granular feed. Then mulch around the base of the tree with well-rotted manure, to help to retain moisture and suppress weeds.

Give figs plenty of water – probably each day during summer. Also during the growing season apply a tomato fertiliser every two weeks until the figs start to ripen.

One of the advantages of figs is that you don't have to worry about pollination; the fruit are seedless and so develop without the need for fertilization.

Except for the very warmest of sites, protect fig plants during the colder months. In autumn, move

A GOOD WAY to grow a fig outdoors is to train it as a fan against a sunny wall. Train two side branches, one for each side of the fan, and as they grow tie in their sideshoots so they are evenly spaced and not crossing.

plants that have been grown in pots into an unheated greenhouse, and return them back outside in late spring. Pack a fan-trained plant with straw, bracken, or even bubble wrap and then cover with horticultural fleece (see page 131). Remove such insulation gradually during late spring.

Dig around the outside of a planting pit every couple of years with a sharp spade to ensure that no roots have escaped.

Repot figs every couple of years even when they have reached their established size. Remove them from their pot, gently prise out their roots from the rootball. Then replant into fresh John Innes No 3 soil-based potting compost.

At harvest time

Cover the plant with a net as harvest time approaches – otherwise the birds, particularly blackbirds, will harvest the crop first.

Figs are ready for harvesting when their skin is soft, sometimes split, and hanging limply from the branch. Occasionally a tear of sugary liquid is secreted from the eye of the fig. When in such condition, pick and eat them raw, straight away.

Otherwise, store the fruit in a dry, cool place, where it will keep fresh for a few days. Figs can also be preserved by drying them on trays in the airing cupboard, turning them once a day for a week.

Training and pruning

Beware of getting fig sap on your skin – it is an irritant. To avoid the sap dripping on you, wear protective gloves and start pruning from the bottom of the plant and work upwards.

It is important to understand how a fig tree produces fruit as this effects how it is pruned. Figs in cool-temperate climates are usually borne in the tips of wood produced the previous season. Embryonic figs

– about pea size – appear in late summer in the growing tips. If unaffected by frosts and cold winters, they will ripen into figs ready for harvesting in late summer the following year. Larger unripened figs that appear in spring won't ripen before the onset of winter, and also won't successfully overwinter. Remove them at the end of summer.

Initial training as a fan

Cut back a single-stemmed plant to about 35cm (14in) to stimulate sideshoots. Train these sideshoots onto a frame of wires secured to the wall, as they develop in the subsequent year.

Remove the central stem from a multistemmed fig and cut back its sideshoots by about one-third. Tie

Recommended varieties

'Brown Turkey'
The most successful fig variety in cool climates in terms of its reliability and popularity. This midseason variety produces a profusion of large, pear-shaped, dark-skinned fruits with a dark red flesh.

'Brunswick'
Another very popular fig variety for outside culture in cool areas due to its hardiness. Midseason 'Brunswick' bears large fruits with yellowish green skin and reddish flesh.

'Panachée'
Slightly more tender than 'Brown Turkey' or 'Brunswick', so 'Panachée' is suitable for only the warmest, sheltered sites. It bears delicate, green-and-yellow, stripy figs with the sweetest, most delicate flavour.

'Rouge de Bordeaux'
One of the finest tasting figs available but needs a very warm, sheltered site to ripen properly. Otherwise, grow in a conservatory or greenhouse. This variety has a deep purple skin with red flesh.

'White Marseilles', syn. 'White Genoa'
Not as well known as it should be, midseason 'White Marseilles' has attractive, pale green to white skin with pale, almost translucent flesh. It is a good variety for growing outdoors.

'Drap d'Or'
A tender, late variety realistically only suitable for a glasshouse or polytunnel, except for very warm, frost free locations. The brown fig with pale, firm flesh has a sweet taste and excellent flavour.

PINCH BACK THE TIPS of branches in early summer to produce compact growth and encourage the formation of a summer crop of figs.

PACK DRY BRACKEN OR STRAW around a wall-trained fig over winter in order to protect the embryo figs from winter frosts. Secure the packing material with wire or twine.

these sideshoots onto wires, spreading them fan-shaped against the wall.

Training an established fan

Prune a fan-trained fig in spring after the frost protection has been removed. The aim is to tie in young shoots, spreading them fan-shaped at an approximate spacing of 15–30cm (6–12in) apart. Cut back excess young shoots to one bud. Remove shoots growing outwards or inwards towards the wall. In early summer, pinch back new growth to five or six leaves, to stimulate the formation of embryonic figs in the tips.

As the plant matures over the years, introduce a system of replacement pruning (similar to peaches; see page 108) whereby the older framework is gradually removed and replaced by younger wood.

Container-grown figs

Figs in pots are best pruned in spring but can also sometimes be pruned in autumn before covering them with frost protection. They are usually grown on a short, single stem (like a standard) with a head of four or five side branches. Occasionally they are grown as multistemmed bushes. To develop such a fig, cut a two- to three-year-old container-grown fig down to the base, in spring. As figs are vigorous, several new shoots will appear from the base.

Choose up to a dozen of the strongest shoots and grow as for a normal container fig.

Except for one task, the pruning principles remain the same whether the fig has one or many stems. This is that every few years on a multistemmed bush you should cut about one-third of the stems back to ground level to ensure a new supply of vigorous young stems.

In spring, remove any dead or diseased shoots. Thin out any branches that are crossing. Ensure that some of the shoots with embryonic figs in their tips are retained as these will produce the fruit in late summer. Cut back the sideshoots to one or two buds on some branches, to encourage replacement tips to produce fruit in the following year.

In early summer, shorten the new growth to five or six leaves, to encourage the formation of tips that will form fruit for the following year.

Pests and diseases

Figs grown outdoors are rarely troubled by pests and diseases, although birds can be a nuisance (see page 58) at harvesting time. Coral spot sometimes infects the branches (see page 60). Red spider mite (see page 58) and brown scale (see page 58) may occur on figs grown in conservatories or greenhouses.

Soft fruit

- Strawberries
- Raspberries
- Blackberries and hybrid berries
- Blueberries
- Cranberries and lingonberries
- Blackcurrants
- Red currants and white currants
- Gooseberries

Carol's fruit notebook

" Most people have a go at growing their own by starting with some really useful things, like potatoes, runner beans, and courgettes. If not initially they very soon progress to strawberries, another easy crop. Even a very ordinary variety of strawberry, grown at home and picked fresh and ripe, is likely to taste better than anything you could buy. Hopefully this will trigger an abiding interest in fruit growing. This is more of a long-term commitment, than a season-by-season activity like planting cabbages. Fruit bushes are permanent fixtures because you don't rotate them in different beds, so they provide an air of permanence and formality.

Soft fruit is utterly luscious and all the more special by being completely fixed in the summer months. Even though you can stagger the harvest by growing early- and late-cropping varieties and thus make the season seem longer – from late spring to early autumn – soft fruit will always be associated in my mind with summer sunshine. Soft fruit bushes can be incredibly productive so you are best served by picking the varieties carefully and nurturing one or two bushes really carefully rather than hedging your bets and growing loads of them tardily.

Decide from the outset if you want all the fruit for yourself, in which case netting early is necessary. While you will be keen to prevent blackbirds gorging themselves without restraint, you should consider also the other creatures at home in your garden. Bees must have unrestricted access to the flowers and up until the point of cropping birds too should make your fruit bushes part of their territory, unless you have rogue bullfinches. Families of tits, for example, will feast on detrimental insects. By the time your jam cupboard and freezer are full, picking the rest of the fruits might become a chore so why not get the birds to help you? More likely though, you will be going round with a red or purple tongue unable to get enough. **"**

Strawberries

"" Before the advent of strawberries being available year-round at supermarkets, the appearance of the first crop of strawberries heralded the arrival of the summer in many countries. The colour, the flavour, the sweetness, and the tanginess all announced that life could be free and easy now. It was a restrained form of sun-worship, a delight worth waiting for. Nowadays, plastic punnets of strawberries are available every week of the year, even though this means they are imported from every corner of the globe. It also means all the strawberry varieties are designed for travelling hundreds, if not thousands, of kilometres and sitting around in fridges for days on end. The result? A tasteless, watery, featureless fruit that fulfils very little and evokes even less.

Luckily, strawberries are easy to grow, and you will be able to see for yourself how much better the sun-warmed, fresh version you grow yourself is. If weather permits, you can leave picking your own strawberries until the selected berries are deep red and fully ripe. Commercial strawberries are always picked under-ripe, and though they are less likely to rot as quickly they will never develop any more flavour when stored, even if evaporation has reduced the water content. There is no concentration of flavour. A ripe berry will still be very juicy, and if you eat it straight after picking it there is no likelihood of it being too dry.

It is worth trying a few different varieties to see which suit your soil and local climate best. In this way you'll find the variety that gives you the best yield, the longest season of ripe berries, and above all else the best flavour for your tastebuds. Personally, I yearn for an intense flavour, rather than mere reliability; I always let "wild" alpine strawberries seed and spread around the garden. Their fragrance and exquisite taste means that when I come across a ripe one it is a delightful treat, either to give to a loved one or to indulge myself. If you can collect enough, try them with freshly squeezed orange juice and a twist of pepper – as they do in Italy. ""

PICK STRAWBERRIES at the warmest time of day. Not only do they taste better, but their beautiful fragrance is at its most intoxicating.

Strawberries
Fragaria x ananassa

These favourite fruits of many people grow on tiny, low-growing herbaceous plants. Their trailing habit makes them ideal for a container or hanging basket. Although these small, red berries don't keep for long and don't travel well, most strawberries in the shops have been flown in from other countries. It is far simpler to grow your own.

The best sites and soils

Strawberries are so versatile they are widely planted outside the fruit garden, either in the vegetable garden or among ornamental plants – all sorts of methods are possible. All they ask for is sun, shelter, and fertile, well-drained soil. Avoid areas prone to frost because strawberries are low growing. Also avoid sites that have previously grown potatoes, chrysanthemums, or tomatoes because they are all prone to the disease verticillium wilt (see page 141). Windy sites will prevent pollinating insects from reaching the flowers. In poor soils grow in raised beds, which improves drainage and increases rooting depth. Alternatively use growing bags (see page 48).

STRAWBERRIES IN GROWING BAGS or other containers are free from soil problems and can be raised off the ground away from slugs. They will also be easier to harvest.

Strawberry plants can successfully be grown under a tunnel cloche to produce an earlier crop by 7–10 days. Make the tunnel cloches, 60cm (24in) wide and 30cm (12in) high, from hoops of galvanized wire covered with clear film plastic. Set the hoops 1m (3ft) apart in the row. In early spring, set the cloche over the plants. Roll up the sides when the plants are flowering to allow pollinating insects access to them.

Strawberries in containers can also be cultivated in an unheated greenhouse, which encourages an even earlier crop, by 10–14 days. In a heated greenhouse or conservatory, it is possible to bring forward their flowering by several weeks, so long as the temperature does not go above 16°C (61°F), because this will inhibit flowering. You will also need to hand pollinate the flowers.

Buying and planting

Strawberries are perennial, herbaceous, low-growing plants with a trailing habit. Traditionally they are grown in rows directly into the garden soil – often referred to as the strawberry patch. They can also be grown as annuals among vegetable plantings and make attractive, low-growing edging plants.

Their trailing habit makes them suitable for hanging baskets. They can also be planted in containers, strawberry planters, and window boxes.

Buy plants from a trustworthy supplier so you know that the crops are what they say they are and disease free. Order plants in late summer so that they can be planted in early autumn.

Strawberry plants bought as cold-stored runners should be planted out from late spring to early summer, and they will fruit 60 days after planting.

PLANTING STRAWBERRIES IN OPEN GROUND

1 MARK OUT a planting line across the bed using a taut string. Alongside it, set a plank with the correct spacings marked 35cm (14in) apart along its length.

2 DIG A HOLE large enough to fit the plant roots along each line, then backfill and firm in, ensuring that the crown of each plant is level with the soil surface.

3 POSITION A FIBRE MAT around each strawberry plant. These will help to prevent weeds and also protect the fruit from touching the ground.

Summer-fruiting varieties are the largest and the most popular strawberries, which most of us associate with summer holidays, outdoor events in summer, and strawberries and cream. They have a short but heavy cropping period over two or three weeks. There are early, mid-, and late fruiting varieties cropping from early to midsummer. Grow them under a cloche or in an unheated greenhouse for a late spring harvest.

Perpetual fruits crop – sometimes called everbearers – produce small flushes of fruits from early summer to early autumn. The crops are not so heavy as the summer-fruiting varieties, but the fruits are smaller, with the plants less likely to produce runners. Perpetual strawberries are useful for extending the season. To concentrate strawberry production in late summer and early autumn, remove the early summer flowers.

Alpine strawberries These plants produce tiny fruits from early summer to late autumn. They are usually red but some varieties are white or yellow. They are very sweet, aromatic, and have superb flavour but are not as juicy as the perpetuals and summer fruiting varieties. Alpine strawberries are only productive for one year and freely seed in the garden. Sow seed in autumn and plant out in spring, or sow in early spring and plant out in late spring.

Planting
Plant strawberries directly into garden soil in late summer for their first crop the following year. Prepare the soil thoroughly by digging to a depth of one spade blade – strawberries don't have a deep

Recommended variety (early)

'Honeoye'
A darkish berry with excellent flavour. Can be susceptible to mildew. Fruits during early summer.

Recommended variety (perpetual)

'Mara des Bois'
A fairly new variety that is well liked for its crop of intensely flavoured berries that are said to be reminiscent of wild strawberries. 'Aromel' is another perpetual variety popular for its delicious flavour.

root system. Remove perennial weeds, then add well-rotted manure to the soil. Level the soil and rake it to a fine tilth. Using string, mark out a planting line. Measure out planting holes 35cm (14in) apart. Dig out a hole large enough to accommodate the strawberry plant. Trim the roots lightly to 10cm (4in) if necessary, then spread them out in the hole. Ensure that the base

EARLY SUMMER is the season every strawberry grower longs for – when they finally get to sample their delicious fruit. Strawberries are at their best when eaten at once.

Recommended varieties (late season)

'Symphony'
A variety from Scotland with attractive, glossy, red fruit and excellent flavour. 'Symphony' is hardy and has good disease resistance, although it can be susceptible to mildew.

'Florence'
A late variety of strawberry with good disease resistance. The large, bright, glossy fruits have good flavour.

Recommended varieties (midseason)

'Elsanta'
The most widely grown commercial variety, it has superb flavour and large yields of glossy, red fruit. Can be prone to disease.

'Hapil'
This midseason variety produces heavy yields of light red fruits. Fruits are firm and have excellent sweet flavour.

'Cambridge Favourite'
A traditional favourite, this variety can have a few disease problems but the fruit is juicy and possesses an excellent flavour.

'Pegasus'
A good, reliable cropper with excellent disease resistance, particularly to mildew and verticillium wilt.

EARLY STRAWBERRY CROPS can be grown under tunnel cloches, as shown, or in a greenhouse. Remember to keep these plants watered while they are covered.

ROLL UP THE SIDES OF TUNNEL CLOCHES during the day while the plants are flowering to give pollinating insects access to the flowers. Such covers can also protect the fruit from bird attacks.

of the crown rests lightly on the surface. Planting at the correct depth is important: if the crown is planted too deeply it will rot; if it is planted too shallowly the plants will dry out and die. Once the plant is at the correct depth, backfill the soil, keeping it off the crown and firming it around the plant using finger tips. Plant any other strawberries in the same way. If planting another row, place it 75cm (30in) away – closer if in a raised bed. Water the plants well. A fibre mat can then be placed around each plant, or you can plant through black polythene.

Plant care

Traditionally flowers are removed in the first year but this is not necessary as you will lose the year's crop.

Water frequently while new plants are establishing themselves in the soil during spring. Also water during dry periods in the growing season. Drip irrigation is the best method of watering as water from overhead can rot the crown and fruits. It can also cause a build-up of botrytis.

During the growing season, give strawberry plants a liquid potash feed – such as a tomato feed – every 1–2 weeks. In early spring, apply general fertilizer at a rate of 50g per square metre (2oz per square yard).

HARVESTING IS USUALLY MUCH EASIER when strawberries are grown in special strawberry planters or other containers because the fruit will be raised off the ground.

A GOOD FLOWERING is required if lots of fruit are to form, and this happens best in full sun in a sheltered site. Assist flowering and fruit set by applying tomato fertilizer.

Weed frequently between plants to prevent any competition for water and nutrients. However, take care not to damage the plants.

As fruits start to develop, tuck straw underneath the fruits and leaves to prevent the strawberries from rotting on the soil. Barley straw is considered to be the best type of straw because it is soft and doesn't pierce the fruit. Otherwise use individual fibre mats if these are not already in position. The straw or matting will help to suppress weeds. Any other weeds that emerge should be pulled out by hand.

After cropping has finished, remove the old leaves from summer fruiting strawberries with secateurs or hand shears. Also remove the straw mulch, fibre mat, or black polythene, to prevent a build-up of pests and diseases, particularly botrytis.

In winter, move container-grown plants in unheated greenhouses outside because they require a cold period in order to fruit well.

Expect strawberry plants to crop successfully for three years before replacing them. Crop rotation is recommended to minimize the risk of an attack by pests and diseases in the soil. It also gives a chance for the soil to rest.

Strawberry plants reproduce themselves by sending out runners from the main plant with baby plants attached to them. These runners compete for water and nutrients and crowd out the main plant. They should therefore be removed at once with secateurs. The baby plants can be rooted and planted out separately (see below) if they have formed a root system, in which case they will fruit the following year.

At harvest time

Pick strawberries when they are bright red all over, ideally during the warmest part of the day because this is when they are at their juiciest and most tasty. Eat them right away; they do not keep well, but they can be frozen.

ROOTING STRAWBERRY RUNNERS

1 GROW ON NEW strawberry plants from the old ones by planting up the runners, which usually arise in prolific numbers from the main plant.

2 PEG DOWN a young plantlet into a small container of fresh potting compost. Use a wire hoop as a peg to keep the runner in direct contact with the soil.

3 AFTER A FEW WEEKS, when the plantlet has taken root, cut the runner from the main plant. Grow on the plantlet as a separate plant.

TUCK A LAYER OF STRAW under the plants to help keep the strawberries clean and free from rot. Remove it after cropping because it can encourage slugs and botrytis.

Pests and diseases

Strawberry fruits are prone to attack by birds (see page 58), and squirrels so cover fruiting plants with netting as the fruits ripen. Botrytis (see page 60), powdery mildew (see page 61), fungal leaf spot (see page 61), and red spider mite (see page 58) can also cause problems, as can the following more specific pests and diseases.

Red core Caused by the fungus *Phytophthora fragariae*, red core is recognizable by the appearance of stunted plants with reddish brown leaves in spring. There is no cure but the fungus thrives in damp conditions, so grow plants in well-drained soil or raised beds. Destroy infected plants and grow new plants in a fresh strawberry patch.

Slugs These cause large, unsightly holes in the fruit, which causes it to rot. Control is very difficult. Scatter slug pellets thinly around strawberry plants to avoid harming pets, hedgehogs, birds, etc. Alternatively, use biological control with Nemaslug and surround plants with slug deterrent barriers. Beer traps (sunken jars of beer that slugs fall into and drown) have limited effectiveness and are considered by many to be a waste of good beer.

Strawberry seed beetle As the name suggests this black beetle, 1cm (½in) long, removes seeds from the outside of the fruit. They also sometimes eat into the fruit itself. Fruits therefore shrivel and rot. Strawberry seed beetles are also attracted by weed seeds, so keeping the strawberry patch weed-free should help reduce numbers. Sinking jam jars into the soil so that they fall in might help to reduce numbers. Avoid chemicals because these beetles feed near harvest time.

Verticillium wilt This fungus causes the foliage on a strawberry plant to wilt. The leaves appear floppy and drooping and the colour changes from green to brown, eventually falling from the plant. In a severe attack, strawberry plants can die within the season. There is no cure available. Immediately the symptoms are spotted, remove the plant and its surrounding soil. Crop rotation helps to avoid this problem, as does never planting strawberries in the same soil twice, nor growing them on sites on which potatoes, tomatoes, or chrysanthemums have been cultivated.

Vine weevil Adult vine weevils eat notches in the edges of leaves, while plump, creamy white larvae with brown heads cause more damage to the roots, on which they feed. This can kill the plants. Using a torch, search for adults at night while they are feeding on the leaves. Dispose of them immediately. Control vine weevil grubs with nematodes (*Steinernema krauseii*), which are added to water and poured around the root area. Also use crop rotation to reduce the risk of attack.

FRUIT NETTING IS ESSENTIAL if birds are a problem, but if you suffer from troublesome squirrels the netting will have to be made from wire.

Carol's fruit notebook

Raspberries

" When I think of raspberries I think of their vibrant colour – red with white and even blue too. When the flesh of the drupelets (the seed-carrying knobbles) is crushed, a flood of translucent juice rushes out, in sharp contrast to the velvety bloom of the undamaged berry. It soaks freely into white sugar, it even completely takes over an ice-cream mixture, and with red currants in a summer pudding, the flesh glows with an inner light.

Raspberries are one of those fruits that make planet Earth a better place to live on. Luckily they grow easily in our gardens, as they cope with cool, wet summers and a wide range of soil types. If you live in a dry part of the world, don't despair. So long as you can provide enough moisture at the base of the plant, and shade from a tree or a building you can still grow raspberries. They survive perfectly well as woodland plants in light shade, and because they have a vigorous habit they will just quietly get on with it. You might not even notice that the fruits have suddenly become ripe and ready to pick. Pulling a ripe raspberry off the core (confusingly termed a receptacle) is very satisfying compared to harvesting many other fruit or vegetables. It will come off in one piece, usually undamaged and perfect and completely ready to eat. Washing picked raspberries seems to go against the grain with me as a light splash bounces off and could never wash off any chemicals and a good drench will damage them and make them go soggy.

Raspberries are a prime candidate for growing organically, to keep them free of toxic chemicals. You can wash off any dirt or cobwebs while the berries are still on the plant and let the sun dry them before they are picked. Raspberries can be cropped into autumn, and still give you a taste of summer, in a last-ditch denial of the relentless march of winter. **"**

LIKE SEARCHING FOR RUBIES amongst dense foliage, the pleasure of raspberry picking is surpassed only by the consumption of your treasures.

Raspberries

Rubus idaeus

A few well-chosen raspberry plants can quickly provide fresh fruit from midsummer until midautumn, and because these fruits are one of the best to freeze, quality fruits can be consumed for much longer. Both summer and autumn varieties are available, each requiring different cultivation techniques to obtain the best yields.

The best sites and soils

Raspberries are native to northern Europe and so are more tolerant of moist soils than many other fruits. Add plenty of bulky organic matter, particularly to sandy or chalky soils with a good thickness of topsoil, prior to planting. This helps them retain moisture during summer when the fruits are swelling and the plants need to sustain their lush foliage. Chalky soils with less than 30cm (12in) topsoil aren't suitable for raspberry cultivation because they require slightly acidic soil, as well as ample moisture. In soils with a neutral or slightly alkaline pH add acidifying materials such as sulphur chips or ericaceous compost.

While moisture is important, raspberries will not tolerate waterlogged soils, especially in winter, as they encourage root diseases and rotting. To improve

POT-GROWN RASPBERRIES

As well as allowing gardeners with balconies and patios to grow these fruits, pot culture also enables the cropping season to be extended as the plants can be moved under cover in spring and autumn.

Pot up raspberry canes in autumn, three to a 30cm (12in) pot, using 50:50 John Innes No 3 and multipurpose potting compost. For an early crop, set summer raspberries into a frost-free spot in late winter; hand pollinate flowers with a paint brush. Conversely, for a late crop, move potted autumn raspberries to a similar spot just before the first frosts. Make sure plants are well fed and watered during summer.

PLANTING RASPBERRIES

1 ADD PLENTY OF ORGANIC MATTER to a trench at least 38cm (15in) wide so the raspberries can grow in moisture-retentive but well-drained soil.

2 ADD SULPHUR CHIPS to the trench if your soil is slightly alkaline. This will lower its pH and deter iron and manganese deficiency.

3 ALLOW YOUR SOIL to settle for a month or two before planting. Space plants at least 30cm (12in) apart, using the soil mark on the stems as a guide to depth.

SUMMER RASPBERRY VARIETIES such as these bear their fruit on short sideshoots, which are produced on the one-year-old canes.

AS SOON AS THE FRUITED CANES have been pruned out, tie in the new canes of summer-fruiting varieties to the sturdy wire supports, spacing them evenly.

drainage, dig in bulky organic matter, such as composted bark or wood chips, along with an equal volume of horticultural grit or pea gravel, to only one spade's depth as this is where the roots grow.

Although raspberries are tolerant of shade, they will crop more heavily and make more sturdy, disease-resistant plants if grown in a sheltered, sunny (but not parched) spot. The flowers, while self-fertile, must be pollinated by insects, so avoid a very windy site unless windbreaks or shelterbelts can be erected. Also, the fruiting side branches of some varieties are very long and may break in the wind.

Buying and planting

Buy only plants that are certified free of viruses because raspberry plants are very prone to such infections, which are spread especially by aphids. Dig up rooted canes for replanting only if you know the plants are healthy and crop heavily.

Summer raspberries require a sturdy support system: run two wires – one 60cm (2ft) high and the other 1.5m (5ft) high – along the length of the row. Autumn raspberries don't need support.

Clear the site of perennial weeds before planting as these are difficult to control once raspberries are established. Plant bundles of bare-root canes in late autumn, spacing the new raspberry plants at least 30cm (12in) apart. Then add a mulch of bulky organic matter, 7.5cm (3in) thick. Avoid mushroom compost (which is too alkaline) or overly rich farmyard manure (which tends to burn off the new shoots as they push through the mulch layer).

Once newly planted canes start to burst into leaf in spring cut them down to 10–15cm (4–6in) in height to encourage more canes to be produced. Tie summer varieties to the support wires ain late summer.

Autumn raspberry canes will bear fruit in their first year, summer raspberries in their second.

Plant care

In early summer, pull up suckers between the rows of summer raspberries, and thin autumn raspberries to 10cm (4in) apart. Cut out fruited summer canes once they've finished cropping and tie in new ones, thinning them to 10cm (4in) apart. Cut autumn raspberry canes down to the ground in midwinter.

In midspring, top-dress both summer and autumn raspberries with a general-purpose fertilizer, then a mulch of low-nutrient organic matter such as garden compost or composted bark chips. Alternatively, top-dress with well-rotted farmyard manure.

At harvest time

The first summer raspberries are ready for harvesting in early summer, whereas autumn raspberries won't mature until late summer. Pick on a dry day. Eat them fresh, freeze them, or make into preserves.

Pests and diseases

Raspberry beetle is the main pest of these fruits. Dried up patches develop at the fruit's stalk end in midsummer, and a small, white maggot, up to 8mm (⅛in) long, is often found inside the fruits. Spray with pyrethrum when the first fruits start to colour and again two weeks later. There are no effective controls.

Cane blight (where new canes brown at the base), spur blight (where new canes develop purple blotches around leaf spurs), and cane spot (where canes develop random purple patches) can all cause individual raspberry canes to die. There is no chemical control but some varieties show good

WHEN ESTABLISHING a raspberry bed it is important to consider bird protection. A fruit cage would be ideal.

resistance (check with your supplier). Prune out affected canes, avoid over-applying high nitrogen fertilizers, and thin out canes sufficiently to deter these diseases, which are more prevalent in still, humid conditions.

Raspberries are especially prone to viruses, which can be transferred via sap-sucking insects. Discard established plants showing symptoms such as stunting, distortion, or irregular leaf yellowing.

BEND OVER THE LONG CANES of vigorous summer-fruiting varieties after leaf-fall and tie them into their support. At bud-break, cut them off just above the higher wire, when any dieback is evident.

ONE-YEAR-OLD SUMMER RASPBERRY CANES are brown at the base, and so are easy to recognize, as the current year's canes are green. After they have fruited, all brown-based canes should be cut out with sharp secateurs or loppers.

AUTUMN RASPBERRY – EXTENDING SEASON

Autumn raspberries bear most of their fruit on the current year's canes, but they can be forced to crop like summer varieties by careful pruning. This allows a single autumn variety to yield both summer and autumn crops, thereby extending the season in the minimum space. Instead of cutting all the canes down to the ground in late winter, shorten a few of them by only one-half. Because these lower sections of cane had not borne fruit in the previous autumn, they will produce fruiting shoots in the spring – much as summer varieties do. Once harvested, cut these canes back to soil level.

HARVEST RASPBERRIES DURING DRY WEATHER to increase their shelf life. Pick over the plants regularly to ensure fruits don't become over-ripe and rotten.

Recommended varieties

'Glen Moy'
This early summer variety bears heavy crops of medium to large berries which have a good flavour. It may also produce a small crop on the new canes, in autumn. The spine-free canes are compact.

'Malling Admiral'
A summer raspberry bearing good yields in mid- to late summer on strong-growing, tall canes, which are best sited in a sheltered spot. The flavour is excellent, and the large berries ripen to deep red.

'Polka'
This new autumn variety ripens two weeks earlier than 'Autumn Bliss', bridging the gap between summer and autumn varieties. It produces very high yields of large, well-flavoured fruits.

'Glen Ample'
Delicious, large fruit are produced in midsummer on this extremely heavy-yielding summer variety with vigorous, upright, spine-free canes. The berries are produced on long, upright stems, making picking easy.

'Leo'
This variety is one of the latest summer raspberries to ripen, producing large, firm fruits with an excellent flavour. The stems are very long, so harvesting is easy. Site in a sheltered position.

'Autumn Bliss'
The short, sturdy canes of this popular autumn variety produce high yields from late summer to midautumn. The fruits are large and deep red with a firm texture and excellent flavour.

Blackberries and hybrid berries

" Picking and eating blackberries from wild and heavily laden bushes are one of late summer's unmissable experiences, as is seeing a dormouse perched on a blackberry bush casually nibbling the ripe fruit, as my husband once did!

Not everyone has the opportunity to go blackberry picking among wild plants, so growing them yourself is the next best thing. And modern cultivated varieties harness that vigour to deliver bigger, juicier berries, so – as long as you can provide enough restraint and support – a bumper crop can be yours.

I like the way wild blackberries reflect their growing season through their size, texture, and flavour, yet many gardeners prefer a reliably large and juicy crop, opting for the improved hybrids such as loganberries, boysenberries, and tayberries. These hybrid berries tend to have more sugar and water in their fruit and so taste sweeter and milder than the wild forms. While they are easier to eat raw, they have less flavour when cooked.

It seems unnatural to me to buy blackberries when they can be picked for free in the wild or grown successfully yourself. Many supermarket blackberries are imported, even flown in from countries with inadequate winters (the cold helps flower buds develop) and where the growers defoliate the bushes with chemicals, then spray on growth regulators to force flowering. Your own blackberries, grown organically, picked fresh, and eaten uncooked are much healthier. In fact, blackberries have recently been admitted to the special group of "superfruits" due to their huge oxygen radical absorbance capacity and an abundance of antioxidants. Unbeatable! "

ONE OF SUMMER'S great pleasures, foraging for blackberries is a wonderful activity and one that shouldn't be rushed.

Blackberries and hybrid berries *Rubus* spp.

Nothing evokes the arrival of late summer quite like a hedge full of ripe blackberries, but there are many improved selections on the wild plant. Cultivated blackberries and their hybrid relatives have much better vigour and productivity, and can be trained into a variety of shapes, making them a very versatile crop in the fruit garden.

In addition to blackberries (*Rubus fruticosus*), many other *Rubus* species and hybrids are invaluable in the fruit garden. Loganberries (*R. x loganobaccus*), tayberries (*R. Tayberry Group*), and boysenberry (*R. ursinus x idaeus*), for example, are all crosses between *R. ursinus* and raspberries, and they produce delicious fruit. In addition to these, other fruiting forms of *Rubus* that are also worth growing for fruit are Japanese wineberry (*R. phoenicolasius*), which produces small, red fruits on extremely bristly, red stems; European dewberry (*R. caesius*), which bears small, purple fruits covered in a grey bloom; and cloudberry (*R. chamaemorus*), which grows well in very cool climates and bears golden-yellow fruits.

The best sites and soils

Blackberries and their hybrids are extremely useful in the fruit garden. Not only do they have high ornamental value (see box, page 152) but their sprawling habit also allows them to easily occupy spaces in the garden such as arches, pergolas, trelliswork, and walls, as well as native hedges. You can allow less vigorous varieties to scramble through large shrubs, although this can at times make access for picking difficult.

Their flowers require insect intervention to be pollinated, so position plants in a sheltered site because they flower relatively early in the year.

PLANTING CONTAINER-GROWN BLACKBERRIES

1 DIG OUT A PLANTING HOLE at least twice the width of the plant's rootball. Then fork over the bottom of the hole to alleviate compaction.

2 TEASE OUT THE ROOTS and cut back to a healthy bud before planting. Set the plant at the same depth at which it was growing in the container.

3 FIRM THE PLANT in with your heel and water it well. Then spread a 7.5cm (3in) layer of bulky organic matter as a mulch around the plant, avoiding the stem.

TRAIN BLACK- AND HYBRID BERRIES against a system of wires to create a framework of annual fruiting branches. These will yield good crops in summer.

SHORTENING ALL SIDESHOOTS that develop from the main stems ensures that plants are kept within bounds and are easy to manage. It also allows sunlight to access the canes.

Blackberries and their hybrids prefer moisture-retentive but free-draining soil, so dig in plenty of bulky organic matter into chalky, sandy, or heavy clay soils prior to planting. While crops can tolerate shade they will be more productive in a sunny, sheltered site. Many varieties, especially the hybrid forms, are extremely vigorous and require at least 3.75m (12ft) between plants when trained against a wall or fence.

Buying and planting

All blackberries and relatives are self-fertile so only one plant is needed to obtain fruit. When buying plants choose from bare-root or container-grown specimens. Thornless varieties make picking less hazardous but their canes require a little more guidance than their thorny relatives. Vigorous varieties need a sturdy support system: use a wall or fence with horizontal wires spaced 45cm (18in) apart, with the lowest wire 23cm (9in) from the ground; or run the wires between two strong vertical posts.

If needed, improve the ground with organic matter well before planting. When planting cut all canes

BLACK- AND HYBRID BERRY PLANTS are often very vigorous and so need to be trained onto a sturdy support, such as this post-and-wire system. Use straining bolts to tighten the wires between the supports.

down to a healthy bud. This may seem drastic but it will ensure your plant throws up lots of vigorous, healthy suckers in spring.

Plant care

Black- and hybrid berries are relatively easy to maintain provided you can keep on top of their vigorous growth. Regularly tie in the shoots of newly planted canes, then, once these reach their first winter, cut back all sideshoots produced on these main canes to 5cm (2in). It is mainly from these fruiting spurs that flowers are formed.

In the second year after planting the crown will throw up yet more new canes from ground level.

Recommended varieties

Blackberry 'Fantasia'
This extremely vigorous, very heavy cropping variety bears fruits of an excellent flavour when fully ripe. The berries can be picked from late summer until the first frosts. Eat them fresh or use for cooking or jams.

Blackberry 'Sylvan'
The numerous fruits of 'Sylvan', which ripen from mid- to late summer, are extremely large with an excellent flavour. Plants are vigorous and thorny, so need sturdy supports.

Blackberry 'Loch Ness'
One of the most widely grown varieties. The thornless canes bear masses of large, glossy, well-flavoured berries. These ripen from late summer until the first frosts, so have a very long harvest period.

Loganberry 'Ly 654'
Thornless canes produce good yields of fruits that are slightly longer than those of a raspberry. The fruits are sharp, juicy, and deep red when ripe, between late summer and early autumn. Use them in cooking.

Loganberry 'Ly 59'
Vigorous 'Ly 59' bears large, quite tart, dark red fruits that have a typical loganberry shape and flavour – ideal for cooking and preserves. The canes crop well in all conditions, bearing fruit in mid- and late summer.

Tayberry Group
This sharp-flavoured berry is very vigorous, producing fruit during mid- and late summer. Allow the fruit to ripen to dark red before picking to develop their full flavour. Use in preserves or cooking.

Loosely bundle these together; insert four bamboo canes in a square vertically around the crown and pull the new canes into the centre; then tie some sturdy twine around the square to hold the new canes gently in place. Remove the one-year-old canes once they have fruited by cutting them into shorter sections with loppers and then extracting them carefully to prevent their thorns snagging on the new canes. Then untie the twine around the new canes and train them along the wires.

Top-dress with a general-purpose fertilizer in midspring and renew the organic mulch, once the soil has warmed up. Make sure the mulch is placed away from the new canes and the crown.

Water young plants during dry summer spells. While mature plants shouldn't need extra irrigation, their fruit size will benefit if the summer is particularly dry.

All blackberries and hybrid berries are grown on their own roots and can be propagated easily by tip-layering young shoots in autumn.

At harvest time

The one-year-old canes will flower, then develop and ripen fruit from midsummer onwards. These berries can be picked as soon as they are ripe, and then either eaten fresh, frozen, or used in jams, jellies, and cooking.

Pests and diseases

Black- and hybrid berries are prone to bird damage (see page 58). They can also suffer from raspberry beetle (see page 146), raspberry spur blight (see page 146), and Eutypa dieback (see page 183). Leafhoppers may occur on plants in sheltered sites; the jumping, light green insects, roughly 3mm (⅛in) long, cause white flecking on the leaves. Control measures are not necessary. Red berry mite may causes blackberry fruit to ripen unevenly, but there is no control for this pest. Blackberry cane spot can cause grey spotting on affected canes, which eventually die. These should be pruned out to ground level.

ONCE THE ONE-YEAR-OLD CANES have borne fruit, cut them out to ground level using loppers or secateurs. Remove them in sections so as not to damage the new canes

TIE THE NEW CANES carefully into position along the wires where the fruited, one-year-old canes had been. Use a figure-of-eight knot and space them out well.

Mulberries
Morus nigra spp.

These handsome trees for the garden are relatively large (up to 9m/30ft tall and wide) so they are only really suitable for large fruit gardens. In such places their gnarled appearance and dense canopy make them an invaluable ornamental addition, and their tart fruits make excellent jams, jellies, and wine.

The best sites and soils

Grow in well-drained but moist soil with a pH of 6–7. Enrich sandy soils with plenty of bulky organic matter, and avoid chalky soils. In exposed or cool-temperate gardens plant mulberries in a sunny, sheltered spot against a south- or west-facing wall. Elsewhere grow them as single specimens.

Buying and planting

Black mulberry (*Morus nigra*) is the main species grown, but white mulberry (*M. alba*) and red mulberry (*M. rubra*) also bear fruit, although it is inferior in quality. Mulberries are self-fertile and pollinated by insects, so only one tree is required to obtain fruit, and they are sold on their own roots rather than as grafted trees. When choosing a new tree, look for one with a strong, tall central leader. Never prune on planting as mulberries bleed sap badly from both root and shoot pruning cuts.

Plant care

Carry out pruning in early winter, when trees are fully dormant. Tip the leader back and remove any lower shoots to create a clear main stem to accommodate the drooping branches when mature. Keep established pruning to a minimum to avoid sap bleeding. Bend over – rather than cut back – all branches to restrict size and encourage fruiting. Prop up spreading branches if needed. Apply an annual top-dressing of general fertilizer in early spring.

At harvest time

Mulberries flower mainly on older wood so trees can take 4–5 years to begin cropping. They flower quite late in spring and thereby often avoid the worst of the frosts. The fruits ripen in late summer and should be picked carefully to avoid crushing them.

Pests and diseases

While virtually problem-free, birds (see page 58) can steal the fruits. Trees may also be affected by mulberry canker, which appears as sunken areas girdling stems and subsequent dieback of the upper shoots. Prune out affected growth in winter.

TAKE CARE WHEN HARVESTING ripe mulberries because their soft fruit can easily bruise and so stain skin and clothes with their rich juice.

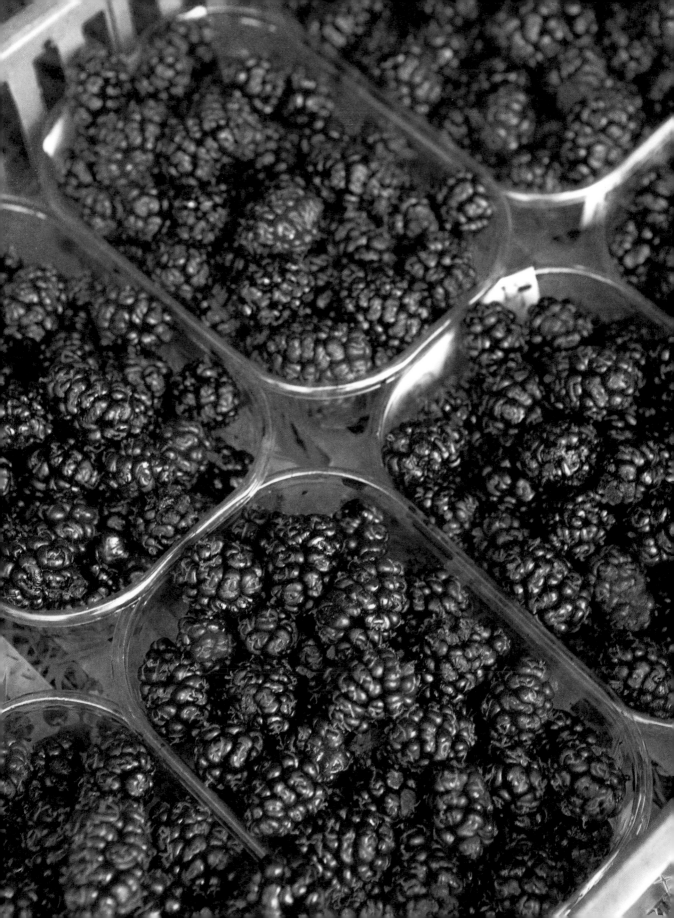

Blueberries

"Blueberries are big, soft, and soppy fruit, with a flared "crown" at the base and with pale flesh like a black grape. They burst onto the scene as a "superfruit" around 2004 and were soon available at supermarkets in tiny plastic trays, almost priced per berry. Nowadays, they are quite likely to have been grown in Chile and held back for months in cold store to ensure a continuous, year-round supply.

Growing your own is simple and rewarding; you can ensure you are eating blueberries at their freshest and most nutritious, just at the time of year when they have the most beneficial impact on your general health. You can keep any surplus berries by freezing them as quickly as possible, having laid them out, dry and not touching, on a flat tray in the freezer. Once frozen, they can be bagged up together for storage.

Why are blueberries so coveted? Unusually among wild types of berries and especially "superfruit" berries, they are very mild and nicely sweet. They could almost have been invented as lazy snack food for office workers to pick at on their desks. Their current claim to fame is for their antioxidants and their anthocyanidins, which can counter inflammation. Their active compounds may also help prevent some kinds of cancer and the advance of Alzheimer's disease. They are by no means a silver bullet, but they are so easy to eat straight from the bush and so handsome in autumn that it's all to the good to grow them.

Another delicious, related fruit is the bilberry. I remember, when I were a girl, striding up Rivington Pike in Lancashire after my mum to pick wild whinberries or "whorts" (from whortleberry), as we called them. They were all *Vaccinium myrtillus*, which are much smaller and denser than blueberries; they are purple all the way through the berry, and much sourer, but after my mum's cooking they were the more flavourful. Her whinberry tarts were the match of any famous French *tarte aux myrtilles*."

THESE LITTLE FRUITS are just bursting with goodness. It's so simple for gardeners to grow them at home and pick them fresh off the bush.

Blueberries *Vaccinium* spp.

These hardy plants require a moist, acid soil, which pot culture can easily provide, and they suffer few pest and disease problems. There are many varieties available, and many are not only highly productive but also provide an ornamental feature because of their glorious autumn colours. The fruits themselves are delicious and extremely high in antioxidants.

The best sites and soils

Plant in moist, well-drained, acidic soil in a sunny, sheltered spot. While blueberries are tolerant of shade, better crops (and autumn colour) are obtained in the sun. The pH should be at least as low as pH5.5 (see box, below right). If your garden soil is very alkaline, grow blueberries in containers of ericaceous compost. This should be loam-based

VACCINIUM CORYMBOSUM AND ITS CULTIVARS are known as northern highbush blueberries and are the most widely grown form of this crop in fruit gardens.

(for example, John Innes ericaceous compost) because it holds its structure better than standard, loam-free ericaceous compost, providing optimum drainage, and it is therefore more suitable for plants that will be in containers for many years.

Raised or sunken beds

Blueberries and other acid-loving crops such as cranberries and lingonberries (see pages 162–65) can also be grown in a raised or sunken bed of acidic materials. Sunken beds are very moisture-retentive so easy to maintain, while raised beds require constant irrigation throughout summer so are more labour intensive. Make the bed, raised or sunk into the soil, at least 60cm (2ft) deep. Line the sides and base with polythene that has been pierced in several places with a garden fork. Fill the bed with loam-based ericaceous compost plus composted bark. If this proves too costly mix together an equal volume of pH neutral or acidic soil, composted bark, and ericaceous compost. Obtain the soil from a reputable topsoil supplier or, if from the garden, discard the top 7.5cm (3in) as this contains weed seeds.

ADJUSTING THE SOIL FOR BLUEBERRIES

To grow well, blueberries require acid soil with a pH of 5.5 or below. In gardens with more alkaline soils, lower the pH to a suitable level with acidifying materials such as sulphur chips or pine needles, unless your soil pH is 8 or above in which case it is simply too alkaline for blueberry cultivation. Instead, grow plants in pots, using ericaceous (acidic), loam-based potting compost. To avoid raising the pH, use rainwater, not tapwater, to irrigate plants, wherever possible.

EACH YEAR REMOVE one or two older stems completely. This encourages the blueberry to throw up new shoots from the base, which are more vigorous and productive.

ALTHOUGH NEW SHOOTS are often vigorous, they generally lack side branching. Encourage sideshoots by removing the tips of such branches to a well-placed bud in late winter.

Buying and planting

Blueberries are very useful fruiting plants, and there are many different forms to provide both fruit and ornamental value to the fruit garden. Their flowers, which appear in early spring, are insect pollinated.

The main blueberry grown by gardeners is northern highbush blueberry (*Vaccinium corymbosum*), of which there are dozens of varieties – all are extremely hardy, have large fruits, and high yields. They also require a significant period of cold to initiate flowers and therefore fruit. Two other forms of highbush blueberry have fruiting potential: *V. ashei*, also known as "rabbit-eyes", which is mainly grown in the southern states of America; and southern highbush blueberries, which are hybrids of the northern and rabbit-eye types, aren't as hardy as the northern types, and crop best in milder parts of cool-temperate areas. There are also the extremely hardy lowbush blueberries, *V. angustifolium* and *V. myrtilloides* (which is native to Canada), and "half-high" blueberries, which are a cross between the lowbush and highbush forms. Other species with fruiting potential include Azores blueberry (*V. cylindraceum*) and bilberry or whortleberry (*V. myrtillus*).

Blueberries are suckering plants that are grown on their own roots so no choosing of rootstock is required. While some varieties can set a fair crop on their own, all yield much heavier harvests if planted near to another variety. Flowering can occur early or late in the spring depending on the variety, so check with your supplier that the plants you want to buy are flowering at a similar time to ensure that successful cross-pollination can occur.

When buying, select plants that have multiple shoots at the base. These should all be tipped back on planting to encourage further side branching. Cut out weak stems completely.

If growing blueberries in your garden soil, add plenty of bulky, acidic organic matter such as pine needles or composted conifer clippings. Avoid well-rotted farmyard manure as this is too rich for the plants and will scorch their fine, fibrous roots. Ericaceous compost is useful to help acidify the soil but its structure is very fine and so it will not help create optimum drainage conditions. Space plants at least 1m (3ft) apart to accommodate their spread – further if more vigorous varieties are chosen.

For pot culture use a container 30cm (12in) in diameter for a small plant, and a half-barrel or similarly larger pot for a larger blueberry plant. Make sure the

BLUEBERRIES FLOWER early in spring, their bell-shaped blossoms being pollinated mainly by bees. Consequently a sheltered position helps achieve the best yields.

COME THE AUTUMN many blueberries will put on an amazing display of autumn leaf colours in a wide range of red and purple hues.

container is either glazed or lined with polythene sheeting (pierced at the base) to avoid moisture loss.

Plant care

Blueberries are relatively easy to look after provided a few key points are addressed, these being soil pH, soil moisture, pruning, and pests and diseases. Ensure the soil has a constant pH of 5.5 or lower, to avoid plants developing lime-induced chlorosis and associated iron deficiency (see page 57). While acidifying materials can be added at planting, their pH levels can rise in time, especially if the surrounding soil has a neutral or slightly alkaline pH. Check the pH of the soil each spring and add sulphur chips if the pH needs to be lowered. This shouldn't be necessary with container-grown plants provided ericaceous fertilizer and rainwater are used to water and feed plants. Apply an annual top-dressing of ericaceous fertilizer to the soil at half the recommended rate and cover it with a 7.5cm (3in) layer of ericaceous mulch material such as composted conifer clippings.

Keep all plants well watered, especially during spring and summer, using rainwater wherever possible. To ensure the plants have water exactly when and where they need it most, lie a seep hose around the plants and cover this with mulch.

Established pruning consists of taking out completely a proportion of the older wood, so use loppers or a saw to remove two or three older stems to the base in late winter. This helps keep plants productive. At the same time tip back vigorous new shoots to a

GREAT AUTUMN COLOUR

As well as bearing fruits, blueberries often exhibit gorgeous autumnal hues in their leaves. This is often expressed most strongly in sunny sites on very acidic soils, or with plants grown in pots, especially if the conditions in midautumn are cold at night and warm in the day with light winds at all times. The varieties 'Spartan', 'Bluejay', 'Tophat', 'Sunrise', 'Berkeley', and 'Grover' are particularly colourful. This makes them excellent additions to a mixed border as well as to the fruit garden.

plump, healthy bud to encourage side branching. Winter prunings of one-year-old wood can be used as hardwood cuttings; cut into 20cm (8in) lengths and insert into a trench of moisture-retentive but well-drained acidic soil so only the top 7.5cm (3in) is above ground. Replant rooted cuttings in autumn.

At harvest time

Flowers appear mainly on one-, two-, and three-year-old wood in spring. Once pollinated by insects, fruits develop and then start to ripen from midsummer onwards, changing colour from green to dusty blue. At this point the fruits can be harvested. Pick over the plants several times as not all the fruit ripens at the same time. The fruits can be eaten fresh; alternatively, they can be dried, frozen, made into preserves, or used in cooking. They are extremely rich in antioxidants and vitamins (especially vitamin C) so have many health benefits.

Pests and diseases

Birds (see page 58) are the main pest of blueberries. Erect taut netting over the plants as soon as the fruits start to show any purple colouration.

IT IS ESSENTIAL TO CONSIDER BIRD PROTECTION before blueberry fruits start to ripen. A tent of taut netting over a sturdy frame is a simple way to do this.

Recommended varieties

'Duke'
Stocky bushes produce good yields of medium to large fruit of excellent flavour. 'Duke' flowers late but crops early so is especially good for northern areas where the growing season is short. Partly self-fertile.

'Tophat'
Self-fertile, heavy-cropping 'Tophat' is a dwarf blueberry. Mature plants attain a height and spread of only 60cm (2ft). The medium-sized berries have a very good flavour. Attractive autumn colour.

'Spartan'
Very hardy, early- to midseason 'Spartan' bears large fruits with a sweet, tangy flavour. To crop well, this variety needs another blueberry variety nearby. 'Spartan' produces some of the best autumn colour.

'Nelson'
A mid- to late-season variety that is very hardy and self-fertile. It was developed for mechanical harvesting. The large fruits and good flavour make it equally useful for the amateur fruit garden.

Cranberries and lingonberries

" Every member of the *Vaccinium* genus is being groomed to become the latest "superfruit". Some are already there, such as blueberries and cranberries, while others are almost there – lingonberries and bilberries. A "superfruit" enjoys a reputation that can be commercially exploited; it is not a scientific fact or even a horticultural consensus. New attributes of all manner of fruit are being discovered daily, and if they directly relate to someone's medical or health concerns they are naturally given immediate importance by that person. "Superfruit" can enter and re-enter the Top 20 phytonutrient rankings endlessly, leapfrogging their rivals with new discoveries. Blueberries were at the top in 2004 but have since been overtaken by Goji berries, elderberries, and cranberries.

So what makes cranberries so special? It seems that some of their active chemicals have anti-bacterial properties. Some attack streptococcus bacteria that would go on to cause dental plaque and tooth decay. (Ironically, cranberry juice, dried cranberries, and cranberry sauce are all heavily sugared to mollify the hugely sour and acidic taste.) Some anti-bacterial chemicals in cranberries flush the kidneys and the urinary tract, and cranberry juice is often prescribed as a diuretic for women.

Whatever the definitive evidence of "superfruit", it is surely a good thing to eat a wide range of fresh fruit regularly, try unfamiliar foods to extend your range, and even grow some yourself. Cranberries and lingonberries are particularly rewarding. When harvested, the fresh, organic fruits will contain their optimum health benefits. Growing a few bushes yourself may also reawaken the lost connection to our foraging ancestors, who rightly valued the nutritious and medicinal bounty that a few wild berries presented. "

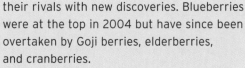

CRANBERRIES form tight mats of creeping stems. Excellent for our health, make sure you repay the favour by regularly maintaining your stock.

Cranberries and lingonberries

Vaccinium, Vaccinium macrocarpon and *V. vitis-idaea* spp.

Both cranberries and lingonberries are evergreen shrubs that are happy in the most seemingly unpromising areas. Preferring acidic, boggy soils they are excellent companions to blueberries, and their sharp flavour makes them an interesting contrast to more conventional fruits and other foods, especially when cooked. They are compact and trouble-free, and offer good yields.

The best sites and soils

Cranberries (*Vaccinium macrocarpon*) and lingonberries (*V. vitis-idaea*) are both evergreen, low-growing, very hardy shrubs that bear spherical fruits. The cranberry is native to North America, whereas the lingonberry is found not only in the alpine regions of North America but also those in Europe and Japan. Both berries offer good autumn colours as well as edible fruit and both require an acidic, boggy soil.

Grow these fruits in containers or in sunken or raised beds, because very few domestic gardens possess ideal growing conditions. Line the pot or bed with plastic, piercing holes in the sides and base so that water is retained but not allowed to stagnate. Fill the pot or bed with John Innes loam-based, ericaceous compost; then top-dress it with a layer, 2.5cm (1in) deep, of horticultural grit.

Position cranberries and lingonberries in the same bed as blueberries, because the soil and moisture requirements of all three crops are very similar. While cranberries and lingonberries tolerate shade, a sunnier position is preferred. Both plants

IF WATERED REGULARLY DURING GROWTH, cranberries are ideal plants for a raised bed or sunken. Line this with pierced polythene and fill with ericaceous compost.

LINGONBERRIES BEAR CLUSTERS of spherical, red berries. They naturally occur in very boggy, acidic sites but the gardener can replicate such an environment at home.

CRANBERRIES MAKE GOOD SUBJECTS for pots where garden soil doesn't have a sufficiently low pH or is not boggy enough to satisfy their cultivation needs.

CRANBERRIES CREATE A CREEPING MASS of stems, which can easily be propagated. Gently fork out healthy stems, together with their roots.

PROPAGATING CRANBERRIES

In midautumn, when the soil is warm and moist, dig up an established clump and gently prise it apart with two garden forks held back to back. Discard the woodier centre and replant the outer, younger divisions. If you don't want to disturb your plant, remove rooted sections carefully from the parent, potting them into a bed or pot of loam-based ericaceous compost topped with grit. Water in well.

(cranberries in particular) have the ability to layer their stems and form a carpet of growth.

Buying and planting

Both cranberries and lingonberries are generally available only as potted plants, each being grown on their own roots and each being self-fertile. Purchase young, bushy plants. If grown in the open ground, set them 30cm (12in) apart. They will eventually knit together to form a groundcover crop. Minimal initial training is needed: on planting, just clip plants back to ensure they remain compact and bushy.

Plant care

Cranberries and lingonberries are relatively low-maintenance as long as their soil requirements are satisfied. Check the pH of soil-grown plants every spring and adjust it with sulphur chips if necessary. If yields are low, apply a liquid ericaceous fertilizer in midspring at half the recommended rate. Water plants with rainwater wherever possible, keeping the soil moist at all times. To encourage plants to spread, maintain a layer, 2.5cm (1in) deep, of horticultural grit or sharp sand on the surface of the bed or pot. Trim over plants as soon as fruits have been harvested to maintain a bushy habit. Every two or three years, thin the stems out to help ensure good air flow and optimum fruit ripening.

At harvest time

The insect-pollinated flowers will appear in spring. Harvest the berries in early or midautumn, before the first frosts. Both fruits are high in vitamin C and are better cooked than eaten fresh because of their astringent flavour. They can also be frozen or dried. Cranberries are often juiced or made into a savoury jelly; make lingonberries into sweet preserves.

Pests and diseases

Lime-induced chlorosis can be a problem on neutral or alkaline soils (see page 57). Verticillium wilt (see page 141) can also be a problem.

Carol's fruit notebook

Blackcurrants

" Blackcurrants are powerful little fruits and are very sour when eaten straight from the bush. To become palatable, so much sugar is needed that these fruits are always eaten very sweet. But beyond the sourness and the sweetness they have such a great intensity of flavour that you can't consume very many of them on their own – they are almost too strong. Balanced with something blander, however,

blackcurrants really come into their own. I was particularly proud of the blackcurrant pies I used to make for my parents-in-law – as well as the tarts, jellies, sorbets, ice cream, and compotes.

We grew our blackcurrants in a fruit cage half way up the garden – or in the birdcage as my mother called it because once a blackbird found its way in and it made no effort to escape the feast of fruit. Even after the blackbirds were sated, Neil and I still had to ferry out the crop in 9-litre (2-gallon) buckets, one in each hand, full to overflowing with shiny, black berries – local flower-show, prize-winning fruits.

Blackcurrants can be very healthy, possessing three times more vitamin C than the same weight of oranges. It has just recently been discovered that these fruits are very rich in flavanoids, antioxidants, and anthocyanins – the phytochemicals that protect against heart disease and some cancers. Almost all the UK blackcurrant crop goes to make commercial blackcurrant drinks. Since a typical drink may contain only 5 per cent of pure blackcurrant juice, commercial breeding has concentrated on improvements to harvesting, and colour and flavour intensity – all to make a little go further. Happily, we now know this also increased the proportion of active phytochemical elements and procured "superfruit" status for the blackcurrant. "

THESE VITAMIN C-RICH berries require a healthy, heavyish soil and should be planted deeply to encourage lots of healthy growth that will produce fruit the following year.

Blackcurrants *Ribes nigrum*

These easy-to-grow bushes produce bunches of dark purple to black fruits in midsummer. They are an invaluable source of vitamin C, and their tart flavour can be used in pies and jams and to make cordials and the popular cassis. The fruits, leaves, and stems all have a powerful, evocative, and unforgettable scent, although it is not to everybody's taste.

The best sites and soils

Like gooseberries and red currants, blackcurrants tolerate a wide range of soil conditions but prefer well-drained, moisture-retentive conditions. They require a richer, heavier soil than gooseberries and red currants to give them the necessary conditions in which to constantly send out strong, healthy young wood each year.

Blackcurrants prefer full sun but will tolerate light shade. Avoid frost pockets – frosts can drastically reduce yields, even on some modern varieties that are later flowering.

Buying and planting

Always buy certified stock to avoid virus problems. One bush should yield about 4.5kg (10lb) of fruit. Grow blackcurrants as stool, or multistemmed, bushes. In small gardens, blackcurrants can be grown in containers. They are not suitable for training as espaliers, cordons, step-overs, fans, or any of the restricted forms (see page 74).

Plant bare-root blackcurrants in late autumn, while containerized plants can be planted at any time of year as long as the soil is not too wet.

A few weeks before planting, clear the soil of all perennial weeds and enrich it with a generous amount of well-rotted manure. Add a compound balanced fertilizer at the rate of 85g per square metre (3oz per square yard). Allow the bed to settle.

Dig out a hole at least twice the circumference of the pot in which the blackcurrant was purchased if not bare-root. Space blackcurrant bushes 1.8m (6ft) apart. Add controlled-release fertilizer on poor soils for individual plants if compound fertilizer wasn't added when preparing the soil.

PLANTING BARE-ROOT BLACKCURRANTS

1 ADD BALANCED FERTILIZER to the bottom of the planting hole, if it wasn't added when the soil was prepared.

2 LOOK FOR THE SOIL MARK on the plant; it should be planted at least 6cm (2¼in) deeper than it was previously.

3 BACKFILL WITH excavated soil enriched with well-rotted manure, then tread the plant in firmly. Water thoroughly.

Set each plant at least 6cm (2¼in) deeper than it was previously, so it develops into a multistemmed stool bush. Deep planting encourages young, vigorous shoots to develop from the base. Use a planting stick (or piece of wood) to ensure that the plant is at the correct depth. Mix the soil from the hole with well-rotted organic manure and backfill the hole. Firm it in well before watering.

When planting container-grown blackcurrants from midautumn until late spring, cut all the stems back to one or two buds above ground level to encourage strong shoots to develop from the base. If planting between early summer and early autumn, wait until the plant is dormant before pruning all the stems.

Plant care

Water blackcurrants during dry periods in the growing season. In late winter, feed with a balanced compound fertilizer at a rate of 100g per square metre (3oz per square yard). Extra nitrogen in the form of sulphate of ammonia can be supplied at 25g per square metre (¾oz per square yard) to encourage the extra growth required of a stool bush.

Hand weed and mulch around the plant in late winter using well-rotted manure to suppress weeds. Avoid hoeing near the base of the bush because the hoe might cut through new shoots developing at the base of the plant.

Prune blackcurrants when dormant – from late autumn to late winter. Bushes fruit on the young wood, mainly from one- or two-year-old stems, and it is important to bear this in mind when pruning. Up to and including the fourth year after planting, remove weak, wispy shoots, retaining a basic structure of 6–10 healthy shoots. After year four, cut out about one-third of the older wood at the base, using a pair of loppers or a pruning saw. This will encourage and make room for younger, healthy wood. Also remove weak shoots and low ones leaning towards the ground.

Repot container-grown blackcurrants every two or three years. Pot back into the same container or one slightly larger. Trim back some of the roots and tease away the old soil replacing it with fresh John Innes No 3 potting compost.

CUT BACK ALL STEMS of newly planted blackcurrants to one or two buds above ground level. If blackcurrants are planted in summer, wait until winter before doing this.

Mulch around the plant in late winter using well-rotted manure or garden compost.

At harvest time

Harvest the fruit on modern varieties such as the 'Ben' series by cutting the strigs (or bunches of fruit) as they turn black. Older types of blackcurrant varieties ripen at different times, with the currants at the top of the strig ripening first. The fruit should therefore be painstakingly picked individually.

Eat fresh blackcurrants within a few days of harvesting. Alternatively, they can be frozen, cooked, or made into jam or jelly. Blackcurrants can also be made into a superb cordial.

Pests and diseases

Blackcurrants are prone to attack by birds (see page 58), so cover the plants with netting as the fruits ripen to prevent birds stripping them of their fruit. Ensure the netting is taut so the birds do not get caught up in it. American gooseberry mildew (see page 183), flower frost damage (see page 57), and

START TO REMOVE UNPRODUCTIVE old wood each year, four years after planting. Thin the remaining stems to create an open habit of young stems.

Recommended varieties

'Ben Sarek'
A good choice for the small garden as this is a compact, high-yielding bush growing only to about 1.2m (4ft) high. It offers resistance to mildew and frost. 'Ben Sarek' produces large berries.

'Ben Gairn'
This compact variety with large, juicy fruit is good for small gardens. It is also one of the earliest to come into fruit and is resistant to reversion.

'Ben Lomond'
An upright blackcurrant with some frost resistance because of its late flowering. Produces heavy yields of large, short-stalked berries, which are ready to harvest in late summer.

'Ben Hope'
An excellent grower with heavy yields of medium-sized, delicious currants. It is resistant to mildew, leaf spot, and gall midge. 'Boskoop Giant' is also recommended but makes a bigger plant so use in larger gardens.

'Ben Connan'
This compact plant is suitable for a small garden. It has resistance to mildew, frost, and gall midge. The berries are large with good flavour.

Jostaberry
A popular blackcurrant x gooseberry hybrid. It is very vigorous, thornless, and has good resistance to mildew, fungal leaf spot, and big bud. The gooseberry-sized fruits have a blackcurrant taste. Grow as a stool bush.

fungal leaf spots (see page 61) and mildew can also cause problems, as can the following more specific pests and diseases.

Big bud mite These mites infest the buds of blackcurrant bushes, causing them to become swollen during winter; eventually they dry up. Big bud mite not only reduces yields but can also spread reversion virus. Pick off infested buds and destroy them as soon as they are spotted. 'Ben Hope' is a resistant variety.

Blackcurrant gall midge Tiny, white maggots feed on the shoot tips of blackcurrants, preventing leaves from reaching their full size; affected leaves dry up and die. Shoot tips can also die back. There is no cure available to the amateur gardener. However, varieties such as 'Ben Connan' and 'Ben Sarek' are resistant to blackcurrant gall midge.

Capsid bugs These green insects suck the sap and cause small holes to appear on the leaves, which sometimes develop reddish brown spots. Spray with pyrethrum as soon as the symptoms are noticed.

Reversion This virus is usually transmitted by big bud mite (see above). It causes the leaves to turn yellow, and flowering and yields are dramatically reduced. There is no cure for this problem and plants should be removed immediately. Always buy certified virus-free plants.

HARVEST BLACKCURRANTS from midsummer onwards, but remember to net the crop if you don't want to share a good deal of it with the birds.

BIG BUD MITE is characterized by the swollen bud shown here, which will eventually drop off. It causes poor yields and must be dealt with promptly.

SOME VARIETIES ARE SWEET enough to eat off the bush, otherwise they are used in cooking. A mature blackcurrant bush should yield about 4.5kg (10lb) of fruit per bush.

Red currants and white currants *Ribes rubrum*

Not only is their fruit delicious when cooked in pies or sauces but these shrubs also have wonderful ornamental qualities. They look superb in midsummer when their branches are laden with strigs of tiny, bright berries. Despite being closely related to blackcurrants, their growth habit and therefore training systems are different and far more similar to gooseberries.

The best sites and soils

White currants and pink currants are basically sports of red currants and should be treated in exactly the same way. (The term red currants in this section refers to all red, white, and pink currants.)

Red currant bushes are hardy plants that thrive in open, sunny positions. Like gooseberries, they are tolerant of moderate shade and so make extremely attractive features when fruiting on a north-facing wall. Avoid frost pockets and exposed windy sites. Prior to planting incorporate rotted organic matter into the soil and add a general balanced granular fertilizer in spring to provide the plant with sufficient potash potassium for optimum fruiting.

Buying and planting

Red currants are suitable for training as open-centred bushes, step-overs, standards, fans, and vertical cordons, because they can be treated like gooseberries (see page 178), rather than like blackcurrants. Each bush will provide about 4.5kg (10lb) of fruit.

Bare-root red currants should ideally be planted in late autumn, although any time in the dormant season will do. Containerized red currants can be planted any time of year, but it is advisable to avoid extremes of weather, such as during periods of drought or when the ground is frozen.

Prepare the ground well, incorporating well-rotted organic matter into the soil. Then plant red currant bushes 1.5m (5ft) apart (see page 46).

Plant care

Keep the area around the plants well weeded. In late winter, feed plants with a balanced compound fertilizer at a rate of 100g per square metre (3oz per square yard), and mulch using well-rotted manure.

During the growing season, water red currants during dry periods. In summer, tie twine attached to canes around the plants to prevent the branches flopping onto the ground from the weight of the fruit, and net the bushes tightly against birds before the fruit starts to ripen.

HARVEST RED AND WHITE CURRANTS with care as they are damaged easily. Separate entire strigs from the bush when all the fruits are well coloured with a glossy sheen.

Formative training as a bush

Start with a two-year-old bush with a short leg trunk and four or five equally spaced branches creating the crown of the plant. As soon as the plant starts to grow, shorten the central leader of the bush (if there is one) back to the highest branch. Then shorten the leader on each branch by one-third: if the plant has an upright habit where the branches lean towards the centre, shorten each branch to an outward-facing bud; if the plant has a tendency to flop

CORDONS AND FANS take up less space than red and white currants trained as bushes, but yields are lower.

Recommended varieties (red currants)

'Jonkheer van Tets'
One of the earliest varieties with heavy crops, large berries, and excellent flavour.

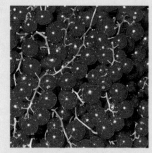

'Red Lake'
A midseason variety producing large, heavy yields. It has long strigs that are easy to pick.

'Stanza'
This heavy cropping, late variety has superb flavour. The berries are much darker than most other varieties once they have fully ripened. Growth is compact so 'Stanza' is good for a small garden.

'Redstart'
A heavy yielding, late variety with an upright habit. 'Redstart' fruits in late summer, producing long strings.

Recommended varieties (white currants)

'White Grape'
An early variety with an upright habit. The pure white, large berries have a better, sweeter flavour than 'Versailles Blanche'.

'Versailles Blanche', syn. 'White Versailles'
Bearing fruit in midsummer, this early variety produces heavy, regular yields of pale white, large berries.

outwards, then prune to inward-facing buds. Cut back to one or two buds any sideshoot that has formed along the four or five main branches. Leave well-placed new branches as future replacements.

Formative training as a standard
The simplest method of training a red currant is to grow it initially as a vertical cordon, supported by a bamboo cane attached to wires. Then after three or four years, when it has reached about 1m (3ft) high, prune the cordon so that four or five branches develop into a crown. Thereafter support the red currant between two stakes and secure in position with tree ties or chain-lock ties (see page 178). Formatively prune such a standard in the same way as a bush (see above). See page 181 on how to train a cordon.

Pruning an established red currant
Red currants fruit on old wood and at the base of new wood, so in summer prune the new growth back to five leaves, to encourage small fruiting spurs to developed on the branches. In winter, prune sideshoots back to two buds and leaders back by about one-third. Cut out any branches growing up through the middle of the plant to create an open-centre bush. Occasionally remove older branches and leave a younger branch in its place.

At harvest time

When the fruit first turns red it is not yet fully ripe, so harvest only once it has sweetened. It is simplest to cut the strigs (bunches of fruit) using scissors. Store in a fridge for a week or two after picking. Alternatively, freeze the fruit or preserve it as red currant jelly. White currants and pink currants make an interesting variation to red currants when used in cooking or as garnish on a plate.

Pests and diseases

Red and white currants are prone to attack by birds (see page 58), gooseberry sawfly (see page 58), splitting (see page 57), and coral spot (see page 60), in addition to the following more specific pests.

Currant clearwing moth A very small moth that looks like a small wasp with a black body crossed with

three yellow bands, and largely transparent wings. Its larvae feed in the stems of blackcurrants, red, and white currants, but it poses little threat.

Red currant blister aphid These pale yellow aphids suck sap on the underside of leaves. The chemicals they secrete cause the leaves to blister and discolour. In winter, use a plant oil wash to control overwintering eggs, or spray plants in spring with an insecticide containing thiacloprid or pyrethrum.

Leaf spot A fungal disease which causes brown spots on leaves. They do little damage, but remove and destroy affected parts to prevent reinfections.

PRUNE SIDESHOOTS back to two buds during winter to keep the plant compact and ensure that growth is concentrated from the spurs.

IN SUMMER, prune the new growth of that year back to five leaves, to encourage the formation of small fruiting spurs on the main branches.

Gooseberries

" You might be fortunate enough to come across a seemingly wild gooseberry bush on a walk alongside a hedgerow, but these days it is becoming increasingly unlikely. Wild gooseberries, feral gooseberries, and escapees from gardens were once viable hedgerow inhabitants because of their robust and tolerant constitution. However, they seem to have been squeezed out by hedgerow clearances and hungry birds foraging earlier in the year because of climate change. Gooseberries are now also rarer in the shops so many people do not know what to do with these fruits.

Yet if you grow your own, you can be prepared for the short cropping season and fully appreciate the gooseberries' potential. They have long featured in the traditional cottage garden, the heavy crop easily justifying the space taken. Cottage gardeners have developed ways to manage the same bush to give two different crops.

In the first instance, most of the young, green fruit - still small and hard - are taken off for cooking with sugar and maybe elderflowers. This can be a one-off picking, or on several occasions over a week or two. The fruit that is left - usually the most handsome and well protected by the branches - can then mature on the bush.

By reducing the crop, the surviving fruits can accumulate all the bush's energy so it is concentrated in a favoured few rather than dissipated thinly among the many - fruit-growing, feudal style. The remaining gooseberries gradually swell up and get softer, even splitting their skins to exude a sweet, fragrant jelly. Although such split skins would disqualify your gooseberries from a gooseberry heavyweight competition, these treasures are memorably delicious eaten raw as dessert gooseberries, still tangy but with as full a flavour as a muscat grape. "

NO LONGER A TYPICAL hedgerow plant, gooseberries come in a range of sizes and colours, including white, green, red, pink, and yellow.

Gooseberries *Ribes uva-crispa*

Ranging from huge, juicy, red dessert spheres to tiny, sparkling, gold drops of sweetness, gooseberries are one of the most underrated fruits in the garden. A bit like collecting marbles at school, there are plenty of different types and colours to choose from including green, white, yellow, pink, and red.

The best sites and soils

Although tolerant of a wide range of soil conditions, gooseberries prefer moisture-retentive yet well-drained soil. Avoid very shallow, dry soils because the roots will dry out quickly, causing problems with American gooseberry mildew (see page 183).

Gooseberries are very much a hardy fruit and do particularly well in some cool-temperate areas, where the fruit slowly ripens on the bush while its flavour develops and matures. Despite very early flowering, they are reasonably resilient to harsh frosts although planting in a frost pocket can reduce yields.

The best thing of all about gooseberries is that they can tolerate some shade and will successfully fruit on a north-facing wall. They can also be grown under fruit trees or in rows under trees in an orchard.

Buying and planting

Heralding the start of summer, gooseberries are one of the first of the main fruits to crop in cool-temperate areas. With well over a hundred varieties, there is a huge range of dessert and cooking gooseberries available as well as more specialized berries such as worcesterberries (small, purple gooseberries with resistance to gooseberry mildew) and jostaberries (a gooseberry/blackcurrant cross, see page 183).

Gooseberries can successfully be grown as bushes – sometimes called "open-centre goblets". They have a short leg (trunk) of 10–15cm (4–6in) and then four

STAKING A GOOSEBERRY TRAINED AS A STANDARD

1 DRIVE IN TWO STAKES, one at each edge of the planting hole, using a post-tamper or sledgehammer.

2 PLACE THE GOOSEBERRY PLANT in the hole, ensuring its rootball is at the same depth as it had been grown in the nursery. Backfill with soil and firm.

3 USE TREE TIES or chain-lock ties to fix the gooseberry plant to the stakes, just below the head of the standard.

or five permanent branches, radiating out from the centre, which carry the fruiting sideshoots and spurs. Their short leg enables better air circulation, helping to prevent diseases such as gooseberry mildew. Expect a crop of 2.5–5.5kg (6–12lb) from a bush.

They can also be grown as standards, which involves growing them on a long leg of 1m (3ft) with a round head at the top. Such standards are grafted onto a rootstock such as *R. odoratum*. Because of its top-heavy nature, support a standard gooseberry just below the head with two posts (see opposite).

A gooseberry can be trained as a fan against a fence or wall, or as a step-over along a border. Watch out for thorns if stepping over a step-over gooseberry.

Cordons are the best method of growing these fruits if you want lots of varieties and colours in the garden. Expect a crop of 1–1.5kg (2–3lb) from a cordon. Stretch two wires – one at 50cm (20in) and one at 1.3m (4½ft) – between two posts and tie vertical canes to the wire at the place where each gooseberry is going to be planted.

Prior to planting, incorporate well-rotted manure into the soil, and add a balanced granular fertilizer to poor, nutrient-deficient soils, applying it at a rate of 100g per square metre (3oz per square yard). Then allow the soil to settle for a few weeks.

Plant gooseberries in late autumn. This will give the plants a chance to establish before the next growing season. Container-grown gooseberries, however, can be planted at any time, although autumn is still best.

Set gooseberry bushes 1.5m (5ft) apart, while jostaberries and worcesterberries, which are very

GOOSEBERRY CONTESTS

Gooseberry growing became popular in the 19th century. Gooseberry clubs were set up all over the UK, but were predominantly in Lancashire. Growers would compete annually to produce the largest gooseberry. Thanks to these clubs more than 3,000 gooseberry varieties have been recorded and more than 150 varieties are still in existence today. The yellow variety 'Montrose' holds the record for the largest ever gooseberry. The gooseberry growers even had a song about their hobby:

Come all ye jovial gardeners, and listen unto me,
Whilst I relate the different sorts of winning gooseberries,
This famous institution was founded long ago,
That men might meet, and drink, and have a gooseberry show.

vigorous, require 2.1m (7ft) spacing. Plant single, vertical cordons 30cm (12in) apart.

Plant care

Keep the area around the base of the plants free from weeds. In late winter, mulch around the base of the stems with well-rotted manure, making sure it is kept away from the stems.

Put taut nets over the plants as the fruits start to appear. Some birds such as blackbirds and pigeons don't wait for them to ripen and will strip a tree in minutes. Also support bushes with canes and twine

Recommended varieties (green goosberries)

'Invicta'
A relatively modern, cooking variety with high yields of large, pale green fruits and some resistance to mildew. It is a vigorous variety with a very thorny habit.

'Greenfinch'
Recommended due to having some resistance to mildew and leaf spot. Its prolific, green gooseberries are best consumed once they have been cooked.

FROM A HEALTHY MATURE BUSH you can expect 3.5kg (8lb) of fruit each season; from a gooseberry cordon about 1kg (2lb). Pick the fruit with its stalk to prevent the skin tearing.

WHY THE NAME?

There are a number of different theories as to why gooseberries are so named. The most popular one is that the thorns look like the foot of a goose. Or perhaps it was because the sharp thorns reminded people of gorse, hence gorseberries. Yet another theory is that the berries made a tasty yet sharp sauce to accompany poultry dishes, particularly goose.

wrapped around the outside of the plants to prevent heavily laden branches snapping and flopping onto the ground.

Remove suckers around the base of the plant as they appear throughout the summer. Tear them off by hand if possible because gooseberries are prone to regenerate from pruning cuts.

Water regularly during dry periods. Container-grown gooseberries often struggle in dry conditions, so carefully monitor their watering requirements.

In late winter, feed with a balanced granular fertilizer at 100g per square metre (3oz per square yard). Avoid feeding the plants with too much nitrogen because this can encourage wispy, sappy growth, which is prone to gooseberry mildew.

Replace a healthy gooseberry bush after 10–15 years, once its regular bumper crops start to fade.

Formative training as a bush or standard

The pruning for a gooseberry trained as a bush or standard is the same and is based on the principle that gooseberries fruit on old wood and at the base of the previous year's wood.

As soon as the plant starts to grow, shorten the central leader (if there is one) back to the highest branch on a two-year-old gooseberry bush with a short leg (trunk) and four or five equally spaced branches. Then cut back the leader on each branch by one-third to inward-facing buds to retain the upright habit of the bush – most gooseberries have a tendency to flop outwards and therefore quickly lose their shape. Cut back to one or two buds any sideshoot that has formed along the main branches.

Recommended varieties (yellow gooseberries)

'Leveller'
A large, yellow dessert gooseberry with one of the best flavours of any variety. A bit of a shy cropper except on good, fertile soils.

'Yellow Champagne'
A classic, yellow culinary gooseberry that is quite hard to come by. Other good yellow gooseberry varieties you might try include 'Bedford Yellow' and 'Early Sulphur'.

IN WINTER, PRUNE the new sideshoots back to one or two buds to concentrate growth from the spurs and keep plants compact. Wear gloves to protect your hands.

IN SPRING, STRONG NEW GROWTH will emerge from the spurs; these will soon bear the flowers, and eventually the gooseberries themselves.

Formative training as a cordon

Train a gooseberry cordon to grow vertically up to a height of about 1.5m (5ft), and have a dominant central stem bearing short fruiting laterals along it.

In the winter after planting, select one leader and cut it back by about one-third. Tie the leader into a vertical cane. Shorten all other shoots growing 10cm (4in) or more above ground level, to one or two buds. Remove any shoots below this height, because, like a gooseberry bush, a cordon is grown on a short leg to keep the fruit off the ground.

In summer, prune the new growth back to about five leaves. Continue to tie in the leader.

The following winter, shorten the leader by about one-third. Cut the growth made the previous year back to one or two buds. Thin out any fruiting spurs that are congested. Remove any dead, dying, or diseased stems on the gooseberry cordon, as well as any weak growth.

Continue summer pruning and winter pruning until the cordon has reached the desired height. Then cut the leader off at the top of the cane.

Recommended varieties (red gooseberries)

'Whinham's Industry'
A dark red, large dessert variety that tastes superb when allowed to ripen fully on the plant. The plant is vigorous with an upright habit. Is more tolerant of heavy soils than other gooseberry varieties.

'Lancashire Lad'
This old favourite, raised in 1824, is a moderately vigorous plant with medium to large berries.

HARVEST GOOSEBERRIES IN TWO STAGES. Before the crop is fully ripe, thin half the crop to use in cooking. Let the remainder sweeten on the bush, then pick them as required.

Pruning established gooseberries

Gooseberry bushes and standards generally require two pruning sessions each year. In winter, create the fruiting spurs by cutting back new growth to one or two buds. Occasionally replace old branches with new shoots. In summer, shorten the shoots back to five leaves when the plant has produced 8–10 leaves – usually in early summer.

On cordons in winter, cut the leader back to one bud above the top of the cane, and prune all new sideshoots back to one or two buds. In summer, prune the new growths each to five leaves when they have reached about ten leaves in length.

At harvest time

Harvest gooseberries in two main pickings. A few weeks before the gooseberries are fully ripe, pick every other gooseberry and use for culinary purposes to put in pies, tarts, sauces etc. Leave the remaining fruit to ripen in the summer sun until the sugars and flavours have fully matured. If time permits, do this second picking gradually over a few days, harvesting as and when the fruits are wanted.

Gooseberries taste delicious when eaten fresh off the bush, making those scratches and cuts from the spiky, sharp thorns all worthwhile. However, they must be eaten within a few days of picking, because they do not remain fresh for long; although they can be stored in a fridge for about two weeks.

The fruit can also be frozen, juiced, cooked, or made into delicious-tasting jam. Some gooseberry varieties are sharper than others and can be used to make an interesting home-made wine, with similar flavours and aromas to a white Loire-style or sauvignon blanc type of wine. The crisp, fresh gooseberry flavours beautifully complement elderflowers, which are in season at the same time.

Pests and diseases

Gooseberry bushes can be attacked by squirrels, moth caterpillars, and birds (especially bullfinches), which eat the buds before they have broken into leaf and also eat the ripe fruit (see page 58). They are also prone to leaf spot (see page 175) and fungal leaf spots (see page 61), as well as to the following more specific pests and diseases.

Recommended varieties (white gooseberries)

'Langley Gage'
The ovoid berries have a silvery, transparent appearance. Bears delicious, very sweet fruits when allowed to fully mature on the bush.

'Careless'
This heavy cropping, popular variety is easy to grow and has an excellent dessert flavour. The fruit is greenish white in colour.

American gooseberry mildew This mildew causes the leaves and stems to appear with a covering of powdery, grey and white fungus. The mildew can also appear on the fruit, causing problems with ripening. Dust with sulphur or spray with systhane fungicide. Gooseberry varieties such as 'Greenfinch', 'Hinnonmäki Gul', 'Hinnonmäki Röd', 'Invicta', and 'Martlet' provide some resistance to American gooseberry mildew.

Capsid bugs These small, pale green, sap-sucking insects destroy plant cells. The adult bugs are up to 6mm (¼in) long and have distinctive wings: the basal two-thirds are coloured and thickened, the outer third is transparent. The wings are folded flat over the body when at rest, so the transparent part of the wings shows as a clear diamond-shaped area at the rear end of the insect. On gooseberries, they cause leaves at the shoot tips to develop small, brown-edged holes. The shoot tips themselves may die. Growth from affected buds is distorted. Examine

susceptible plants from late spring, and if any capsid bugs or symptoms are seen spray with pyrethrum.

Eutypa dieback Caused by *Eutypa lata*, this fungus causes branches to die back and occasionally kills the whole plant. Fruits shrivel up and the leaves turn brown and fall off. Remove and destroy any infected wood.

Gooseberry sawfly An attack of gooseberry sawfly larvae can strip a plant of leaves in days. Look out for pale green caterpillars with clear black spots that devour the leaves. Regularly inspect plants by looking on the underside of leaves. Spray with pyrethrum at the first sign of the caterpillars or of feeding damage (see also page 58).

Potash deficiency Gooseberries regularly suffer from potash deficiency, which shows up as a brownish edge around the leaf. Apply sulphate of potash at 15g per square metre (½oz per square yard) in late winter.

AMERICAN GOOSEBERRY MILDEW covers the leaves and sometimes the fruit. It can affect the harvest, but resistant varieties are available such as 'Invicta'.

GOOSEBERRY SAWFLY can strip whole bushes of their leaves in serious infestations. Watch out for their pale green, black-spotted, caterpillar-like larvae.

Recommended varieties (other types of gooseberry)

Worcesterberry
This small, purple gooseberry is resistant to gooseberry mildew, while a hybrid of worcesterberry and gooseberry is 'Black Velvet', which bears high yields of dark red berries.

Jostaberry
This hybrid is very vigorous, thornless, and has good resistance to mildew, fungal leaf spots, and big bud mite (see also page 170). The fruits have a blackcurrant taste. Grow as a stool bush (see page 168).

Vine fruit

- Grapes
- Kiwifruit
- Melons

Carol's fruit notebook

" Melon and grape plants may seem completely different from each other; one is an annual curcurbit, the other a long-lived vine, but they both share a questing, vigorous habit that responds well to training. It is easy to take imported melons for granted because they can be cheap and plentiful, and are an easy way to buy in the water and sunshine of another country. But to grow them in a cool-temperate climate is a challenge, where there certainly is the water – it's just the sunshine that is in short supply. Nonetheless, you only need one long, hot summer in such a region to convince yourself it is worthwhile; obviously it would be nice to know at the outset how the weather will be. After selecting a suntrap in your garden or greenhouse, the next most important thing is to choose a melon variety that will fruit early and so get a long chance to ripen, as 'Minnesota Midget' or 'Petit Gris de Rennes' can do outdoors in cool-temperate areas.

Kiwifruit also fruit on vigorous vines, but left to themselves they would make all leaf growth and barely any fruit. Decisive pruning is effective and necessary, even several times a year. The vines are very robust, and no harm comes to them.

Grapevines create more inhibition in the pruner, if only because the stakes seem higher. You can even have a vineyard in your garden, but you do need an awful lot of space. The attraction is that you can grow wine grapes outside – and you can always use up under-ripe grapes in the wine you will make. Dessert grapes have to be grown under glass in cool-temperate areas, and this can present its own challenges. The roots are best in soil outside the greenhouse; the branches benefit from a few weeks of cold in early winter but then need the extra warmth and shelter of covered protection in mid- and late winter, then open access to insects for pollination in spring and for fresh air in summer. A fandango but quaintly fulfilling. **"**

Carol's fruit notebook

Grapes

"" Growing grapes might seem like a serious business – a first step that ends up with the wine buff deconstructing a mouthful of vintage St Snobbysomething-Very-Special. It is true that both grape-growing and wine-making require enormous attention to detail, but don't let that put you off. It is entirely up to you as to how much trouble you want to go to.

I have a white muscat grapevine that scrambled over my old greenhouse on the outside. Some years the blackbirds and wasps had the sour grapes all to themselves; other years the timing with the weather came right and we shared bunch after bunch of the most

sweet, perfumed, and exalted grapes imaginable. One year I made the surplus into grape jelly that kept in the fridge for two years and was used instead of sugar, elevating any cooked fruit – such as damsons, plums, or apricots – to the sublime. My husband now intends to leave the roots in place outside and train the vine through the wall to the inside of the replacement greenhouse – the classic arrangement – but the vine might decide otherwise.

Despite human intervention and wine technology, the quality of each year's crop is dependent on the minutiae of the past three seasons' weather. This is why grape-growing and wine-making are as much an art as a science. Just when France seemed to have lost its crown as the wine producer par excellence, science discovered "The French Paradox", whereby drinking red wine daily ameliorated the effects of a rich and fatty diet. The active chemicals are found in the skin and seeds of black grapes, especially muscadine types, so the good news for those who dislike red wine, like myself, is that a daily glass of claret is not the only way to prevent heart disease. Instead you can drink your own black grape juice, which you can freeze, or eat your own sultanas and raisins by drying seedless grapes. Avoid eating fresh grape skins, however tempting, if you have candida. ""

NOT ONLY ARE GRAPEVINES ornamentally valuable for training up walls and over arches, but the fruit can be juiced and fermented to make your own 'domaine' wine.

Grapes *Vitis vinifera*

Fancy growing your own chardonnay? Well it's easy, and small rows of vines can be planted in the tiniest of gardens. Their climbing habit means they can be trained up walls, on trellis, or over arches. There is one essential ingredient to making fine wine – plenty of sunlight – in order for the grapes to ripen properly.

The best sites and soils

There are basically two types of grapes: dessert and wine. Dessert grapes require a greenhouse or conservatory if they are to ripen properly and produce large, sweet, and juicy berries. In some cases the dessert vines can be planted outside but have their trunk and stems trained inside under glass. The benefit of this cultivation method is that the vine doesn't require as much watering as an all-indoor one, because it receives rainfall. Dessert vines can benefit from extra heat supplied from early spring to a temperature of about 16°C (61°F).

Wine grapes are suitable for outdoor growing and produce aromatic yet small and acidic bunches of tightly clustered grapes that although palatable are not sweetly flavoured. Choose a warm, sheltered sunny location, such as a south- or south-west-facing wall or fence. If planting a row of vines, then a south-facing slope is required. Such a slope angles the grapevines towards the sun, and so like solar panels they soak up the rays of sunlight. Avoid planting in frost pockets as the young shoots emerging in late spring can get damaged. Also, grapes are not suitable for planting at high altitude.

Grapevines grow on a wide range of soils – famous vineyards around the world are situated on soils ranging from the chalk hills of champagne to the gravelly soils of Bordeaux, and the Barossa valley in Australia ranges from sand to heavy, red-brown clay. What these places have in common is that the soil is well drained, because vines struggle in waterlogged conditions. Avoid rich, fertile soils, which can produce too much luxuriant, vegetative growth at the expense of fruit production.

It is possible to have your own mini-vineyard in your back garden or on your allotment on a plot 6m (20ft) long by 5m (16ft) wide. A back garden is usually more sheltered than an open field or allotment. Space three rows 1.5m (5ft) apart, with five vines in each row set 1.2m (4ft) apart. Each mature vine

PLANTING A CONTAINER-GROWN GRAPEVINE

1 DIG A HOLE into prepared soil just in front of a single vertical cane attached to the wire support.

2 PLACE THE ROOTBALL into the hole, angling the main stem toward the vertical cane.

3 TIE THE MAIN STEM to the vertical cane and lowest wire using string or garden twine in a figure-of-eight loop.

should produce enough grapes to produce one bottle of wine. Therefore, such a vineyard should supply you with 15 bottles of wine a year.

Buying and planting

Before buying, take the plant out of its container to look at the condition of the roots, checking that they are not potbound. If buying in summer, ensure the foliage is a healthy green, and not yellow. Make sure that the vine you buy is an outdoor variety if you are planning on using it for wine-making. Glasshouse/dessert varieties will not ripen outside.

Preparing the ground

Dig over the soil and break up any compacted soil. Add a bucketful of grit to the planting hole on heavy, clay soils. The vine roots should be encouraged to seek out their own nutrients from deep down in the soil, so do not add manure or compost. Nor should fertilizer be added to outdoor grapevines – the individual flavour of wine is based very much on the unique soil characteristics of a place derived from its natural nutrients in the soil.

Planting methods

Guyot system The most popular method of growing wine grapes is to train them outside in rows, using the guyot system. A single guyot involves training one fruiting arm along the wires, while on a double guyot two fruiting arms are laid along the wires one in each direction away from the trunk of the vine.

On open ground, secure the wires between stout wooden posts that have been supported with struts at the end of each row, to give them extra strength. For a long row of vines, place intermediate support posts every 4m (13ft). Between them fix two single fixed wires, with the lower wire trained at 45cm (18in) above the ground and the upper wire at 65cm (26in); the wires can be nearer ground level if they are in a frost-free area. Above these two fixed wires, attach three sets of parallel wires at 1m (3ft), 1.2m (4ft), and 1.5m (5ft). These parallel wires need to be adjustable so that they can be loosened and tightened when tucking in the growing shoots during spring and summer. To make the parallel wires adjustable, attach chain links that can hook onto straining bolts in the end posts. In the

GRAPE VINES ARE USEFUL for quickly covering bare walls or fences, and they provide shade if grown over a pergola. Some varieties have attractive red leaves in autumn.

AUTUMNAL FOLIAGE

Grapes' large, attractively shaped leaves can provide a stunning display of autumnal colour including crimson, purple, bronze, and pink, adding extra interest to a vertical space such as a wall, fence, or trellis. They also create colourful cover when trained across pergolas.

Some of the most colourful autumnal-foliage varieties of grape include: *Vitis* 'Brant', *V. vinifera* 'Purpurea', *V.v.* 'Dornfelder', *V.v.* 'Dunkelfelder', and *V. coignetiae*.

GUYOT SYSTEM

1 TIE IN NEW FRUITING ARMS to the lowest fixed wires in winter. These replace the fruiting arms of the previous season, which are removed prior to tying in.

2 REMOVE ALL OTHER STEMS except for one or two stems in the centre, which should be cut back to two or three buds. The fruiting arms should each form an arc.

intermediate support posts insert hooks over which the parallel wires can be lifted up and down as the vines grow during the season.

Vines can be planted at anytime, but the best time is in spring. Place vines 1.5m (5ft) apart along the row, and tie vertical canes to the wires at every individual vine. Set the rows 1.5m (5ft) apart. After planting, prune the leader back to just above the height of the bottom wire. This will encourage buds to break just below the cut. Remove any other shoots growing from the plant.

Cordon vines This is a useful method of growing lots of varieties in a small space. This system can be used for dessert grapes indoors or outdoor wine grapes. Plant individual grapevines 1m (3ft) apart, and train them up single, vertical canes attached to a system of wires spaced 30cm (12in) apart.

Creating a guyot-trained vine

Formative pruning

In the spring after planting, as the buds are starting to develop into shoots, select three or four new shoots and tie two shoots – one in each direction – to the two low, fixed wires to form the arms of a double guyot; these will become the fruiting arms of the vine. The remaining one or two shoots are spares, which can be tied up vertically. Remove any shoots that appear further down the trunk. Prune both of the vertically trained shoots so they form spurs of two or three buds; the new growth that comes from these will be used to replace the fruiting arms next year.

In the following winter, select four new shoots as potential replacements for the fruiting arms. The shoots should ideally come from the lowest buds of

Recommended varieties (dessert grapes)

'Schiava Grossa', syns. 'Black Hamburgh' and 'Trollinger'
A superbly flavoured, black variety that produces good, heavy yields. It requires an unheated greenhouse.

'Muscat of Alexandria'
This white grape variety with excellent flavour is a muscat type of grape requiring a little bit of heat to do well. 'Muscat of Alexandria' benefits from hand pollination.

3 TUCK OR TIE IN ALL NEW GROWTH to the parallel fixed wires. Remove any buds or shoots that develop low down on the trunk.

4 REMOVE ALL NEW GROWTH that appears above the top wire. Shorten any sideshoots that grow from the new branches to one leaf.

the spurs that were created the previous year. Remove the rest of last year's growth. Shorten the new fruiting arms to 8–10 buds and cut out all sideshoots that formed on them. Tie these two new arms down to the low, fixed wires to form an arc. If either break, tie in one of the spare shoots. Once the new arms are in place, cut back the spare shoots to two or three buds.

In the following summer, tuck all new growth between the parallel wires. Pinch out their tips when they reach the top wire. Shorten any sideshoots that grow from the new shoots to one leaf.

In the next winter, repeat as for the previous winter, replacing the fruiting arms with new shoots and leaving one or two spurs near the trunk with two or three buds on each.

Pruning an established guyot-system vine

During each dormant season, continue to replace the the fruiting arms, using the same method as in the final winter of formative pruning. Select the fruiting arms either from a shoot produced by the spur(s) left from the previous year, or from one of the lower shoots off the previous year's arm. Never select water shoots (shoots coming directly off the trunk), because these are rarely fruitful. Also, if the trunk grows above the bottom wire as the vine gets older, select a spur from below the bottom wire to ensure that the trunk doesn't continue to get too high.

During the growing season, remove buds or stems that appear low down on the trunk of the vine. This process is called "bud rubbing" and is important as these water shoots will deprive the plant of necessary nutrients and water.

'Buckland Sweetwater'
An easy variety to try. White 'Buckland Sweetwater' provides early season, high yields and good flavour. Its lack of vigour makes it suitable for a small greenhouse, and it may need extra feeding.

'Foster's Seedling'
High-cropping, white 'Foster's Seedling' has superb flavour. Its large bunches of juicy, sweet grapes ripen early and should be eaten quickly after picking, to savour their full flavour.

CORDON GRAPES

WHEN THE BRANCHES ARE BARE (left), you will see how much your vine has grown over just one season. As for guyot vines, much of this new growth on cordon vines will have to be removed in winter; prune it all back to two healthy buds (right) and tip the leading shoot back by one-third.

In summer, pinch out the growing tips or use a hedge trimmer to cut the tops of the vines. If a row gets too high and crowded it will shade the plants in the neighbouring rows.

In mid- to late summer, shorten sideshoots (produced in the leaf axils of the fruiting arms) back to one leaf to get more sunlight into the canopy and improve air circulation. Remove green bunches of grapes that won't ripen in time for the autumn harvest. Also in late summer, thin out some of the foliage using a pair of sharp secateurs, to expose the remaining grapes to sunlight.

Creating a cordon vine

Formative pruning

In early winter after planting, prune back the leader by about one-third. Shorten any lower growth back to one or two buds.

In summer, tie in the leading shoot to the vertical cane with soft twine and shorten the main other shoots to five or six leaves. Prune back any sideshoots on these main shoots to one leaf.

In the following winter, tip the leader back by about one-third and prune back the other shoots to two buds.

Recommended varieties (white wine grapes)

'Müller-Thurgau' syn. 'Riesling-Silvaner'
Yields are high and flavour good with a riesling, aromatic-style flavour. In cool-temperate areas, however, it often does not ripen wood well, and it suffers from botrytis.

'Seyval Blanc' syn. 'Seyve Villard 5276'
A mid- to late-ripening hybrid with good disease resistance, particularly to powdery and downy mildew. It is a reliable cropper and is useful in blended wine or sparkling ones.

AFTER PRUNING, only the basic stem and spurs of the cordon remain (left), but in spring this soon resprouts to form new shoots bearing flower trusses. Cut back these shoots to five or six leaves beyond a flower truss (right), and cut back any sideshoots that grow back to one leaf.

In the following summer, continue to tie in the leader to the vertical post. Prune back other shoots to five or six leaves. Shorten any sideshoots on these main shoots to one leaf. In the next winter, repeat the pruning actions from the previous winter. Some of the spurs that have formed will have started to become congested; thin them out so that only one or two shoots remain.

Pruning an established cordon vine

In winter, tip the leader back by about one-third and shorten the other main shoots to two buds. Thin any crowded spurs back to one or two shoots. When the vine is at the desired height, cut back the leader to one bud. Thereafter to retain the cordon at that height, cut the leader back each year to one bud above the top wire. Where fruit has formed, summer pruning is the same as in formative pruning (see left) but on shoots on which fruit is growing, cut back to two leaves past where the fruit is forming.

Plant care

In their first year after planting, water grapevines during dry periods. Once fully established, those in the cool-temperate regions shouldn't need watering, because their deep-rooting system makes them drought tolerant.

'Phönix'
Increasing in popularity is this hybrid variety with 'Bacchus' parentage. It has some disease resistance and makes a wine of good quality. The distinctive 'Bacchus' aroma is pleasantly noticeable.

'Chardonnay'
This early ripening, dark golden grape tastes good when eaten as well as being a useful variety for making wine. It has a powerful, highly scented aroma that can overpower other varieties in a blend.

Remove all flowers for the first couple of years after planting, to prevent overcropping on young vines. Allow about three bunches of grapes on a three-year-old vine and about five on a five-year-old vine – a few more if growing well.

Suppress weeds and retain moisture by placing stones or gravel around the base of the plants. White gravel is useful because it reflects sunlight back into the canopy of the grapevine, while black gravel or recycled slate is also suitable as it absorbs the heat from the sunlight, helping to warm up the soil. Avoid mulching around the vines with manure, because this encourages surface rooting and contributes to luxuriant vegetative growth.

Encourage grapevines to send their roots downwards to seek out their own nutrients, but do treat nutrient deficiencies individually depending on the type of soil. Grapevines can be prone to magnesium deficiency, which can be treated with a foliar feed of Epsom salts, or lime-induced chlorosis, which can be improved with a liquid tomato fertilizer. Do not apply a general granular feed each year.

In the greenhouse

Ventilate the greenhouse or conservatory on bright days during spring and summer, and wet down the floor and staging, except when flowering and when the fruit are ripening. Pollination during flowering in late spring requires dry conditions. Gently shaking branches can help spread the pollen and therefore aid pollination.

Ensure that you water the plants frequently in the growing season, and as the vines start to grow feed them with a high potash liquid fertilizer, such as

ON CORDON VINES, allow just one bunch of grapes to develop on each lateral branch. Remove all others so that the vine concentrates its energy into those remaining.

tomato feed, at the rate that is recommended by the manufacturer.

Thin out individual dessert grapes on the bunches to allow the berries to ripen fully and to improve air circulation. Use scissors to remove berries when they are small, removing about one in three per bunch.

Dessert grapes require a period of dormancy, so keep the greenhouse unheated until early spring. If this isn't possible because the vine is being grown with other crops that require heat, then move grapevines in containers outside.

Recommended varieties (black wine grapes)

'Pinot Noir'
A classic, world-famous grape that requires a cool climate to properly develop its flavours. It is prone to botrytis so avoid damp conditions.

'Regent'
This hybrid boasts the desirable characteristics of good disease resistance and the potential to make a good-quality wine. It provides good yields, and the grapes have high sugar levels.

At harvest time

Grapes are ready for picking when they feel soft to the touch and taste sugary. The skins on white grapes often change from deep green to a translucent yellow and they become much thinner. The best way for an amateur to tell when wine grapes are ready is by tasting them – only when they're at their sweetest, containing maximum sugar, will they be ready. Cut them in bunches with each stalk still attached.

Although wine grapes can be eaten fresh, they are better when crushed and made into wine. Dessert grapes are best consumed as soon as possible after harvesting, but they will keep for about two weeks if stored in the fridge. If dessert grapes have been grown for exhibiting at shows, be careful not to damage the bloom while picking them.

Pests and diseases

Grapevines are prone to attack by glasshouse red spider mite (see page 58), rabbits (see page 59), mealybugs (see page 59), brown scale, woolly vine scale (see page 59), botrytis (grey mould) (see page 60), downy mildew (see page 60), and powdery mildew (see page 61). Birds (see page 58) and wasps attack fruits as they ripen, so protect them by wrapping the bunches in muslin bags or old nylon tights (see page 59). Magnesium deficiency (see page 57) can be a problem in some gardens.

Phylloxera The sap-sucking insect *Phylloxera vastatrix,* which is not found in Britain, attacks the foliage and roots of grapevines. It decimated the French wine industry in the 19th century, so vines are now grafted onto resistant American rootstocks, to avoid the problem.

Shanking In this disorder, some grapes in a bunch fail to colour up properly, and the grapes then begin to shrivel and lose their flavour. It typically affects vines under cover and is often caused by drought or waterlogging, which damages the roots.

Weedkiller damage If you are using weedkillers in the garden, this task should be done only on still days. Grapes are very sensitive to weedkiller damage, so keep any spray well away from your vines.

THIN OUT INDIVIDUAL DESSERT GRAPES from bunches for a really professional crop of large and juicy, evenly developed fruit. Support the bunch with a forked twig while you thin.

POWDERY MILDEW affects the fruit as well as the leaves on grapes indoors and out. Resistant varieties are available, but it can be avoided by adequate watering.

Kiwifruit

" Kiwifruit are a real marketing success story: the "national fruit of South China" remarketed as a New Zealand delicacy, mainly grown and exported by Italy, and introduced into the United Kingdom by two leading supermarkets.

I remember the first kiwifruit I ever ate, back in the 1980s; my young daughter had eaten one at a friend's house and they had become a playground craze. "You just eat them like this." Without her youthful daring I steeled myself for the first bite of the furry "egg" in anticipation of the juicy reward. The bright green flesh was definitely sweet, sharp, and refreshing, but the hairy skin was a real struggle. We always peeled them after that.

The initial rush of sour juice in the first mouthful is soon softened by a fruity sweetness and a wet texture – a kind of firm jelly. No wonder the Chinese have a lot of popular folk names for them, and the original commercial nickname was "Chinese gooseberry". It is easy to imagine that all that intense juice is delivering more than your daily dose of vitamin C – and what a great way to fight off the first colds of late autumn.

Female kiwifruit trees, if pollinated from a male tree, can be very abundant in fruits as well as in vigorous, robust growth. So in your own garden, if you have the space, you can grow your own supplies of this really useful, nutritious fruit.

"Actinid" enzymes in the juice can tenderize other ingredients, but if left too long this can go too far, especially in any milky recipe. This same enzyme, rather than the hairs on the skin, can cause mild irritation in the mouth, even extreme allergic reaction in some people. But for most of us, growing our own kiwifruit is a wonderful way to keep healthy and enjoy a real burst of succulent fruitiness. "

KIWIFRUIT VINES are rampant growers, but you'll be rewarded with a delectable sweet and sour harvest.

Kiwifruit *Actinidia deliciosa*

Some gardeners are surprised to discover that kiwifruits grow in cool-temperate climates. These vigorous climbers not only provide excellent screening but, if properly trained, will supply an abundance of fruits, too. Their trouble-free nature makes them an excellent addition to the fruit garden but they must have plenty of space in which to grow.

The best sites and soils

Kiwifruits are vigorous, deciduous plants that need a lot of room and plenty of sun to crop well. While plants will happily scramble over small buildings and through trelliswork, they will crop much better if trained and pruned correctly.

Although plants are tolerant of temperatures as low as -8°C (18°F) while dormant and not in leaf, the new shoots are vulnerable to frost damage so plant them against a sunny, south- or west-facing wall where plants can be easily shielded from late frosts. Such a position also encourages maximum cropping.

Grow in well-drained but moisture-retentive soil. During summer their generous canopy of large leaves requires plenty of moisture, as do the fruits when they start to swell. However, kiwifruit roots are damaged by wet, cold winter soils.

Buying and planting

Kiwifruit varieties are either all-male, all-female, or self-fertile (see recommended varieties, page 201). While self-fertile plants will set fruit on their own, all-female varieties will only set fruit if pollinated by a self-fertile plant or a male variety (see box, opposite). Male plants bear male flowers, but these do not develop into fruits.

When buying plants choose those with a strong main stem especially if you are growing as an espalier or on a free-standing structure. Allow at least 3m (10ft) between plants. Shorten the leading shoot by half, and tie in the resulting growth.

You can train a self-fertile kiwifruit as an espalier against a sunny wall. This ensures sunlight reaches the developing fruits and also ripens and hardens up new growth ready for winter. Run horizontal wires

PLANTING A CONTAINER-GROWN KIWIFRUIT

1 DIG A HOLE at least twice the width of the kiwi rootball. Add a base dressing of general-purpose fertilizer and lightly mix it in using a garden fork.

2 PLACE THE KIWI in the middle of the hole. Check that the top of the rootball is at soil level, using a board or cane, then gently tease out any spiralling roots.

3 BACKFILL THE PLANTING HOLE with garden soil, firming it in gently with your heel. Water the plant in well and apply a mulch 7.5cm (3in) thick.

FEMALE AND MALE FLOWERS

Although some kiwifruit varieties are self-fertile and need only insects to pollinate their flowers, most plants are dioecious, which means they bear either all-male or all-female flowers. On such varieties only the female plants will bear fruits, but these must first be pollinated by the flowers from a male plant such as 'Tomuri' to set a crop. Identifying female and male flowers is important to ascertain whether your kiwifruit will bear fruits or not, especially if inheriting a single plant in a garden. Female flowers have a white central stigma that is multibranched and star-shaped, whereas male flowers bear numerous pollen-bearing, yellow-tipped anthers.

FEMALE KIWI FLOWERS each have a pure white stigma while the anthers are incomplete.

MALE KIWI BLOOMS can be recognized by their feathery, yellow-tipped anthers.

roughly 38cm (15in) apart; these need to be very sturdy to hold the weight of a mature plant.

Kiwifruits can also be trained over arches, pergolas, and other structures as a feature. Ensure you can access such plants freely to carry out pruning, which will make plants more productive.

To grow a separate male and female plant on a free-standing structure, erect two sturdy, T-shaped posts, 2.1m (7ft) tall and 1.5m (5ft) wide, so they are at least 3m (10ft) apart. Run five strong wires between the horizontal supports. Plant a male at one post and a female at the other, shorten their central leader and tie in, then remove all the sideshoots.

FRUITS DEVELOP FROM THE LEAF AXILS of one-year-old shoots, and so their numbers can be increased by pruning to develop fruiting spurs that bear just such growth.

USING A FIGURE-OF-EIGHT KNOT, tie in new shoots as they appear if a productive plant is required. Left to its own devices a newly planted kiwi will quickly become unruly.

IN WINTER CUT BACK well-placed, healthy, new shoots to 12–15cm (5–6in). These make useful replacement growths for old, unproductive spur systems.

AT THE SAME TIME THIN OUT some of the older spurs, which in time become unproductive. Such winter pruning will also encourage good air flow around the fruits.

Plant care

Apply a top-dressing of high potash fertilizer, such as sulphate of potash, in late winter and a more balanced feed in early spring. In midspring, once the ground has warmed slightly and the soil is moist, surround the kiwifruit with a mulch of bulky, well-rotted organic matter to a depth of at least 7.5cm (3in). This will help suppress weeds, retain soil moisture, and keep the extensive root system cool.

Water young plants regularly during their first two growing seasons. More established plants require less watering but yields will be significantly increased if plants are watered thoroughly during dry spells.

The most important factor to consider when growing kiwifruits is pruning, because if left to their own devices plants will quickly take over their allotted space and focus on leaf rather than fruit production.

Initial training of an espalier

To create an espalier framework with a self-fertile variety cut the leading shoot just above the lowest horizontal wire to encourage both left and right sideshoots to form. As these develop tie them onto the wire. Repeat this process as the leading shoot develops until five or six tiers have been established. As the tier shoots develop, remove their tip when they fill their allotted space and pinch out any sideshoots they produce to four or five leaves. These will develop into fruiting spurs that will flower and fruit in subsequent years.

Initial training on a free-standing structure

When the central shoot reaches the top of its support, train it along the horizontal wires, removing the tip when it reaches the end of these wires. Allow the central shoots to develop sideshoots along the horizontal wires, thinning these out to roughly 50cm (20in) apart. Train the sideshoots to the outer wires, then remove their tips. These sideshoots will form permanent fruiting arms. Pinch back any shoots that

KIWIFRUITS ARE VERY VIGOROUS and look attractive grown over arches and pergolas. Ensure that you can access plants easily to prune them, because this keeps them productive.

arise from them to four or five leaves. These will flower and fruit in subsequent years.

Pruning an established kiwifruit

Flowers are borne in early summer along the length of one-year-old wood and at the base of new shoots, rather than on older wood. Therefore, pruning can be quite drastic each year once a framework of branches has been established. This will ensure a succession of new, fruit-bearing growth is produced.

As vines mature the spur systems can become congested. During winter thin these out and periodically train in new shoots to replace them, cutting these shoots back so they are 12–15cm (5–6in) in length, to encourage new spurs to form.

Also summer-prune established, fruiting vines by shortening shoots with fruits developing at their bases, to five or six leaves past the last fruit. This will divert energy into the developing fruits (there is no need to thin out the fruits). Once harvested cut this fruited shoot back to 5–7.5cm (2–3in), to develop a spur system.

At harvest time

Kiwifruit plants bear flowers in early summer, and if successfully pollinated these develop into furry fruits that ripen during early autumn. Finish off ripening the fruit, which is generally not soft when picked, by storing it, often with apples. Then consume the softened fruit raw or place it in a pierced, clear plastic bag and put in a refrigerator. Kiwifruits will keep this way for 6–8 weeks. The fruits can also be made into preserves.

ONCE VINES BEGIN TO BEAR FRUIT, cut back the fruiting shoots to five or six leaves to divert energy into the fruits and allow sunlight to penetrate the canopy. In this way the plants can benefit from the extra heat supplied by the sun during this critical stage of fruit maturation.

Pests and diseases

Kiwifruit are usually free from attack by any significant pests or diseases. Glasshouse red spider mite (see page 58) may attack plants in hot, dry summers. Birds and wasps aren't a problem on kiwifruit because the fruits don't ripen fully on the plant.

Recommended varieties

'Hayward'
This variety bears only female flowers, but when fertilized these develop into large fruits, up to 7.5cm (3in) long. The vine is vigorous and healthy, and the fruit flavour is a good balance between sweet and tart.

'Jenny'
For those who only have room for one kiwifruit plant, this self-fertile variety is ideal. The plant is vigorous, and its hermaphrodite flowers, when pollinated by insects, bear numerous well-flavoured fruits.

Melons

Cucumis melo

The sweet melon is a tender annual vine with climbing or scrambling growth. There are three main groups: honeydews (firm yellow flesh, weak scent, keeps well), cantaloupe (ribbed, rough fruit, orange-coloured flesh, most likely to succeed in cool climates), and musk (yellow- or green-netted skin, green- to orange-coloured flesh, only worthwhile under glass).

The best sites and soils

Choose a warm, sunny spot in humus-rich, well-drained soil and high humidity. The soil must be light so that it will warm quickly in spring, and deeply cultivated to allow roots to grow down for moisture. On heavier soil, use raised beds because the soil will warm up more quickly.

In cool-temperate climates, grow melons in a greenhouse or in a warm, protected microclimate, such as against a very sunny or sheltered wall or under cloches or frames and black plastic mulches. Only in warm-temperate climates will melons grow successfully without protection or shelter.

Buying and planting

Always choose a variety that suits your climate so you are not disappointed. For cool-temperate climates, melons such as 'Sweetheart' and 'Ogen' are reliable. For greenhouses and warmer climates, a wider range of varieties is available.

It is possible to buy seedling melons, either by mail order or from your local garden centre, much as you can buy young tomato or courgette plants. Failing this, they are quite simple to grow from seed.

Sow in early spring for growing crops under glass, and midspring for outdoor crops. Sow as many as four seeds in a small pot, water well, and place in a heated propagator at 20–25°C (68–77°F) in a well-lit site. Sow an extra pot in case of failure – you can always give these away if they all germinate.

Germination should occur in less than one week, after which the compost should be kept moist but not saturated. Once three or four leaves have formed, remove the plants from the propagator and grow at 18–20°C (68–70°F). If you can't provide

GROWING FROM SEED

1 FILL A SMALL POT with seed or general potting compost and firm it down gently into the container.

2 SOW UP TO FOUR SEEDS per pot. Lie the seeds on their side and then label and date the pot.

3 COVER THE SEEDS with a thin layer of vermiculite. Place in a warm, well-lit place while the seeds germinate.

GROWING BAGS ARE IDEAL for the cultivation of melons. Plant no more than two plants per bag, and in a greenhouse tie their stems onto bamboo canes, for support.

TRAIN A MELON VERTICALLY in a greenhouse to make the most of the space. The framework needs to be strong, with horizontal bars or wires to support the lateral branches.

these conditions, buy young plants from a garden centre later in the season.

If planting outside, dig plenty of well-rotted organic matter into the planting site. Then, in late spring, gradually harden off plants for outdoor cultivation. At the same time place cloches or frames and black plastic mulches over the prepared area, to warm the ground in advance.

In early summer, plant in the final positions, setting each melon so the top of its rootball is just below soil level; space them 60cm (24in) apart. Do not plant too deeply because this encourages rotting. Before transplanting into pots or growing bags in a greenhouse, water the compost the day before and leave it in the sun to warm up to help avoid transplant problems. Set two melon plants in each standard-sized growing bag or one plant per 30cm (12in) pot filled with multipurpose compost.

Plant care

In the very sunniest weather, shade indoor crops with netting or a whitewash on the glass. Keep well watered at all times and feed with tomato fertilizer at weekly intervals. Also pinch out the growing tips to encourage the sideshoots, which will bear the fruiting flowers.

ONCE THE FRUIT IS GRAPEFRUIT SIZED, support it in a net made from recycled materials, such as an old sack, bag, or tights, to stop it breaking the lateral branches.

When plenty of flowers have formed, open up part of the greenhouse, cloche, or frame to allow pollinating insects access to the flowers. At the same time, remove any fruits that have already formed, because they inhibit subsequent fruiting, and pinch out the sideshoots at one or two leaves past the

CANTALOUPE MELONS ARE CHARACTERIZED by their ribbed, rough skin and sweet, orange-coloured flesh.

pollinated flowers. Once the fruit has reached golf-ball size, thin out to leave two to four per plant. As the fruit swells, it may need supporting in a net as it can get quite heavy once it grows beyond the size of a cricket ball. Fruits ripening on the soil may need to be lifted off the ground using a piece of wood to prevent rotting and encourage even ripening.

Let outdoor melons form no more than four fruit; greenhouse melons can ripen up to six before the end of the season.

Late varieties may need protecting with fleece during the first cool nights of autumn, while the melons finish ripening during the warmer daytime.

At harvest time

Early varieties start to ripen from midsummer, and the later varieties not until late summer or early autumn. When melons are ready to be harvested, they emit a strong scent and start to crack and soften around the stalk.

IDENTIFYING FEMALE AND MALE FLOWERS

A melon plant produces both male and female flowers. These are easy to distinguish because the female flower has a swollen base underneath the petals that, once fertilized, will become the actual fruit. The male flower just has a thin base under the flower. Male flowers are the first to appear each year, and as the plant grows and the weather warms up you will begin to notice female flowers starting to develop. In a greenhouse, it may be necessary to hand pollinate the flowers. To do this, remove a male flower and brush its pollen onto the centre of each female.

A FEMALE MELON FLOWER has a swollen base (right), which is the unfertilized fruit, while the male (left) does not.

Ripe melons can be stored in the fridge for a few days. Take them out of the fridge at least two hours before eating them to let them warm up and develop their full aroma and flavour. Before serving, cut each melon in half, scoop out the seeds, and cut it into wedges or chunks. Melons combine well with Parma ham or other tangy, salty meats and cheeses, as well as herbs and spices. Try using pepper, chilli, ginger, or mint.

Pests and diseases

Water frequently when the fruit swells to avoid splitting, and to deter powdery mildews (see page 61). Remove promptly any leaves that are affected with powdery mildew. Damp down periodically to deter glasshouse red spider mite (see page 58), and apply biological controls if either red spider mite or whitefly (see aphids, page 58) are seen.

Greenhouse crops attract the same pests year after year (such as red spider mite, whitefly, and aphids), so ensure that the greenhouse is thoroughly cleaned and disinfected each autumn to prevent them overwintering. Biological controls can work very well, too, if introduced before plants are heavily infested.

WATER YOUR MELONS OFTEN and feed them weekly with tomato fertilizer when they are in growth. This encourages strong growth that is more resistant to pests and diseases.

Melons are also prone to attack from slugs and snails (see page 141) as well as from more specific pests and diseases.

Cucumber mosaic virus This infection is fatal, so destroy plants that show the classic symptoms – a mosaic pattern on the leaves and stunted or deformed growth – to prevent the virus spreading. Wash your hands before handling healthy plants.

Recommended varieties

'Durandal' (musk)
This variety bears small fruits with netted skin striped with green. The flesh is sweet and orange in colour. Other musk melons to try include 'Blenheim Orange' and 'Hero of Lockinge'.

'Earlidawn' (musk)
Good yields of fruit with netted, green skin and sweet, orange-coloured flesh. As the name suggests, it ripens early. In cool climates, musk melons need the protection provided by a greenhouse.

'Ogen' (cantaloupe)
A very popular variety, like 'Sweetheart', for a cold frame or unheated greenhouse. The light green skin matures into a golden yellow and features a very light netting. The sweet flesh is highly recommended.

'Fastbreak' (cantaloupe)
This early cropper is high yielding and disease resistant. The fruits of 'Fastbreak' have netted, pale green skin and nicely sweet, orange-coloured flesh.

Nuts

- Almonds
- Cobnuts and filberts

Carol's fruit notebook

" When you've taken the plunge to grow your own fruit, it is a small step to consider growing your own nuts. Cobnuts and filberts come from the hazel, a small hedgerow and woodland tree common in cool- and some warm-temperate regions. You might first notice it in early, early spring when the male catkins, or lamb's tails, hang down, vibrating in the breeze like a lamb's tail shaking excitedly as it feeds from its mother.

We have a line of hazels forming a hedge at the back of our house, like a sheltered wind tunnel so the male pollen is easily spread to the female catkins nearby. Although we curb its growth slightly each year by cutting out a bundle of twiggy pea-sticks in spring, sometime soon we are going to have to take the plunge and cut all the branches back to the base. This drastic coppicing should rejuvenate the stool (the base of the tree), and new branches will emerge from ground level, untangled and vigorous. Such drastic pruning seems a very easy and vernacular thing to do, probably because it is so traditional and familiar.

I adore almonds, either as a daily treat or a desert-island luxury – marzipan, nougat, or cantuccini – you name it. Such a tree is simple enough to grow if you have free-draining soil and a south- or west-facing wall. Unfortunately I have run out of south-facing walls to grow one up against, so if I am denied the breathtaking beauty of an almond tree in blossom it will prompt me to be more altruistic. I will plant something else for posterity if I can find a suitable place.

A walnut tree may do very well; the "king of trees", if left to mature, becomes a magnificent, free-standing specimen, and the walnuts are a bonus. Where it might be possible to protect a small almond tree in blossom against a nasty late frost, a walnut would probably escape and happily be left to its own devices, but it would take maybe ten years to fruit properly, whereas an almond tree would have fruited within four or five years. "

Almonds *Prunus dulcis*

Sweet almonds make attractive additions to the fruit garden. The trees stay relatively small so can be easily placed, and they produce pink flowers very early in spring. They crop best in a sunny, sheltered spot, where their nuts are often produced in abundance. These can be stored for many months so are an invaluable addition to the fruit garden.

ALMONDS FLOWER BEAUTIFULLY in early spring, and here you can see them with all that remains of the previous year's unharvested crop.

The best sites and soils

Grow in well-drained, humus-rich soil against a south- or west-facing wall. Failing this a sheltered, sunny spot would be sufficient. Avoid exposed, windy sites or frost pockets.

Buying and planting

Almonds are either partly or fully self-fertile, but even self-fertile varieties seem to crop more heavily when planted with another almond variety. Most trees are grafted onto 'St Julien A', which produces a mature tree 5–6m (16–20ft) tall and wide, and is the rootstock commonly used for peaches. On very free-draining soil, use almond rootstock, which produces a tree of much the same size.

Train an almond tree as an open-centred, free-standing tree or as a fan. For the best-quality nuts opt for a fan if you have a suitable wall. When purchasing a tree to be trained as a fan, choose one with a strong left and right sideshoot originating at much the same point off the main stem. A free-standing tree should have three or four strong sideshoots arising from the main stem, with a clear trunk to a height of at least 38cm (15in). In both free-standing trees and fans the sideshoots should be at a wide angle, because narrow ones tend to make weak unions and can also collect water, which can lead to decay and bacterial canker infection.

Plant a bare-root almond in late autumn. Although a container-grown tree can be planted at any time of year, this job is still best done in spring or autumn.

Plant care

As flowers appear so early in the year, hand pollination (see page 106) may be necessary to set the fruit, especially if the weather is inclement during the flowering period.

In late winter, top-dress with a high potash fertilizer such as sulphate of potash, then apply general-purpose fertilizer in early spring. To retain soil moisture in summer, which is essential for healthy nut development, maintain a layer, 7.5cm (3in) thick, of bulky organic matter such as well-rotted garden compost or farmyard manure around the root zone; avoid the mulch touching the almond's trunk directly to deter rotting of the collar. Top up the mulch in midspring, once the soil is warm and moist.

Prune while the tree is in full growth during late spring or summer to avoid potential infection by silver leaf fungus and bacterial canker. Train an almond fan formatively in much the same way as for a peach (see page 107), because it fruits mainly along the length of its one-year-old wood.

PRUNE ALMONDS IN SUMMER to deter infection by silver leaf or bacterial canker. Like cherry trees, free-standing almonds need little pruning once established.

MAINTENANCE PRUNING includes removing dead, diseased, or damaged branches, as well as those that are crossing. Aim to achieve a tree with healthy, well-spaced branches.

Established pruning of an almond fan is also as for a fan-trained peach (see page 108).

To formatively prune an almond as a free-standing tree, follow the advice given for acid cherries (see page 118); do so also when pruning an established free-standing tree (see page 119).

At harvest time

Nuts ripen in late summer (there is no need to thin them), when the outer husks crack open. Harvest, remove the outer husks, lay the nuts in a sunny, dry place for a few days, then store them in a rodent-proof shed until required.

Pests and diseases

Almonds suffer from peach leaf curl (see page 109), bacterial canker (see page 59), silver leaf (see page 61), and glasshouse red spider mite (see page 58). Squirrels aren't much of a problem but you should pick up all fallen nuts along with those on the tree.

Recommended varieties

'Ingrid'
An almond/peach hybrid with good vigour and some resistance to peach leaf curl. Robust and hardy, the attractive, pink flowers are followed by an abundance of hard-shelled nuts with a good flavour.

'Mandaline'
Self-fertile 'Mandaline' is an excellent pollinator for other varieties, which only set a mediocre crop when grown on their own. Its nuts are of a high quality.

Cobnuts and filberts

Corylus avellana and *C. maxima*

Cobnuts and filberts are two tree species that bear not only nuts but autumn colour and harvestable wood as well. The trees' ability to be coppiced ensures that they can be kept within bounds, and their tolerance to shade means they are more versatile than many other crops in the fruit garden.

The best sites and soils

Cobnuts and filberts are happy in a wide range of soils provided these are of pH6.5–7.5 and well drained. On heavy clay, incorporate plenty of bulky organic matter into the soil prior to planting.

Both cobnuts and filberts are monoecious, meaning that a tree will bear separate male and female flowers. The tiny female flowers are star-shaped and red, whereas the male flowers are pendulous catkins 2.5–7.5cm (1–3in) long. Both are produced extremely early in the year – often in late winter and early spring – and so it is essential that trees are positioned in a sheltered site away from frost pockets if a good yield of nuts is to be obtained.

Choose a sunny site. Although these trees will grow happily in half or full shade, the more shade they experience the lower the nut yield, so bear this in mind when positioning your plants.

The trees make useful informal hedging in a fruit and vegetable garden – the lower half of the main stems can be cleared of sideshoots so that the ground underneath the canopy can be planted with shade-tolerant crops such as alpine strawberries, salad leaves, and *Rubus tricolour*. This also makes coppicing an easy task because the stems have already been partly cleared of growth.

Buying and planting

Cobnuts and filberts are two species of tree characterized by the papery outer husk that

COBNUTS AND FILBERTS are quite ornamental, with autumn foliage and late winter catkins. In a woodland garden, where it is shaded, the nut yields will be lower.

COBNUTS OFTEN HAVE short, outer husks, which leave the nut itself partly exposed.

surrounds the nut. With cobnuts the husk only partly covers the nut, leaving the tip exposed, while the husk of filbert varieties often encloses the nut completely. Cobnuts and filberts are grown on their own rootstock. All varieties yield useful timber as well as nuts, and some also have attractive, purple foliage, flowers, and fruits so are highly ornamental as well (see recommended varieties, page 212).

Even though all varieties are self-fertile, some varieties produce only a few male flowers and are therefore best planted with others that are more floriferous. Group different varieties together for maximum nut numbers, because the trees are wind-rather than insect-pollinated.

Trees are best grown as multistemmed specimens with the lower half of the stem cleared of all sideshoots, to make harvesting and weeding simpler. When buying, choose a plant that has been pruned back hard to create multiple stems near the base; if

FILBERTS CAN BE IDENTIFIED by their long, papery husks, which often cover the nut completely. They are varieties of *Corylus maxima*.

no such plant is available, prune the plant you buy back hard on planting, to encourage the new shoots.

Plant in winter, spacing trees at least 5m (16ft) apart to allow the spreading canopies to develop fully. On planting, cut these stems back by half (know as brutting) their length to encourage sideshoots to form.

Plant care

Apply a bulky organic mulch to a depth of 7.5cm (3in) in midspring, to help young trees establish, and keep these trees well watered during dry spells. Mature trees don't require extra irrigation.

Apart from regular pruning to encourage new, nut-bearing wood, cobnuts and filberts can be left to their own devices. Yields will be increased, however, if a top-dressing of general-purpose fertilizer is applied in early spring,

Nuts will develop on established plants along the length of one-year-old wood and on fruiting spurs. To encourage the production of new, more floriferous growth on established trees, remove older, thicker stems; these can be used for hurdles or plant supports. Do this in late winter when the trees are

STRONG, NEW SHOOTS can be broken – but not detached – half way along their length in late summer. Such "brutting" encourages flowers and suppresses vigorous growth.

Recommended varieties (cobnuts)

'Cosford Cob'
This well-established variety produces thin-shelled nuts with a sweet flavour. The tree is vigorous and upright and yields moderately but reliably. 'Cosford Cob' is a good pollinator for other varieties nearby.

'Gustav's Zeller'
A vigorous, healthy, and upright variety, with reliable, relatively heavy yields. The nuts, while relatively small, are of very good quality. They are produced early in the season.

'Fuscorubra'
Highly ornamental and productive 'Fuscorubra' bears purple foliage and flowers – the emerging male catkins being especially eye-catching. The tree also produces heavy yields of good-quality cobnuts.

'Pearson's Prolific'
Compact and healthy, this variety produces a regular and moderately heavy yield annually. The nuts are round and medium to large in size, and they possess a good flavour. Is an excellent pollinator.

flowering, because in the process their pollen is likely to be dislodged from the male flowers and transferred to the females on the remaining stems.

In late summer, break some of the new shoots in half and leave hanging on the tree; this encourages flower buds to form in autumn. In winter, shorten these "brutted" stems to 10–12cm (4–5in).

At harvest time

Harvest cobnuts and filberts just as the nuts and husks begin to turn yellow in late summer. If left on the tree after that they will often be stolen by squirrels, yet if picked too early the unripe nuts will shrivel in storage. Once harvested, lay the nuts out on a rack in a sunny, dry spot for two weeks until the husks turn brown and papery. At this point pick over the nuts and discard any showing signs of nut weevil attack (see above right), or any other evidence of damage. Place the remaining nuts on slatted trays or in net bags and store them in a cool, dry, rodent-free building until needed.

SQUIRRELS are the main pest of cobnuts and filberts. Deterrents have variable results, so it is best to harvest the nuts as soon as they are ready to remove temptation.

Pests and diseases

Cobnuts and filberts are generally free of major diseases but three pests can cause serious problems.

Nut weevil The grubs feed inside cobnuts and filberts. Round exit holes may be seen in the shells. There is no pesticide available.

Hazel big bud mite Widespread, but rarely has a damaging impact on the plant so it can be tolerated.

Squirrels are very agile mammals and so are difficult to control. The best advice is to pick the nuts as soon as they are ready.

Recommended varieties (filberts)

'Butler'
This variety produces heavy yields of large, round, high-quality nuts and therefore is widely grown commercially. The filberts are light brown and possess a strong, distinctive flavour.

'Gunslebert'
Robust and vigorous 'Gunslebert' produces regular, heavy yields of medium to large-sized nuts with a distinctive, strong flavour.

'Kentish Cob'
One of the most popular varieties, this nut is a filbert despite its name. The tree is vigorous and produces heavy, regular crops. The nuts are long with a good texture and excellent flavour.

'Purpurea'
The flowers, nuts, and foliage are all deep purple in colour, making 'Purpurea' an extremely eye-catching, highly ornamental tree. The leaves age to green and the fruits are of a good quality.

Unusual fruit

There are numerous other plants that provide gardeners with fruits, some that can be found in the garden and others in the hedgerows. Many provide excellent-quality fruits for fresh consumption or for use in pies, preserves, or liquors. A conventional fruit garden can usefully accommodate these crops to create a more diverse harvest.

Cape gooseberry This tender perennial bears numerous small, round fruits, orange when ripe, with a delicate bitter-sweet flavour. The fruits of cape gooseberry (*Physalis peruviana*) are borne within papery calyxes, and these can be folded back when the fruits are eaten. Sow seeds under glass in early spring and transplant to a cold frame, polytunnel, or greenhouse in late spring. Plants are naturally quite spreading so stake them. Damp down the self-fertile flowers to assist pollination. Harvest in late summer and early autumn. It is susceptible to red spider mite (see page 58) and glasshouse whitefly (see aphids, page 58).

Chokeberry Red chokeberry (*Aronia arbutifolia*), black chokeberry (*A. melanocarpa*), and purple chokeberry (*A. x prunifolia*) are all fully hardy, deciduous shrubs that bear pea-sized fruits. The berries of black chokeberry in particular have very high levels of antioxidants. Grow in moist, neutral to acid soil in sun or half shade. The self-fertile flowers appear in spring and the fruits ripen in late summer. These shrubs also have excellent autumn colour and are valuable for that reason alone. Eat the astringent fruits fresh or use them in pies and preserves.

Elderberry (see photo opposite). Both delicious flowers and fruits are provided by elderberry (*Sambucus nigra*). While garden plants can be grown it is also possible to forage from hedgerows – this plant freely occurring in the wild. Make sure, however, that you have identified it correctly because many other hedgerow plants have similar flowers. In your own garden, plant elderberry in a sunny site

and prune out older stems periodically in winter to keep the tree compact. Pick the creamy flowers when open to create elderflower fritters, champagne, and cordial. The fruits, which ripen in late summer, can be harvested to make preserves and wine or be dried.

Fuchsia In good summers some fuchsias produce grape-sized fruits, reddish purple in colour, which have a pleasant, mild taste. While all garden fuchsias have the ability to produce edible fruits, some species, such as *F. corymbiflora* and *F. excorticata*, are more productive for cultivation as fruiting plants. Position potted fuchsias in the sunniest, most sheltered spot in your garden to encourage fruits to form, and avoid deadheading the flowers. The fruits ripen in late summer and early autumn, and can be eaten raw or used to make jams or jellies.

Goji berry Goji or wolfberries (*Lycium barbarum* and *L. chinense*) are hardy, deciduous shrubs that can be grown in a wide range of soils in a sunny site. It is essential to source plants that have been raised within the European Union. Clusters of small, purple, self-fertile flowers in late spring are followed by oval, orange-red berries, 2cm (¾in) long. These can be eaten fresh, made into juice, or dried and eaten as snacks as well as steeped to make a "tea". The berries are high in vitamin C and antioxidants.

Huckleberry This tender annual belongs to the potato family. Raise garden huckleberry (*Solanum melanocerasum*) by seed – always purchase from a known source because this plant looks very similar to

CAPE GOOSEBERRIES (left) bear berries encased by papery shells, while chokeberries (right) bear pea-sized fruits that ripen in late summer just in advance of the autumn foliage.

GOJI BERRIES (left) are fast becoming popular as a nutritionally rich, dried fruit. Huckleberries (right) are like a blueberry but tarter and with a more crunchy texture.

OLIVES (left) are harvested at the green stage or left to ripen and turn rich purple. Passion fruit (right) has a sweet, runny flesh and crunchy seeds that can be scooped out.

PINEAPPLES (left) are borne on top of a long flower stalk. Pomegranates (right) are quite an exotic fruit, full of tiny "berries" that are packed within the leathery flesh.

deadly nightshade, which has poisonous fruits. Sow in individual 7.5cm (3in) pots in early spring under glass. Pinch out the tips of the seedlings when plants are 12cm (5in) tall, to encourage side branching. Plant out in a greenhouse, polytunnel, frame, or cloche in a sunny, sheltered spot. Harvest the purple, pea-sized fruits from late summer onwards, when they make a useful addition to pies or preserves.

Olive The frost hardy olive (*Olea europaea*) is native to the Mediterranean. It is popular as a garden tree in cooler areas, where although tolerant of a few degrees of frost it is best grown in a pot so it can be moved under cover during more harsh winter weather. Plant olives in gritty, free-draining potting compost and position in a sheltered, sunny site. Trees can be pruned in late spring to keep them in shape. The fruits are borne from self-fertile flowers and ripen in early autumn. To make them edible, soak the fruits in brine – a lengthy process that renders this tree more useful as an ornamental than a fruiting tree.

Prickly pear These come from the cactus *Opuntia ficus-indica*, originally from south-western North America, but now widely established in hot countries all over the world. They are unmistakable with their large, oval, prickly pads. Prickly pears are not reliably hardy below 10°C (50°F) so need a hot, dry climate to really thrive – especially if their fruits are to ripen. These develop from bright orange-yellow spring flowers. It is possible to grow prickly pears in pots in a greenhouse in cool climates, but they will not

develop their full potential and it would be a challenge to get them to bear good fruit under such conditions. The spiny fruit should never be touched with bare hands until the spines have first been removed as they severely irritate the skin. Commercial varieties have spineless fruit, but it may be difficult for amateurs to source them. The pulp inside the fruit is sweet and full of hard, edible seeds.

Oregon grape A hardy evergreen shrub often grown as an ornamental plant in gardens, oregon grape (*Mahonia aquifolium*) is tolerant of a wide range of soils and half shade. Its clusters of bright yellow flowers, borne in early spring, are followed by pea-sized, purple fruits with a grey bloom, which ripen in midsummer. These fruits have a sharp but pleasant flavour and can be eaten fresh or made into jams or jellies. Prune wayward or old stems down to the base immediately after flowering to keep flowering and fruiting productive.

Passion fruit The passion fruit grown as an edible fruit is *Passiflora edulis*. This requires a minimum temperature of 16°C (61°F), so grow it in a greenhouse, polytunnel, or conservatory. Position this climber in a sunny spot and feed it with high potash liquid tomato fertilizer in spring and summer. Harvest the egg-shaped, purple fruits when they begin to shrivel on the plant. Prune sideshoots back to two or three buds in midwinter, just before plants come into growth. The hardiest passion fruit, *P. caerulea*, produces lots of orange fruits in good summers but these, while edible, aren't particularly palatable.

Pineapple This tender, evergreen perennial needs a minimum of 15°C (59°F) at all times and will only bear fruit after a long, very hot summer. Grow pineapple (*Ananas comosus*) in containers in a greenhouse, conservatory, or polytunnel, keep barely moist in winter, and water well and feed with high potash liquid tomato fertilizer in spring and summer. Mature plants will develop a central flower spike in midspring; this will swell and ripen by mid- to late summer. Harvest once the fruit emits a ripe perfume. Propagate pineapples by suckers.

Pomegranate Another plant that requires a long, hot summer to ripen its fruit is the pomegranate (*Punica granatum*). Either grow this frost hardy, deciduous shrub or small tree in a pot of John Innes No 2 compost and move it under cover for winter, or plant it in free-draining soil against a sheltered, sunny, south- or west-facing wall. Red, funnel-shaped, self-fertile flowers in late spring are followed by spherical fruits. To help them ripen, cover outdoor plants with a cloche on cold nights. Prune wayward shoots in spring and feed during summer with high potash liquid tomato fertilizer.

Rosehip Raw rosehips are a great source of vitamin C and they can also be used to make syrup and jelly. The best roses to grow for their hips are *Rosa rugosa* and *R. canina*. Grow these roses as a hedge or as free-standing plants, and ensure their dead flowerheads are retained on the plant so hips can develop. Harvest in autumn once the hips have softened but before the first frosts. Prune in winter when roses are dormant; thin out old or congested stems if compact plants are wanted (which makes the hips easier to harvest). These species roses are less prone to diseases than many rose varieties.

Sea buckthorn The sea buckthorn (*Hippophae rhamnoides*) is a deciduous, large, thorny shrub which, while fully hardy, deciduous, large and thorny shrub. It is often planted along coastlines because of its tolerance to salt-laden winds. Both male and female plants are required to obtain berries. Flowers are borne in spring and, on female plants, these are followed by pea-sized, bright orange fruits, which are high in vitamins (especially vitamin C) and antioxidants. Pick the fruits in midautumn. Although exposing the fruits to frost makes them less astringent and so more edible when fresh, they are better mixed with other fruits as a juice or used as a cooking ingredient. Good female varieties include 'Leikora', 'Juliet', 'Hergo', 'Askola', and 'Frugna', while useful males are 'Matt', 'Pollmix', and 'Romeo'.

Sloe These round, black fruits are borne on blackthorn (*Prunus spinosa*) – a thorny, large shrub or small tree often found in mixed native hedgerows. Because blackthorn flowers very early in the year, harsh frosts can cause a plant to lose all its flowers, and therefore fruiting potential. Consequently if you grow one in the garden, site it away from frost pockets. Plants are happy in a wide range of soils and sites, and don't require any pruning other than to remove dead, diseased, or damaged growth. Pick sloes during midautumn, then make them into sloe gin by mixing the fruits with an equal volume of gin and adding sugar to taste; steep until Christmas.

ROSEHIPS (left) are used to make syrups and jellies, but not eaten raw. Sea buckthorn fruits (right) are also too acidic to eat raw, and they are suitable for cooking or as flavourings.

SLOE BERRIES (left) look delicious but are unpalatable raw, while prickly pears (right) look offputting with their coating of barbed spines, yet they are delicious fruit.

Pollination chart

Flowers need to be pollinated to set fruit, and for some crops, such as strawberries and raspberries, all that is required is pollinating insects. Some fruits, however, bloom collectively over long periods and only varieties that flower at the same time can pollinate each other. Each of these crops has been divided into pollination groups, depending on the time its individual varieties flower.

Apples

Traditionally there are seven pollination groups for apples. Trees should be chosen from the same group or from ones either side as flowering periods usually extend into each other.

Group 1 'Gravenstein' (triploid), 'Vista-bella'

Group 2 (requires group 1, 2, or 3) 'Beauty of Bath', 'Devonshire Quarrenden', 'Egremont Russet', 'George Cave', 'Idared', 'Lord Lambourne', 'McIntosh', 'Reverend W. Wilks', 'Saint Edmund's Pippin'

Group 3 (requires group 2, 3, or 4) 'Arthur Turner', 'Blenheim Orange' (triploid), 'Bountiful', 'Bramley's Seedling' (triploid), 'Charles Ross', 'Cox's Orange Pippin'**, 'Discovery', 'Elstar', 'Falstaff', 'Fiesta', 'Granny Smith', 'Greensleeves', 'James Grieve', 'Jonagold' (triploid), 'Katja' (syn. 'Katy'), 'Kidd's Orange Red'**, 'Peasgood's Nonsuch', 'Red Devil', 'Redsleeves', 'Rosemary Russet', 'Scrumptious', 'Spartan', 'Tom Putt', 'Wealthy', 'Worcester Pearmain'

Group 4 (requires group 3, 4, or 5) 'Ashmead's Kernel', 'Autumn Pearmain', 'Claygate Pearmain', 'Cornish Aromatic', 'Cornish Gilliflower', 'Cox's Pomona', 'D'Arcy Spice', 'Ellison's Orange', 'Gala', 'Golden Delicious', 'Golden Noble', 'Howgate Wonder', 'Laxton's Superb', 'Lord Derby', 'Pixie', 'Tydeman's Late Orange'

Group 5 (requires group 4, 5, or 6) 'Gascoyne's Scarlet' (triploid), 'King of the Pippins', 'William Crump', 'Newton Wonder', 'Suntan' (triploid)

Group 6 (requires group 5, 6, or 7) 'Court Pendu Plat', 'Edward VII'

Group 7 (requires group 6) 'Crawley Beauty' (which flowers exceptionally late; although it is partially self-fertile, the planting of crab apples nearby should increase yields dramatically)

** 'Cox's Orange Pippin' is incompatible with 'Kidd's Orange Red' despite being in the same group.

Cherries

There are six pollination groups for sweet cherries and five for acid cherries. Some varieties are self-fertile (sf) and will set fruit on their own; others are partly self-fertile (psf) and will set some fruit on their own but are better if cross-pollinated with another variety; and some varieties are totally self-infertile (si) so won't set a crop unless cross-pollinated.

Sweet cherries All cherries listed in this book are in group 4: 'Bigarreau Napoléon' (si), 'Lapins' (sf), 'Stella' (sf), 'Summer Sun' (sf), 'Sunburst' (sf)

Acid cherries 'Morello' (sf) is in group 5

Pears

There are three main pollination groups for pears.

Early 'Louise Bonne of Jersey', 'Packham's Triumph'

Mid 'Beurré Hardy', 'Black Worcester', 'Concorde', 'Conference', 'Durondeau', 'Jargonelle' (triploid), 'Joséphine de Malines', 'Merton Pride' (triploid), 'Fertility', 'Williams' Bon Chrétien'

Late 'Beth', 'Catillac' (triploid), 'Doyenné du Comice', 'Glou Morceau', 'Improved Fertility', 'Onward'

Plums, damsons, and gages

These tree fruits are divided into five pollination groups. As for cherries, varieties can be self-fertile (sf), partly self-fertile (psf) or self-infertile (si).

Group 1 Gage: 'Jefferson' (si)

Group 2 Gage: 'Denniston's Superb' (sf)

Group 3 Bullace: 'Small Damson' (sf). Gage: 'Golden Transparent' (sf). Plums: 'Czar' (sf), 'Laxton's Delight' (psf), 'Opal' (sf), 'Pershore' (sf), 'Sanctus Hubertus' (psf), 'Victoria' (sf)

Group 4 Bullace: 'Golden' (sf). Damsons: 'Farleigh Damson' (psf), 'Prune Damson '(sf). Gage: 'Cambridge Gage' (psf), 'Oullins Gage' (sf)

Group 5 Plum: 'Blue Tit' (sf), 'Marjorie's Seedling' (sf)

Glossary

Annual A plant that lives for one year only.

Anther The male, pollen-bearing part of a flower, often borne at the tip of a long filament.

Bare-root A tree or shrub sold without soil on its roots.

Basal cluster The lower cluster of leaves on a branch or stem.

Base dressing A fertilizer added to the soil before planting.

Biennial bearing Where fruit is borne every two years instead of each year.

Biological control Way of controlling pests using predators and parasites instead of chemicals.

Bleeding The loss of sap from branches after damage or pruning.

Brutting The fracturing of young shoots to restrict growth.

Bud A protrusion on a stem containing embryonic leaves. On bud break, in spring, the bud swells and opens. Fruit buds also contain flowers and they often differ in shape to leaf buds.

Calyx a cluster of green, petal-like leaves that surround the base of a flower.

Canes Straight stem of cane fruit like raspberries and blackberries.

Cloche A structure made of glass or plastic used to protect or accelerate the growth of early crops.

Collar A point on the main stem where the roots and stem meet.

Cool-temperate Temperate regions lie between the tropical and arctic regions. They are further subdivided: warm-temperate areas lie either side of the tropics and include Mediterranean climates; cool-temperate areas, like northern Europe, lie below the arctic regions.

Coppicing The practice of cutting all stems back to ground level in order to promote regeneration.

Cordon A tree or bush trained against a support to form a single rod or stem. U-shaped cordons have two stems. The stems of oblique cordons are set at an angle.

Cross-pollination The transfer of pollen between two separate plants of the same species.

Cultivar A word derived from the contraction of "cultivated variety" to specify that a variety arose in cultivation rather than in the wild. In this book, "variety" and "cultivar" are used interchangeably.

Dioecious Of a fruit or nut that has male and female flowers on separate plants. For example the kiwifruit, which has male and female plants.

Embryonic fruit The fruit in its earliest stage of developement.

Ericaceous compost Lime-free potting compost with a pH below 7, suitable for plants, like blueberries, that need acid soil.

Espalier A tree or bush trained against a support with an upright trunk from which horizontal lateral branches arise to create a tiered effect.

Family tree A fruit tree onto which several different varieties have been grafted onto the same rootstock. It is useful in small gardens where two or more varieties are required for pollination, but there is only space for one tree.

Fan A tree or bush trained against a support, with branches splayed out to form a fan-shape.

Feathered maiden A young fruit tree, usually in its first year after grafting, with branches along its length. Each branch is sometimes referred to as a feather. *See also* maiden whip.

Festooning The practice of training fruit tree branches horizontally in order to increase the yields of fruit.

Forcing The practice of accelerating plant growth and fruit production by manipulating the growing environment.

Free-standing A bush or tree grown without any support such as a stake or fence.

Graft union A slightly swollen section on a plant stem where the scion and the rootstock have been grafted together and fused.

Hardwood cutting A method of plant propagation using woody stems.

Heel in Planting a bare-root tree in a temporary location when soil conditions aren't suitable for a permanent planting.

John Innes A suite of potting compost recipes invented by the John Innes Horticultural Institute, each one designed to suit particular needs.

Lateral A stem or branch arising from a main stem or leader. *See also* sublateral.

Leader A primary branch from which lateral branches are produced. Central leaders form the main stem or trunk at the centre of the plant.

Maiden whip A young fruit tree, usually in its first year after grafting, without branches. *See also* feathered maiden.

Monoecious Of a fruit or nut that has separate male and female flowers but carried on the same plant. For example, hazel trees.

pH A scale that is used to measure acidity and alkalinity of a soil. It ranges from 1 (acid) to 14 (alkaline) with 7 being neutral.

Perennial A plant that lives for many years.

Pollination The transfer of pollen from the anther to the stigma which, if successful, leads to flower fertilization and fruit set.

Pyramid *see* spindle.

Rootstock The lower part of a grafted fruit tree or bush onto which the scion or top part is joined. The rootstock is used purely for its roots. The type of rootstock chosen controls the vigour of the tree or bush.

Runners Surface-running stems that grow from a parent plant. Runners bear young plants at the end, which root into the soil. Strawberries have runners, and they can be separated to create new plants.

Scion The above-ground part of a grafted fruit tree or bush, which joins the rootstock.

Seep hose A hose with pinprick holes in it. These allow moisture to seep out of the full length of the hose for irrigation.

Self-fertile A plant that is able to pollinate its own flowers.

Self-infertile A plant that is unable to pollinate its own flowers and depends on the presence of another tree of the same or closely related species nearby. Also known as self-sterile.

Sideshoot *see* sublateral.

Softwood cuttings A method of plant propagation using young and soft, unripened growth.

Spindle A compact tree form that retains its central leader. The tree is trained in a cone shape so sunlight can reach fruits both at the top and the bottom of the tree.

Spur A short branch or network of branches of a fruit tree, bush, or vine. Spurs bear an abundance of fruit buds and therefore carry the flowers and fruit.

Spur thinning Pruning to thin out a congested system of fruit spurs. This encourages good air flow around the fruits, deterring pest and disease attack and encouraging even ripening and fruit size.

Standard A tree or bush grown on an upright, leafless trunk.

Step-over A compact form of apple or pear tree with a single clear stem to a height of 40-60cm (16–24in). This terminates in a horizontal stem, which bears fruit.

Stigma The female part of a flower, which receives the pollen. *See also* pollination.

Stone fruit Trees or shrubs belonging to the cherry family, including peaches, nectarines, plums, damsons, and almonds.

Strig A cluster or string of currants.

Sublateral A sideshoot arising from a lateral stem. *See also* lateral.

Sucker Any shoot that arises directly from the root or rootstock of a woody plant.

Tip-layering A method of plant propagation where tips of stems are made to root while still attached to the main plant.

Top dressing Fertlizer applied to the soil after planting.

Variety *See* cultivar.

Water shoot Young branches that arise directly from a bare stem or trunk.

Index

Page numbers in **bold** refer to main entries. Those in *italics* refer to picture captions

ACKNOWLEDGEMENTS

Special thanks to all those who have contributed to this book.

Thanks to Carol Klein for her time, enthusiasm and energy, and to Neil Klein for his constant support.

Text written and compiled by: Carol Klein, Simon Akeroyd, Lucy Halsall, and Simon Maughan

Edited by: Joanna Chisholm

RHS: Jim Arbury, Andrew Halstead, and Beatrice Henricot

RHS Publications: Susannah Charlton, Lizzie Fowler, Simon Maughan, and Rae Spencer-Jones

Photography Credits

All photographs copyright Torie Chugg, apart from:

MAIN PHOTOGRAPHS

Jim Arbury: 107b

GAP Photos: Maxine Adcock 161tr; Dave Bevan 58bl; Elke Borkowski 20, 22; Suzie Gibbons (design Rita Armitage) 12; John Glover 76b, 125t, 160b, 165tl, 197; Marcus Harpur 65t; Geoff Kidd 77; Howard Rice 34; S & O 65b; Friedrich Strauss 14, 107t; Rachel Warne 189; Mel Watson 17b; Rob Whitworth 114b

Garden World Images: Dave Bevan 39l; Jacqui Dracup 39c

iStockphoto: Claude Dagenais 64; FhF Greenmedia 36; Jivko Kazakov 187; Jennifer Sheets 154; Serge Villa 23

Marianne Majerus Garden Images: Karen Grosch 18; Marianne Majerus 206, 210; Wyken Hall, Suffolk 19

Paul Jasper (www.jaspertrees.co.uk): 68

Photolibrary: David Cavagnaro: 211b; Neil Holmes 97b

Photoshot/NHPA: Stephen Krasemann 163

Shutterstock: Canoneer 89; Brittany Courville 204t; Hannamariah/Barbara Helgason 117; Igors 113; Varga Levente 208; D McKenzie 27; Gordan Milic 211t; Orla 90t; Massimiliano Pieraccini 110; Dennis Albert Richardson 123b; Thomas Smolek 104; John Swithinbank 120;

Clive Simms: 164

VARIETY AND FRUIT TYPE BOXES

Alamy: Holmes Garden Photos, Neil Holmes 190bl; David Hosking 101tl; Malcolm McMillan 212bl; John Swithinbank 125cl, 125bl

Jim Arbury: 70tcl, 70bcr, 90bl, 101bcr, 109bl, 111bl, 170br, 174bl, 174cr, 180br, 181bl, 181br, 183br, 201bl

Blackmoor Nursery (www.blackmoor.co.uk): 109tr

Burpee (www.burpee.com): 205cr

DEFRA National Fruit Collection, Brogdale: 71cl, 99bl, 182bl, 182br

Derek St Romaine: 108bl, 180bl, 191br

GAP Photos: Christina Bollen 109tl; Mark Bolton 192br; Paul Debois 170cl; John Glover 152cl; FhF Greenmedia 97tr; Clive Nichols 130bl; Friedrich Strauss 201br; Rachel Warner 101tr; Jo Whitworth 93bl

Garden World Images: Dave Bevan 183bl; Liz Cole 130tl; Glenn Harper 119br; Glenda Ramsay 205bl; Trevor Sims 119tl; C Wheeler 205br

iStockphoto: Roger Whiteway 213tr

Paul Jasper (www.jaspertrees.co.uk): 70bl, 71tl, 71cr, 72bcr, 72br, 73tcl

Marianne Majerus Garden Images: Andrew Lawson 119bl; Marianne Majerus 108tl, 130br;

Marshalls Nursery (www.marshalls-seeds.co.uk): 101bcl, 101tcr, 111bl, 138tr, 193bl, 194br

photolibrary: Steven Morris Photography 193br; Emma Peios, The Citrus Centre 125cr; Howard Rice 72tcl, 97br, 109br; Mick Rock 194bl

Photoshot: Photos Horticultural, Michael Warren 125tl, 130cl, 190br, 191bl, 212cr

RHS Herbarium: 73tr, 73bcr, 73br, 93br, 137bl, 138bl, 147cl, 152tr, 174tr

RHS Wisley Fruit Department: 70tl, 71br, 119cr

Seaspring Photos: 170tr

Shutterstock: Gavrila Bogdan 217cr; David Bukach 215cr; Elena Butinova 216r; Maslov Dmitry 215cl; Stale Edstrom 217l; Fotocrisis 215l; Filip Fuxa 217r; Benjamin Howell 122tr; Karin Lau 122br; Robyn Mackenzie 216cl; Microgen 215r; Photooiasson 216l; Inacio Pires 122tl; Ivaschenko Roman 217cl; Jerome Scholler 216cr; Fred Sgrosso 122bl; Andriy Solovyov 97tl; Liz Van Steenburgh 97bl

Clive Simms: 125br, 130tr, 130cr, 161bl, 174br, 213cl, 213br

Mike Sleigh/RHS Herbarium: 205cl

Suttons Nursery (www.suttons.co.uk): 209br

Graham Titchmarsh/RHS Herbarium: 70bcl, 70tcr, 70br, 71tcl, 71bcl, 71tcr, 71bcr, 72tl, 72bcl, 72bl, 72tr, 72tcr, 73tl, 73bcl, 73bl 73tcr, 98tl, 98bl, 98tr, 98br, 99tl, 99tr, 99br, 101tcl, 101bl, 101br, 106bl, 108tr, 108br, 119cl, 119tr, 138tl, 138cr, 138br, 147tl, 147tcr, 147cr, 152tl, 152bl, 152cr, 152br, 161cl, 161cr, 170tcl, 170bl, 170cr, 174tcl, 174cl, 179, 192bl